Reclaiming
the Body

The Christian Practice
of Everyday Life

David S. Cunningham
and William T. Cavanaugh, series editors

This series seeks to present specifically Christian perspectives on some of the most prevalent contemporary practices of everyday life. It is intended for a broad audience—including clergy, interested laypeople, and students. The books in this series are motivated by the conviction that, in the contemporary context, Christians must actively demonstrate that their allegiance to the God of Jesus Christ always takes priority over secular structures that compete for our loyalty—including the state, the market, race, class, gender, and other functional idolatries. The books in this series will examine these competing allegiances as they play themselves out in particular day-to-day practices, and will provide concrete descriptions of how the Christian faith might play a more formative role in our everyday lives.

The Christian Practice of Everyday Life series is an initiative of The Ekklesia Project, an ecumenical gathering of pastors, theologians, and lay leaders committed to helping the church recall its status as the distinctive, real-world community dedicated to the priorities and practices of Jesus Christ and to the inbreaking Kingdom of God. (For more information on The Ekklesia Project, see <www.ekklesiaproject.org>.)

Reclaiming the Body

Christians and the Faithful Use
of Modern Medicine

THE CHRISTIAN PRACTICE OF EVERYDAY LIFE Series

Joel Shuman
and Brian Volck, MD

Brazos Press
Grand Rapids, Michigan

Published by Brazos Press
a division of Baker Publishing Group
P.O. Box 6287, Grand Rapids, MI 49516-6287
www.brazospress.com

Printed in the United States of America

Library of Congress Cataloging-in-Publication Data
Shuman, Joel James.
    Reclaiming the body : Christians and the faithful use of modern medicine / Joel Shuman and Brian Volck.
        p.   cm. — (The Christian practice of everyday life)
    Includes bibliographical references and index.
    ISBN 1-58743-127-0 (pbk.)
    1. Medicine—Religious aspects—Christianity. 2. Health—Religious aspects
—Christianity. 3. Medical ethics. I. Volck, Brian, 1959– II. Title. III. Series.
BT32.S482 2006
261.5′61—dc22   2005021597

Contents

Introduction

■ In a literature and medicine course one of us teaches to fourth-year medical students, classes begin with a writing prompt relevant to the book or story to be discussed. Like their teachers, our students punctuate more pedestrian efforts with moments of penetrating insight, however unintentional. One prompt, now discarded, asked them to describe how and with whom they hoped to die. Almost without exception, their essays were the antithesis of what they'd witnessed in the hospital. Death takes them placidly, painlessly, and almost by surprise, without time for suffering or unwanted reflection, though beloved friends and family happen by in time to receive touching farewells. Intrusive technological fixes are nowhere to be found, and bodies never falter before the mind or—perhaps more importantly—the will. Able-bodied octogenarians pass an idyllic afternoon of tennis, terrific sex, and fine wine, then sleep between soft sheets, to be discovered next morning, smiling and dead. Like pornography, it's thoroughly utopian and cliché-ridden.

Before the rise of biomedical science, Westerners imagined death differently. The thought of dying without careful preparation terrified the average Christian. Something more than personal comfort or pain was at stake: the fate of the soul itself. By way of literary illustration, consider Hamlet's father's ghost, demanding revenge upon Claudius, not only for stealing his throne through murder, but for doing so as he slept:

> Cut off even in the blossoms of my sin,
> Unhous'led, disappointed, unanel'd,
> No reck'ning made, but sent to my account
> With all my imperfections on my head.
> O, horrible! O, horrible, most horrible! (act 1, scene 5)

Later, with perfect opportunity to slay Claudius alone in prayer, Prince Hamlet reconsiders, sheathing his sword for a more opportune moment:

> When he is drunk asleep, or in his rage,
> Or in th' incestuous pleasure of his bed,
> At game a-swearing, or about some act
> That has no relish of salvation in't. (act 3, scene 3)

Somewhere between Shakespeare and the medical school class of 2005, the mental furnishings of death changed. Now is not the time to review the history of this shift or examine sixteenth-century theological debates over extreme unction, sacramental confession, and judgment. We're more interested in the medical students who are, we suspect, not much different from other North Americans on the fashionable side of forty. Unlike their nonmedical colleagues, however, these students are quite familiar with the machinery of hospitalized death, which makes their studied silence about technology eerie. Are we reading too much into their death fantasies to see a devil's bargain with their technologized profession? Medicine and its machines will keep their arteries clean, joints limber, and genitalia perky until that inevitable moment of decline, then suddenly step back, keeping a respectful distance while the vigorous pass mildly away. Religious conviction, or its more consumer-friendly cousin, "spirituality," rarely makes a show in these dreamy deaths. A single student marveled at the prospect of "finally leaving my body," a startling comment for someone entering a profession dedicated to body maintenance and repair. We suspect no one in the class noted how far from the Nicene Creed's "resurrection of the body" his statement fell, but shared religious conviction is too much to suppose in a pluralistic society, and theological language—as distinguished from statements of "personal belief"—is no more welcome in medical schools than are seminars in chiropractic.

This book is an attempt to reframe that relationship, to ask if theology as lived in the church has something to offer anyone who has had or will have an encounter with the medical establishment. What if, for instance, the things we say in church about God, the body, or our relationships and responsibilities to each other have real consequences beyond church doors? What if they were more than mere whistling in the dark, private comforts in a heartless world?

We are not interested in current fads regarding spirituality and belief as health-and-wellness techniques. One of us has already coauthored a book critiquing this phenomenon.[1] Rather than trying to cram religion into a pigeonhole left momentarily vacant by the medical industry, we ask what theology has to say about medicine, our bodies, and our health.

This is not an exercise in medicine-bashing (one of us *is* a physician!) but rather an opportunity to view the turf medicine typically claims for itself from a new vantage, that of a people who are called to be different. It does not surprise us that many doctors dismiss such critiques as ill informed and benighted: physicians have a clear stake in maintaining medical prestige. What astonishes us is how often people of faith, and particularly clergy, accept such brush-offs. When George Bernard Shaw wrote, "All professions are conspiracies against the laity," the target of his barb was medicine, not religion.[2]

Perhaps we would do better by saying more about what this book is not. This is not a standard book of medical ethics seen from a Christian perspective. We will not be considering individual medical dilemmas—abortion, euthanasia, stem cell research, and so forth—examining them philosophically and arriving at recommended responses. In fact, as we argue in chapter 6, this individualized approach gets things exactly wrong. Nor are we endorsing an alternative Christian medical establishment, complete with hospitals, machines, and friendly staff all operating under the official fish-symbol seal of approval. We return instead to the theological traditions of the church in order to reimagine the relationship between Christians and the enterprise named medicine. Thus, our approach, when we turn to practical matters, will be necessarily more suggestive than prescriptive, although to those who assume the medical industry "gets it right," our stories and illustrations will seem annoyingly out of bounds. In any case, those hoping to find a five-year plan for the re-Christianizing of medicine must look elsewhere.

But, before we get to the stories we offer as alternatives to the constricted way most of us now imagine medicine and health, we attempt to lay some groundwork, drawing on the central *theological* convictions of historical Christian tradition. By *theology,* we mean the ways in which those communities gathered to follow and participate in the life of Christ have understood God's identity, action, and powerful presence among God's people. By *ecclesiology,* we mean the ways in which those gathered peoples have understood how to be church, to be gathered by Christ in order to live differently and more fully. In a world more comfortable with individual "seekers" pursuing private "spiritualities," such communal understandings may seem peculiar at first, even unnatural. Given the propensity for humans to envision themselves each as the psychic center of the universe, community may well be unnatural, but it is the way the church hands on to us the traditions it received from those who came before. The word *tradition* comes from a Latin root *(tradere)* meaning "to hand over." The word *treason* has the same origin. We have a choice: to receive and pass along what has been carefully handed down from generation to generation to us, or to hand it over to those who care nothing for the past or the people we are. Twenty-first-century Westerners have been taught to see tradition as confining and undemocratic. In G. K. Chesterton's words, however, tradition is "democracy extended over time," a practice that recognizes that we, in our particular moment in history, cannot claim a monopoly on truth.

We approach our subject in what might appear to be traditional medical fashion, by describing what we take to be the current illness: most North American Christians approach medicine without much consideration of its relation to their theological convictions. We then explore the pathogen we take to be responsible for the current illness: what the New Testament calls the "powers and principalities," those structural and institutional entities from which we derive so much good, yet which entrap us in designs we come to regret—much like the technological dilemmas our medical students imagine they can avoid. Having examined the problem and its mechanisms, we consider the most effective ways of combating the disease, beginning by reimagining the body in its many theological meanings, and by considering practices that both embody and reinforce these convictions. We conclude with several chapters considering particular cases, illustrations of ways in which these convictions and practices may be lived out. We have no illusion that these illustrations are exhaustive, as if we could catalog the limits of the Spirit's action in human life. We sincerely hope our readers will surprise us with new ways of living out the truths toward which we gesture.

Of course, the "medical structure" we outline above is offered tongue in cheek. In our experience, it is anything but standard medicine to consider the body a gift or to consider theologically understood communal practice as more important than the dogmas of individualistic "scientific" medicine. After all, unstated assumptions marble medical doctrine like fat in a thick, cholesterol-laden steak, and the person who questions such assumptions might as well advance Galen's theory of humors for all the hearing he's likely to receive. As one of our students recently put it, "my colleagues don't get it when I tell them that we, as medical students, are learning as much a belief system as we are a knowledge system." It is the business of medicine to obscure the ways in which it is a belief system, particularly with the currently fashionable emphasis on "evidence-based practice." Only in the margins of the hospital, inhabited by the "soft sciences" such as the ethics committee and the diversity department, are such observations permitted. Our perceptive student saw the magician behind the curtain at a much earlier age than either author of this book, and that gives us hope. She spoke from the vantage point of a student, educated in philosophy and rhetoric, with a way of narrating the story she was living as other than the prefabricated one medicine as scientific industry was trying to sell her. If she maintains her stance of resistance, she will be an oddity within the profession, a sore thumb likely to be struck repeatedly with institutional hammers. We flatter ourselves to think theologically minded medical practitioners are equally odd and vulnerable. We invite you to join us on our exploration of medicine as if God, which is to say, theology and the church, actually mattered. If the Christ we claim as Savior calls us to be all thumbs, who are we to argue?

1

Doctors and Christians

■ A friend of ours recently wrote that "God sometimes comes up when we get sick,"[1] which strikes us as something of an understatement. In few other places in contemporary North America is God's name so frequently invoked as in the hospital, yet there are few places where God makes less of a difference in the way things are done. To be sure, there are as many prayers in hospitals as there are in foxholes, and even hospitals without religious affiliation have staff chaplains, but those lucky patients who, health insurance permitting, may choose among competing hospitals are more likely to select one for the reputation of its physicians, its convenience, or its national ranking than for its spiritual resources. At a time when research touts the beneficial health effects of generic "spirituality" and intercessory prayer,[2] the deity invoked in the hospital resembles the god-idea in any technology-dominated field: either a god of the gaps, a last resort turned to when "rational" means have been exhausted, or god-as-technique, one therapy among many in the "holistic" arsenal of the modern health care team.

In practice, God becomes the guy in the sky appealed to when we are worried medicine alone will be insufficient, or that nothing else will work. No wonder families get nervous when clergy calls in the hospital room. Though Roman Catholic official understanding of the sacramental anointing of the sick has returned to a communal practice of healing rather than merely the "last rites,"[3] some Catholic families still debate whether it's "too early" to call a priest. North American hospitals often make concessions to the peculiar needs of Catholics, but many Orthodox and Protestants, if they request clergy, must accept a "one denomination fits all" approach, where an elderly Mennonite, a Southern Baptist family with a sick newborn, and a Unitarian awaiting heart surgery may all receive "spiritual consolation" from a Methodist chaplain fresh from seminary, clad not in a clerical collar, but in the white coat of medical authority. Whether Jews, Muslims, or Hindus have anyone from their respective traditions to call on in hospital is, at best, unlikely. Nor can a patient assume a chaplain who shares her or his religious tradition will speak in that tradition's language. Psychiatrist and author Robert Coles tells of a friend, a Catholic physician hospitalized with terminal cancer, who was visited by a priest more intrigued by the doctor-patient's ability to "cope" than by his religious life.[4] By limiting the conversation to matters of "feeling," "spirit," "stress," and "thoughts . . . for discussion," the priest, in the patient's eyes, showed more concern for the man's psyche than for his soul. "He comes here with a Roman collar, and offers me psychological banalities as God's word!"[5]

The point we wish to make is not that families don't care about "the big questions" or that all clergy in hospitals are shallow psychobabblers. Far from it. Many families we've met in hospitals have a deep, if sometimes vaguely held, belief in God's action in their lives or impending deaths, and most hospital clergy are thoughtful, extraordinarily faithful people challenged daily by terrible suffering. Yet these two groups—patients, along with their families, on the one hand, and clergy on the other—rarely communicate until the doctors' bag of magic (and the best technology always gives the appearance of magic) looks empty. By the time the chaplain is called, which as often as not happens as he or she is talking to another family in equally dire straits, there's scarcely time for family and chaplain to learn one another's names, much less their respective life stories. Like the "service attending physician" seeing patients whose regular doctor lacks hospital admitting privileges, the chaplain has a lot of ground to cover in a very brief time. The chaplain must first track the patient down—no simple feat in the warrens of a modern hospital—and verify the names of the patient and family, the diagnosis and condition, and the religious tradition, if any, of those involved. *Then* comes the task of identifying the particular "spiritual concerns" of patients and determining the degree to which they actually seek to embody these concerns in their daily lives. If a grieving wife identifies herself as Lutheran, does that mean she attends services weekly and regularly staffs the inner-city soup kitchen, or that she last saw the inside of a church at her wedding twenty years ago and hasn't seriously thought about God since her confirmation? From the point of view of the chaplain, this probably ought to make a difference,

14

but does it? Indeed, is it realistic to expect it will? If our own conversations with the families of the sick and dying are at all representative, what many people want when sickness threatens or death is at hand is a way to make sense of what is happening, or some reassurance that God will make it all come out right in the end. A conversation deserving a lifetime of action and contemplation must necessarily be condensed into a few minutes, hours, or, at most, days. For families suddenly aware that they need "spiritual guidance," there's never enough time. Overworked clergy, pulled in several directions at once, find themselves having to "make do" in matters of the spirit.

Not so when it comes to doctors. Insurance permitting, we want the best doctor, the latest technology, the newest medication. The same friend we quoted above noted this difference some years ago, writing that "no one really believes that an incompetently trained priest might threaten his or her salvation, since no one really believes that anything is at stake in salvation; but people do think that an incompetently trained doctor might in fact do them serious harm. People no longer believe in a God that saves, but they do believe in death, and they know they want to put it off as long as possible."[6] To accuse people of "not believing in a God that saves" is a bit harsh, but an anthropologist studying self-identified Christians in contemporary hospitals would discover scant evidence to the contrary. Little in the behavior of hospitalized Christians suggests a concern with much more than the doctor's realm; namely, this life and its prolongation, limited, if at all, only by issues of cost and "quality." Indeed, some Christians exhibit a greater obsession with this life to the exclusion of other concerns than do many non-Christians, fueling accusations that all this talk about a life to come with a loving deity is so much whistling past the graveyard. And in the unlikely event we act as though there are more important concerns than our own lives, we're still reluctant to challenge medical "experts" when our understanding conflicts with theirs.

Authority and Its Discontents

How do we account for such timidity, such unwillingness to act with respect to matters we, as Christians, claim are of ultimate importance? Among the many interrelated forces one could propose—secularization, the privatization of belief, or the rise of technological medicine, for example—we wish to examine most closely the problem of authority. Whatever claims North Americans make about the sincerity of their religious beliefs, we remain remarkably pragmatic people, more obviously concerned with the results of certain practices than with their meaning. Since most of us understand health as an unquestioned and even a supreme good, we

15

can't imagine asking what health might be *for,* what ends health might serve. That endlessly quotable movie *The Princess Bride* (1987) parodies the assumptions keeping us from asking such questions: when the prince describes his busy schedule of murder and warmongering, the unexpectedly concerned count (and chief torturer) replies, "Get some rest. If you haven't got your health, you haven't got anything."[7]

To the extent we see health as the most important thing, the greatest good, we understandably look for the person best able to provide us with that good, or at least the best person our medical insurance permits us to see. Once we find ourselves in the doctor's office, though, we are on the doctor's turf (or perhaps it would be better to say, on the turf of modern medicine), no matter how much the language of medicine has changed to suggest a contractual relationship similar to that of taking one's car to the shop.

Particularly in the United States, the word *authority* carries enormous baggage, and the American habit of questioning authority is far too complicated and contradictory to be reduced to a bumper sticker. The Anglo-European experience in colonizing what became the Eastern Seaboard was defined in many (but certainly not all) instances by an escape from a resented authority—often the British crown—and the establishment of a new, more local authority—with the blessing and protection of that same British crown—often in the name of "freedom." The "freedom from," which looms large in the American psyche—freedom from religious persecution, from taxation without representation, from federal encroachment upon "states' rights," or from the systematic racial oppression of "Jim Crow"—assumes a complementary "freedom to"—freedom to relocate, freedom to revolt from tyranny, freedom to secede, or freedom to vote and change laws.[8] Yet political theory within what is known as the liberal tradition, from Hobbes and Locke to Rawls, Nozick, and Rorty, assumes a negotiable line between the freedoms of the individual and the authority of the state.[9] By elevating the sovereign, his "Leviathan," as the last, surest protection against the war of all against all, the seventeenth-century philosopher Thomas Hobbes defined the political bargain that has characterized liberal politics since: the individual must surrender a certain amount of authority in order to guarantee her or his freedom. One could argue that all subsequent liberal theory is a gloss on Hobbes, an ongoing tug-of-war between individuals who demand freedom and the government necessary to preserve it. Just so, in both practice and theory, the very freedom celebrated in the act of questioning authority assumes there must be some form of authority for us to have any freedom at all. In the crudest possible modern terms, we recognize authority because without it we can't get what we want.

16

Governments aren't the only institutions to which we willingly cede authority in the expectation of "getting what we want." To the extent we trust doctors at all, we believe doctors know things we don't about our bodies and the means to make or keep them healthy. That is, we trust doctors to be knowledgeable technicians providing us with something we want: our health. However diminished physician authority has become in recent years, doctors retain an almost clerical aura, something like priests of the religion of medicine.[10]

What remains hidden, then, behind all the talk about patient choice, the importance of informed consent, and the primacy of patient autonomy, is that the scope of medical conversations is still determined by the particular concerns and technological power of medicine. In effect, what medicine offers to its "consumers" is a menu of technological responses to the problems and limitations of the body. Though that menu increasingly recognizes the power of patient interest—what is now referred to without irony as "consumer demand"—the selections making it up are still decided upon by medicine.

Not that the captains of medicine are all power-hungry despots. Indeed, much of what drives modern medicine is an admittedly noble concern to "eliminate suffering" and increase the individual's control over his or her life. This has been an explicit aim for much scientific and technological advancement at least since Francis Bacon's *Novum Organum* (1620).[11] That these claims sound so benign and noble—so "Christian," in fact—is, we think, a big part of the problem. By assuming medicine and Christianity are pursuing the same things—which, coincidentally, happen to be things we want, such as health, the power to choose, and an able-bodied, painless death—Christians transfer even more authority from their religious community to medicine, reinforcing one of the least-appreciated phenomena in Christianity since the Reformation—the growing amnesia that Christians can and should think, speak, and act differently than the rest of the world.

But why should Christians act distinctively when there seems nothing inherently Christian about going to the doctor? Religious traditions make occasional pronouncements about medical things, but these are usually matters at the margins of understanding—such as the obscure beginnings or the final moments of life—and so only minimally under medical control. In practice, however, most decisions come down to what medicine has to offer and what the patient or his or her family wants. Despite an increased awareness of patients' "spiritual issues," physicians like to believe they offer the best medical care they can to all patients, regardless of religion, generally accepting that certain privately held, "nonscientific" positions, such as the Jehovah's Witnesses' prohibition on blood transfusion, may limit what the doctor can accomplish. Yet in spite of its willingness to accommodate such beliefs, medicine cannot help but see their consequences as tragic.

Contemporary North American culture, which exalts technology and highly specialized knowledge as the latest, surest means to "get what we want," reserves to the private sphere that vague, if increasingly consumer-driven, enclosure known as "spirituality."[12] Though spirituality is frequently described as "that part of our lives that gives us meaning," or "the repository of our deepest convictions," its exile to the purely private makes it dependent upon and secondary to the "publicly responsible" practices of reason and technology. In a variation on Maslow's hierarchy of needs, spiritual concerns become a pleasurable afterthought to be indulged in once more practical matters are accounted for.[13] This need not, and often does not, take the form of crass materialism. Many of the recent cultural developments we find appealing—a heightened concern for where and how our food is grown and prepared, the recovery of pedestrian-accessible urban neighborhoods, or the small but growing demand for high-efficiency, low-emissions automobiles—demonstrate that personal preferences may congeal into a public force. Yet these continue to take the form of market responses to consumer demands.

And medical practice has changed to fit this overall scheme. Adding a chiropractor to an orthopedic office, offering "complementary medicine" as part of a "total package," and becoming conversant in matters of herbal medicine, qigong, and homeopathy are more a shrewd response to "loss of market share" than the consequence of a collectively chastened medical ego. Yet, with a new respect within medicine for the "spiritual dimension" of health care and a broadened and spiced-up menu of medical techniques providing the patient with that much more choice, who can complain?

Christians and Doctors

Christians, for starters—or so we'd like to suggest. While Christians have squandered, through two millennia of shameful behavior, their claims to the moral high ground, it nonetheless seems quite a fall-off for those who profess to worship the Lord of the Universe to settle for a role as consumer interest group. The early Christian martyrs, who accepted death rather than offer incense to the gods or kill in the emperor's name, would be appalled at our false humility. Before the Emperor Constantine and his successors confused matters, Christians understood that their worship of the crucified and risen Christ changed everything they did and made them distinctly odd in a world used to doing things otherwise.[14] We modern Christians, for whom religious belief has only as much significance as we choose to give it, are less prone to see ourselves as distinctive. As

18

in the hospital scenarios we presented earlier, it's often only in the moments when "the normal ways of doing things" fail—such as when death is imminent—that we grasp for meaning through distinctively Christian means.

Put another way, many self-described Christians realize only very late that their Christianity calls them to understand their personal stories and the larger story of their faith *theologically,* to see that God, and even more surprisingly, the church, are important characters in a tale larger than the aspirations or desires of any single person. Getting Christians to invite the right characters into their story is, in part, what we hope to encourage. But before that, it may help to demonstrate why we think Christians *can* include such oddities as God and the church in the deceptively simple tale of going to the doctor.

Remembering Who We Are and How We Got That Way

How might Christians reimagine the encounter between patient and physician? As we've suggested already, any Christian reimagination should include a requirement to think theologically. Christian theology (from the Greek for "God-speak") is a language, and it demands, as any language, that we learn some vocabulary and grammar before saying anything important.

Where, then, do we begin? First, Christians do well to remember the particularly Christian story of how they got to be who they are. This may seem an odd way to talk about identity, but because our identities are established over time, we think it essential that each Christian learn to tell his or her story, not in isolation, but as a contingent, dependent story, part of the much larger story of God's redemption of creation through the particular, gathered people we call "church." The name Christians give to the practice of bringing a person into that story is "baptism."[15] Early Christians did not see baptism as a mere hazing ritual or club admission procedure, but as a complete transformation of identity. Newly baptized persons were called "neophytes"—the Greek means "newly planted"—(1 Tim. 3:6), members of "a new creation" (2 Cor. 5:17 NRSV), and "partakers of the divine nature" (2 Peter 1:4). The identity a Christian puts on at baptism cannot be understood in isolation; through the ritual of baptism (the immersion of a body into water or the pouring of water over a body[16]), what were once individual bodies are incorporated into the one body of Christ (1 Cor. 6:15, 12:27). The varied people gathered into this body, which is Christ's, also become members of one another (1 Cor. 12:12–13; Eph. 4:25). The First Letter of Peter describes new believers as "living stones" building a "spiritual house" (1 Peter 2:5), but

19

the author also reminds his readers that with new identity comes a new allegiance: "you are a chosen race, a royal priesthood, a holy nation, God's own people, that you may declare the wonderful deeds of him who called you out of darkness into his marvelous light" (1 Peter 2:9). This suggests that after our baptism, we can't simply go on doing things as we've always done them. The enormous story into which our baptism welcomes us makes equally enormous demands. Responsibilities come with the gift of this new identity.

Learning these new responsibilities begins with learning to see differently. Baptism transforms our vision and allows us to see other persons—indeed, all creation—as part of the story we now inhabit (2 Cor. 5:16; Eph. 1:9–10; Heb. 1:1–3). This story tells us that creation is full of good things, and God so cares for this creation and for us as a particular part of that creation that we needn't be anxious for our life or health as long as we seek to serve God (Gen. 1:31; Matt. 6:25–33). The goods of creation, we learn, are always subordinate to our love of and service to God (Rom. 1:19–23; 1 Cor. 8:5–6). This subordination of the goods of this world to the service and glory of God is a constant theme in Christian teaching.[17] Among these many created goods is our life itself and the health in which we hope to enjoy it. Health, in other words, is a good, but not *the* Good. Margaret Mohrmann, who is a theologian as well as a pediatrician, comments on the proper place of health in the lives of Christians:

> Health can never be anything other than a secondary good. God is our absolute good; health is an instrumental, subordinate good, important only insofar as it enables us to be the joyful, whole persons God has created us to be and to perform the service to our neighbors that God calls us to perform. Any pursuit of health that subverts either of these obligations of joy and loving service is the pursuit of a false god. Health is to be sought in and for God, not instead of God.[18]

Speaking of health as a potential "false god," or idol, is part of the strange language we learn upon entering God's story, reminding us that God's good creation has become alienated from its Creator. Through what the Christian tradition has described as "the fall," we, and the goods of the created order, no longer serve God in the ways God intended.[19] Contrary to the way we often live, none of the secondary goods we seek in this life are pure, or unalloyed. Rather, they are "alloyed," partial goods. Like us, they are fallen and in need of redemption. As Christians, we acknowledge that all redemption comes as a gift of the crucified and risen Lord through the power of the Holy Spirit, and not through any effort on our part. We cooperate with that redemption through our faithfulness to God. One of the characteristics of this faithfulness is a right ordering of created goods, or rather a right ordering of our love for these goods, which is simply to say we must learn to love and use them properly.[20] Faithful Christians act so that the higher goods—the highest good being God alone—are loved and pursued with greater fervor than the lesser. Insofar as God grants them the ability to do so, faithful Christians (and Jews, too, since these injunctions are grounded in the Hebrew scriptures) direct their efforts to the love of God first, then to love of neighbor, with all other goods subservient to these (Deut. 6:4–5; Lev. 19:18; Matt. 22:34–40; Mark 12:28–34; Luke 10:25–28).

To order properly our love for created goods, we first acknowledge their origin in God. Second, we recognize that these goods are never ends in themselves, but good *for* something. That something, Christians believe, is not determined by individual preference or will, or achieved through our own effort. Rather, by the power of the Holy Spirit and through practices formed by the story of the people Israel—and most particularly through the person of Jesus—the people gathered as church learn properly to appreciate the real but still subordinate goods of the created order.

Third, practices like caring for the sick of the community must be embraced, embodied, and sustained. Nothing so subtle and complex as the proper ordering of our loves can be learned first in the abstract and only later put into practice, just as few piano students spend their first years exclusively studying music theory, or approach the piano keyboard only after they have mastered the concepts of harmony, melody, dynamics, and rhythm. Even as the piano student learns music kinesthetically, through "doing" the music not just with the fingers, but with proper posture, arm position, and preferably—if the beginning musician wishes ever to sight-read—with eyes on the page rather than watching his or her fingers, the Christian embodies his or her faith, living out in the flesh, through word and act, the substance of the Christian story.

The New Testament Letter of James makes clear that the life of faith must consist in bodily acts: "If a brother or sister is ill-clad and in lack of daily food, and one of you says to them, 'Go in peace, be warmed and filled,' without giving them the things needed for the body, what does it profit? So faith by itself, if it has no works, is dead" (James 2:15–17).[21] Matthew's Jesus, in describing the last judgment, tells us we encounter him decisively through what the church has come to call the "corporal acts of mercy" (Matt. 25:31–46), and Luke ends the Emmaus story with the extraordinary claim that the resurrected Lord was made known to the travelers, less through Jesus's "opening" of the scriptures than by a bodily action, that he had been "known to them in the breaking of the bread" (Luke 24:35). The practices of the church, then, are not ritualized relics some people once considered edifying. They are, rather, schools in themselves, teaching us what we cannot learn otherwise.[22] We learn how to be in the world as Christians by doing the things Christians are supposed to—and sometimes actually—do.

How Christian Community Shapes Our Encounter with Medicine

What does all this theology have to do with medicine? First, we suggest, Christians should always understand themselves as part of a gathered people, integral parts of a community called the Body of Christ. In other words, we never really go to the doctor alone. This will take some getting used to, since so much of the medical profession (or, as it seems increasingly appropriate to call it, the medical industry or the medical-industrial complex, even though such terminology strips medicine of much of what makes it good) assumes the doctor-patient relationship is an encounter between individuals.[23] That we continue to think in this manner when patients and physicians are constrained by third-party payers, government regulations, hospital networks, and technological quirkiness seems almost charming, a nostalgia for an idea whose time has long since passed.

But there is something even more basic alerting us to the foolishness of "autonomous individualism" in matters of health: the inherent dependence of the human body. A careful consideration of the body reminds us that it is not simply a biological phenomenon, but a social one as well. Animal bodies need oxygen, water, energy in the form of food, and appropriate shelter; humans, it seems, also need social interaction, touch, and communication.[24] Wendell Berry notes:

> Our bodies are involved in the world. Their needs and desires and pleasures are physical. Our bodies hunger and thirst, yearn towards other bodies, grow tired and seek rest, rise up rested, eager to exert themselves. All these desires may be satisfied to honor the body and its maker, but only if much else besides the individual body is brought into consideration. We have long known that individual desires must not be made the standard of their own satisfaction. We must consider the body's manifold connections to other bodies and to the world.[25]

What we learn from this, Berry asserts, is that "the community—in the fullest sense: a place and all its creatures—is the smallest unit of health and that to speak of the health of an isolated individual is a contradiction in terms."[26]

For Christians, that community is necessarily Christian in character, understood and acted out in Christian terms. As we hope to demonstrate in later chapters, this community should have as much to say about why we seek medical care and the results we seek from that care as should the assumptions of modern medicine. Of course, Christians, at least

Christians in industrialized North America, are not used to consulting their "community" before making an appointment with the doctor. We're quite used to making that decision on our own, for our own reasons, and to achieve our own ends. This, we suggest, is a behavior we must unlearn, however slowly and with what will certainly be some discomfort. At the very least, we might begin to ask if the reasons we are seeking "health care" recognize our dependence upon and debt to the community or if they are rather purely individual and even potentially "anti-communal." Getting an annual checkup or taking a sick child to the doctor to care appropriately for his fever, headache, and sore throat would certainly recognize such a relationship, since the health of persons, as understood by the community, is one of the goods of that community. Visiting the cosmetic surgeon about bothersome wrinkles or requesting a medication for "personality enhancement," however, may be more problematic.[27] Yet it is particularly important we learn to think and act this way in simple, less urgent matters, since there will be precious little time to learn how in a real emergency. It is when we are sick and potentially near death that having been trained to act properly matters most.[28]

Whether sick or seeking to remain well, Christians never encounter the medical industry as individuals in search of a peculiarly efficacious means to achieve our own ends, nor do we cede to it sole authority to decide how and why certain things should be done or not done. Especially when we are sick, we approach medicine as part of a suffering people hoping to remain faithful to our Creator, reserving to the gathered community of which we have been made members the right to judge the aims and means of medical practice in the light of the crucified and risen Jesus we worship.[29] Through our shared practices, even the significance of our bodily illness is interpreted communally, as David Power observes:

> In the sacrament of the sick what is at stake is the sacramentality of sickness itself, or perhaps it would be better to say, the mystery which is revealed in the sick person who lives through this experience. In other words, the accent is not on healing, nor on forgiving, nor on preparing for death. It is on the sick person, who through the experience discovers God in a particular way and reveals this to the community.[30]

As we will explore in greater detail later, the ill person and his or her community strengthen each other. Inviting Christians to understand health and illness theologically does not mean we should understand them abstractly. The mutual strengthening we have in mind includes such mundane tasks as driving a friend to the doctor's office, picking up medication or dropping by with a meal, and sitting at a bedside, which can be all the more faithful if done in respectful, compassionate silence

23

than if filled with cliché-ridden theobabble. Megan McKenna notes how much better we witness the life of the crucified by sharing each other's pain as it is actually lived than by explaining it away:

> We must, in the face of life, hold each other's hands, find some sense of belonging together, of being in communion truly. What we celebrate in the sacraments must be celebrated in the flesh first or else the ritual will be shallow, full of the taste of ashes and death rather than the Spirit and life. What we celebrate in community must find a home in our daily life. If we anoint and strengthen life and lift up the sufferings of those in our communities, we must resist death in all its forms and stand against the forces of destructiveness and despair that each of us faces. We must lay hands on people in the world with words of comfort if we lay hands on them in church and expect healing and wholeness in our communities. Suffering is the way to God; it is the way of the cross. We must embrace the passion of Christ, which continues to lift up to God the world and make it holy by embracing it with tenderness and love.[31]

There is no point in pretending any of this is easy, and it is certainly not "nice."[32] Anyone who cares for the very old or the very ill is quickly disabused of such sentimentality. Caring for the sick calls us deeper into the lived mystery of the body, not only in the person or persons we care for at the time, but—by small steps and in ways difficult to describe without actually having lived them—in all creation:

> If we lay hands on those who come before us, anoint them with oil, and pray for their healing in body, mind, and soul, we are called to extend that prayer and action to all, especially those who most need such love, care, and compassion. Pastoral care is ongoing, enduring, consistent, delicate, hard, and often repulsive. Physically caring for the sick, the dying, and the old is not easy, but it is being a "balm for all wounds" (Etty Hillesum). We all have a tendency to romanticize about such hands-on care until we are face to face with it. We imagine the great consolation and explain away the drudgery, mess, and smell.[33]

This is difficult work, especially if we hope to sustain it throughout a lifetime. We need a lot of help—yet another reason why our gracious God gathers us together as a church. We are all sinners (present tense), as wounded, dense, and cowardly as the apostles Jesus gathered around him.[34] By grace—never by our own effort or will—we are better as a gathered community than as the sum of our separate selves. We search for healing together and bring one another into the story of God's healing action through the smelly acts of bodily care.

Many New Testament stories illustrate the search for healing as a communal act, or at least as an encounter where the person in need of healing is accompanied by family or community representatives. One of the most interesting is the presentation to Jesus of the paralytic in Capernaum, where the man's friends, undeterred by the crowd surrounding the house where Jesus is staying, remove part of the roof and lower the man to Jesus on a pallet (Mark 2:1–12). When the sick are brought to him, Jesus is not afraid to touch the unclean, nor is he ashamed of the facts of the body in his healing ministry, using his own saliva to heal (Matt. 8:2–4; Mark 1:40–42, 7:33–34, and 8:23–25; Luke 5:12–14). Even Gentiles bring their ill to Jesus, as in the story of the Capernaum centurion and his servant, and the Canaanite (or Syrophoenician) woman (Matt. 8:5–13, 15:21–28; Mark 7:24–30). John's Gospel even provides an interesting counterexample, in which the paralyzed man lying on his pallet by the pool claims he has "no [one] to put [him] into the pool when the water is troubled." This is, at the very least, a strange response to Jesus's question, "Do you want to be healed?" For the crippled man, there seems to be no real hope of healing without a community to assist him (John 5:2–9). However foolish his answer may sound to modern ears, he knows something we would do well to learn ourselves.

Seeing the Practice of Medicine with Christian Eyes

Living as members of a gathered community has other consequences, too. If we are graced to be better as a gathered community than as the sum of individual selves, then our shared judgments ought to be similarly graced in comparison to our "personal values." The judgments we learn through the practices of the community we enter—in this case, the community called the body of Christ—are not merely "private matters," conventional wisdom to the contrary. North Americans in particular have been taught that religious thought is a kind of gasoline best kept securely away from the fire of politics. While we agree that Christians should *not* demand the government be Christian, this is not because we think religion is an inherently dangerous, irrational force. Rather, we understand as Augustine did sixteen centuries ago that the governments of the City of Man are crude, debased, and inappropriate instruments for bringing about the reign of God.[35] That reign is brought about only by God, of course, who chooses in God's own time how and when to make use of our faithfulness. Put another way, we believe that a proper Christian politics does not involve electing the right kind of people to high office or basing secular law on the Ten Commandments, but in being faithful Christians in a community of shared faith and practice.[36]

The same is true about the relationship between Christian communities and the practice of medicine. A Christian "takeover" of the American

25

Medical Association would almost certainly make matters worse than they already are. The strength of Christians is and should be in the faithfulness of the community willing to bear one another's burdens. The wisdom of the gathered community enables us to make judgments about the proper place of health and "health care" in our shared lives. We're not used to doing this, either, since most of us have come to see medicine as an honorable, if overpaid, profession that has, of late, become more attentive to giving "health-care consumers" what they want. While we are pleased that some physicians have surrendered at least part of their god complex and are more willing to respect what the patient thinks than simply to write prescriptions and expect compliance,[37] we suspect this only confuses matters for Christians. The consumer model to which medicine seems to be uncritically adopting presumes that providing what the patient wants—that is, customer satisfaction in matters of health—is the measure of success.

We hope we've already shown why this should not be the case for Christians baptized into the body of Christ. For us, health—and presumably "health care" as well—is a good subordinate to the love and service of God first and then of our neighbor. We are rightly concerned about health only insofar as our health permits us to, in the old formulation, "know, love and serve the Lord." Part of the difficult and lifelong process of conversion is learning again and again that what we want is often neither what we need nor what God wants for us.[38] Fortunately, we aren't asked to do this alone, but in a community—sinful, flawed, and usually confused, which seems to be the way Jesus prefers it, judging from his choice of disciples.

So, in response to the problem of authority, we propose the Christian community, humbly reserving to itself the right to judge modern medicine on the community's terms rather than on medicine's.[39] We use the word *humbly* with care, realizing on the one hand that the church's judgments are provisional and must themselves be constantly judged in the light of Christ's truth, while on the other hand knowing how timid and deferential the gathered community has become in the face of "experts." The community called the church errs both in failing to acknowledge and atone for its own sinfulness and in lacking confidence that it has something crucial to show the world.[40] We must, then, walk the narrow ledge between these two mistakes, drawing on the best parts of our shared tradition and stories, as embodied in our life together. From this position of humility and authority, we can begin exploring what judgments we might bring to our encounters with modern medicine. In the following chapter, we will argue that if we are properly to understand (and so make faithful use of) modern medicine, we must understand it as being one of what the New Testament calls "powers and principalities."

26

2

Naming the Power of Medicine

■ In the previous chapter, we suggested that one of the problems we face when trying to make sense of modern medicine is our culture's pervasive ambivalence toward authority. We are a people who resent and resist authority—unless, that is, we believe we may be able to use it to get what we want. Yet in our more reflective moments, we may want to wonder where those wants come from, and whether their achievement is worth the cost.

Questions about authority imply questions of power. Some philosophers go so far as to claim that power is an irreducible aspect of all human relationships, a point we're unprepared to challenge here. In every human interaction, the imposition of one party's will upon another is forever potential, if not already present. This is no less true in modern, liberal cultures (like our own) than in totalitarian societies. In cultures like ours, the powerful achieve legitimacy not so much by coercion as by cooption, persuading others that they, the powerful, are stewards of knowledge and skill to be exercised for the good of all.[1] We confer authority upon people and institutions we regard as powerful, in other words, largely because we believe they know things we do not about the way the world is or could be—things that will make our lives better.[2] This is especially true of the complex constellation of practices we call modern medicine.

Volumes have been written about the power medicine wields in modern societies.[3] We cede a tremendous amount of power to physicians and other representatives of the medical industry, not simply because we are afraid of illness or do not like to be ill, but also because we are convinced these folks, and these alone, know things about our bodies that are essential to our well-being. We believe that they have in their hands, drugs, and machines the very power of life and death. This high regard, as we noted in the first chapter, frequently is not misplaced, for these women and men do nearly magical things for us, preserving our lives and helping us function better than we would or could without their help.

At the same time, however, we are often deeply ambivalent about granting so much power to medicine and its representatives. Our ambivalence arises not so much because we mistrust these particular women and men, but because in entrusting our lives to them, we become acutely aware of our vulnerability. In our weakest moments, we discover a troubling dependence upon a group of relative strangers whose presence in our lives is mediated by a complex and usually faceless bureaucracy, and that dependence frightens us.

This is an important enough point to make again, more explicitly: our discomfort with the power of medicine is not primarily a suspicion of the abilities or motives of the women and men who represent the profession to us. To be sure, there are plenty of physicians, nurses, and therapists with questionable characters, swollen egos, and pathetic communication skills, but probably no more than among lawyers, clergy, plumbers, or college professors. Many of the people who care for us when we are sick are not only highly skilled, but kinder and more compassionate than the rest of us. And yet we are often curiously uncomfortable, if not with them personally, then with the power they represent.

The full social power medicine wields in modern societies is far greater than the sum of the power possessed and exerted by the individual wills of its representatives, and our discomfort with that power is based on something more than a mistrust of physicians and nurses. What causes us discomfort, we suggest, is medicine itself, where *medicine* names not simply a group of professionals trained in a set of practices of caring for persons who are sick, but also a mysteriously animated social force. We experience this force as much more than the sum of its practitioners, their tools and techniques, and the bureaucracy that mediates our access to them. We experience it as palpable, as practically alive. When we begin to understand medicine in this way, we see that it seems to possess a kind of creative power. We find, in short, that medicine creates its own world. Those wishing to benefit from medicine's power are expected to live in medicine's world and obey its rules, and because that world is often very different from the one to which we are accustomed, we feel ourselves ill at ease there.

Perhaps the best way to get a sense of what we mean by this claim is through a disturbing short story by Lorrie Moore, "People like That Are the Only People Here: Canonical Babblings in Peed Onk."[4] Moore tells the story of two relatively sophisticated, middle-class parents who discover that their toddler son has a malignant kidney tumor. As they go through the necessary steps of arranging his medical care, they find themselves pulled into a strange new world. When the parents first learn of their child's illness, they are shocked and overwhelmed by vulnerability. Contemplating the very real possibility of her son's death, the Mother asks, "From where will her own strength come? From some philosophy? From some frigid little philosophy? She is neither stalwart nor realistic and has trouble with basic concepts, such as the one that says events move in one direction only and do not jump up, turn around, and take themselves back" (*PIT,* 219). She is, in other words, very much like most of us, who seldom have or care to take time to contemplate our own fragilities or those of the persons we love.

The only refuge the parents can find from the terror of their vulnerability is in the self-assured expertise of the medical personnel they encounter while seeking treatment for their son's illness, a refuge they share with a "community" of others enduring similar trials. "In the end," thinks the Mother, "you suffer alone. But at the beginning you suffer with a whole lot of others. When your child has cancer, you are whisked away to another planet: one of bald-headed little boys. Pediatric Oncology. Peed Onk" (*PIT,* 224).

The narrator's blunt language here is, no doubt, carefully chosen. For while Peed Onk offers the parents a respite from the worst of their terror, they do not experience it as unequivocally benevolent. The Mother soon discovers that Peed Onk is not simply an impromptu community of mutual support, not merely a place in a hospital, but a kind of parallel universe. It is a world with its own language and logic (i.e., its "canonical babblings"), its own ritual practices, and its own social expectations, and those not initiated into its mysteries cannot hope to understand it. "You wash your hands for thirty seconds in antibacterial soap before you are allowed to enter through the swinging doors. You put paper slippers on your shoes. You keep your voice down. A whole place has been designed and decorated for your nightmare. Here is where your nightmare will occur. We've got a room all ready for you" (*PIT,* 224).[5]

Those who inhabit Peed Onk assume a likeness to each other that exceeds the facts of their common vulnerability and concern for their children's good. Not only do they dress alike and speak a common, quasitechnical language, they appear to be playing roles, as if they are actors and actresses in an elaborate drama, one that is sometimes tragic, sometimes comic, always poignant. One of the Mother's friends observes, "Everyone is so friendly here. Is there someone in this place who isn't doing all this airy, scripted optimism—or are people like that the only people here?" (*PIT,* 243).

The taking on of roles in this universe is so parallel that there is no need for personal names. We meet the generically named "Mother," "the Baby," "the Husband," "the Oncologist," and "the Surgeon," while only two patients and one father on Peed Onk retain recognizable names. Connections to the "outside world" are bizarre, fragmentary, and alienating: hospital-provided "courtesy line" calls to friends who recommend having another child as "an heir and a spare"; Christmas carols bearing an eerie resemblance to the theme from *The Exorcist* playing over the waiting-room speakers; and fretful nights alone in a tackily appointed lounge named after the ukulele-strumming pop singer Tiny Tim.

The way the world of Peed Onk pulls on the parents and tries to press them into its mold leaves them—especially the Mother—feeling strangely conflicted. She is, on the one hand, grateful for the knowledge and skills of its practitioners and the help they give to her son—the alternative, after all, would be that her baby would die, within months or perhaps even weeks. On the other hand, she senses something is amiss with the "reality" in Peed Onk, something she cannot quite articulate. "'It's Modern Middle Medicine meets the Modern Middle Family,' says the Husband. 'In the Modern Middle West'" (*PIT,* 222). The Mother, newcomer to the world, will not accept it. When offered the opportunity by one of her son's physicians, the oncologist, to forgo the standard regime of postoperative chemotherapy in favor of a more conservative, albeit experimental, approach, she seizes it with grateful enthusiasm. She is relieved to be free, at least for a time, not simply from the specter of a therapeutic regimen that would leave her son sick and bald and vulnerable to infection, but from an alien world that controlled her by insisting she be someone she neither was nor was prepared to be.

Gods and Doctors

Moore's story interests us not because it roundly condemns modern medicine—it does not—but because it portrays a conflict we think Christians should be open to experiencing when they enter the world of modern medicine. In that world, as we observed in the first chapter, God's name is frequently invoked, but seldom in ways that might enable Christians to live more faithfully in the midst of illness. A recent article in *Newsweek* magazine reports on the increasing space given to God in the medical world, noting that more than one-half of American medical schools now offer courses dealing with matters of spirituality. In that article, one of the leading physician advocates of a more religiously sensitive medicine suggests that given the "growing body of evidence" that faith can play a significant role in the recovery and maintenance of health, "keeping spirituality out of the clinic is irresponsible."[6]

We are reluctant to dismiss this claim, but we find it contributes little to our concern to make possible a more faithful Christian use of medicine. To the extent that religious behaviors have been shown empirically to contribute to better health, medicine has enlisted those behaviors in the service of its own projects. Most of the current literature dealing with faith and medicine seems to suggest that spirituality (or religion) should be brought into the world of the clinic and retooled, when and as necessary, to fit and serve the purposes of that world. Christians, in the meantime, have mostly been content to have their tradition so named and enlisted, grateful for the validation, or at least the attention.[7] Yet we believe this gets matters backward. It is Christianity that ought to be naming medicine, harnessing its power in the service of being a community faithfully witnessing to the work of God in the world.[8] For only as Christians learn properly to name the world and the things in the world can we make proper use of those things. And only as we make proper use of the world can we hope truly to flourish.

Naming Medicine among the Powers and Principalities

What we are suggesting is that if Christians are to make faithful use of the abundant resources of modern medicine, they must first learn properly to name modern medicine. By *naming,* we mean to identify medicine properly as belonging in a certain way to the realm of created things. We maintain that modern medicine may accurately be understood and named as being among, or at least analogous to, what the authors of the New Testament (Paul in particular) call the "principalities and powers."[9] To name medicine in this way is not to demonize it, but to harness it as an instrument helpful in the pursuit of the ultimate human good of friendship with God, a good achieved through our learning properly to love and especially to *worship.*

Although the New Testament authors' use of the language of principalities and powers is anything but univocal—Walter Wink calls it "imprecise, liquid, interchangeable and unsystematic"[10]—it is thematically consistent. The language derives from the thought world of Jewish apocalyptic and is predicated on the conviction that the world as we experience it day to day is, because of its alienation from its Creator and its subsequent corruption, in the process of "passing away." Ultimately, this age—this "present darkness," to use a biblical image—will disappear and will be replaced by the new age of God's reign. In the meantime, it is the task of those gathered together by God to live, to the extent possible, as citizens of the new age. Paul, in 2 Corinthians 5:17, names this age the "new creation," whose members are to bear witness to God's work of effecting the kingdom of God that is to come. Lives so lived will in many ways make Christians appear strange, however, because the world—that is, the part of the creation that refuses to recognize God's reign—remains under the control of false gods of its own making. As Flannery O'Connor once warned, "You shall know the truth, and the truth shall make you odd."

31

One way the notion "principalities and powers" functions within this scheme is to describe the seen and unseen, personal and impersonal institutional forces that provide necessary order, or "structure," making possible a common human life during the time preceding the consummation of God's redemptive work.[11] Governments, bureaucracies, and any other highly organized form of human activity may properly be counted among the powers. John Howard Yoder offers an especially clear account of this way of understanding the biblical usage, which we shall follow:

> The most fruitful illustration of the complexity of this language for the modern reader would probably be a meditation on the variety of meanings of the word "structure" as it is currently used in American English. Sometimes it refers to a particular network of persons and agencies able to make decisions or exert pressure, as in the phrase "power structure." When this term is used it may refer to a group of persons who are known or can be found. . . . Other times the "power structure" is not so visible but one is no less sure that it is there. . . . Yet other times "structure" is present only in the mind of the one analyzing it. . . . In all these ways and more we could add, *the concept "structure" functions to point to the patterns or regularities that transcend or precede or condition the individual phenomena we can immediately perceive.*[12]

The biblical authors appear frequently to associate the powers and principalities with evil, and even with demonic activity; it is the powers, Paul implies at one point, that were responsible for the death of Jesus (Col. 2:15). Yet, it is important to note, especially in the context of our work in this book, that these same authors regard the powers neither as absolutely good nor as inherently and irretrievably evil.[13] According to Walter Wink, the New Testament tells the story of the powers and their role(s) in the world as "a drama in three simultaneous acts: The Powers are good, the Powers are fallen, the Powers will be redeemed."[14] The powers are good because they are part of God's good creation. The author of the letter to the Colossians includes the powers among those things owing their existence to the will of Christ, explaining "in him [Christ] all things in heaven and on earth were created, things visible and invisible, whether thrones or dominions or rulers or powers—all things have been created through him and for him" (Col. 1:16). God has made the powers to serve God and God's creatures by preserving a relatively just and sometimes peaceable order in the realm of created things. Apart from them, we may assume, things would not function as they should, and we would not be able to discover or pursue goods in common; as John Howard Yoder puts the matter, there is a very real way in which "we cannot live without them."[15]

At the same time, however, neither can we fully live with the powers, at least not as faithful citizens of God's reign.[16] Along with the rest of creation, the powers are fallen, alienated from the Creator and so from the Creator's intent for them. The origin of this separation is human sin; disordered human desire—itself a kind of "power"[17]—leads us to be idolators, to love creatures after the fashion and with the intensity with which only the Creator is properly to be loved. And the powers, to the extent they possess something like consciousness, are more than happy to receive our adulation, and so to participate in our fallenness. Says G. B. Caird, "Men had exalted that which was secondary and derivative into a position of absolute worth, and by accepting their worship the rulers had become involved in their sin."[18] The powers, because of the obvious goods they seem to bestow on human societies, assume in human consciousness a quasi-divine status. This adulation in turn corrupts the proper worship of the God of Israel, Jesus, and the church.[19] Women and men are not simply dependent upon, but bound—enslaved, if you will—by and to the fallen powers. As Yoder explains,

> They thereby enslaved man and his history. Man is bound to them; "slavery" is in fact one of the fundamental terms used in the New Testament to describe the lost condition of man outside of Christ. To what is man subject? Precisely to those values and structures which are necessary to life and society, but which have claimed the status of idols and have succeeded in making men serve them as if they were of absolute value.[20]

The influence of the powers on human consciousness and human life is therefore not necessarily violent; rather, it frequently takes the form of deceit and seduction, of persuading women and men that the powers control access to and determine human flourishing. And because in our fallen state our understanding of flourishing is forever becoming entangled in the grasp of egotism[21]—that is, injudicious self-love—we are readily so persuaded. As Hendrik Berkhof puts it, "in contrast to the chaos, to which our enmity toward God has condemned us, life under the Powers is tolerable, even good."[22] We willingly cooperate with the powers' pretensions toward divinity, in other words, because of the apparent short-term benefit our idolatry accrues to us, not the least of which is that the powers allow, and sometimes enable us, to continue living. The powers offer us life; yet the life they offer may ultimately be at cross-purposes with our well-being, because it is predicated on a lie.

The alternative to the idolatry that is bondage to the powers is the proper worship of God. By *worship* we mean not simply what Christians do in church on Sunday mornings, but the entire orientation of lives that have been shaped by the repeated retelling and reenactment of the Christian story on Sunday mornings.[23] Lives formed by the proper worship of God do not presume to destroy the powers, or to ignore them, but rather to make proper use of them, treating them to the greatest possible extent as having been rendered subject again to God through the life, death, and resurrection of Jesus of Nazareth.[24] According to the author of Colossians, it is through the cross that Jesus "disarmed the rulers and authorities and made a public example of them, triumphing over them in it" (Col. 2:15 NRSV). Thus, we find at the very center of Christianity a kind of irony. In the very act through which the powers thought they were ridding themselves of the One whose life afforded the profoundest of challenges to their authority, he breaks their idolatrous hold over humanity.

> He "made a public example of them." It is precisely in the crucifixion that the true nature of the Powers has come to light. Previously they were accepted as the most basic and ultimate realities, as the gods of the world. Never had it been perceived, nor could it have been perceived, that this belief was founded on deception. Now that the true God appears on earth in Christ, it becomes apparent that the Powers are inimical to Him, acting not as His instruments but as His adversaries. . . . Obviously, "none of the rulers of this age," who let themselves be worshipped as divinities, understood God's wisdom, "for had they known, they would not have crucified the Lord of glory" (1 Corinthians 2:8). Now they are unmasked as false gods by their encounter with very God; they are made a public spectacle.[25]

The powers' ultimate destiny is to be redeemed by the cross of Jesus of Nazareth. In the meantime, however, the chief Christian task with respect to the powers is to resist their seduction, for in spite of their having been defeated, the powers continue to refuse to assume their proper, subordinate place in the overall scheme of things.[26] Such resistance, however, by no means precludes Christian association with the powers. "Therefore the believer's combat is never to strive *against* the Orders, but rather to battle for God's intention for them, and against their corruption."[27]

For Yoder, this means one thing, namely, that "the very existence of the church is her primary task." For that existence "is in itself a proclamation of the Lordship of Christ to the powers from whose dominion the church has begun to be liberated." Jesus has defeated the powers, and by her faithful existence as the body of Christ, the Christian community demonstrates that defeat to the world.[28] Berkhof perhaps puts this best when he says, "By her faith and life the Church of Christ labels the dominion of the powers as *un-self-evident.* She is the turnstile which shuts off all return to the unconscious taken-for-grantedness of the former cultures."[29]

Learning to Resist and Harness Medicine's Power

Two tasks remain to be completed in this chapter. First, we must show some of the ways modern medicine may legitimately be counted among the principalities and powers; and second, we must suggest a general scheme, to be elaborated upon in subsequent chapters, for a Christian resistance to and harnessing of the power of modern medicine. Berkhof's remark about the importance of Christians' interrogating and overcoming the "taken-for-grantedness of the former cultures" provides a good place to begin the first task, for it reminds us that medicine, like every other aspect of the secular culture within which we exist as Christians, is not simply "there." In spite of its remarkable accomplishments and its generally benevolent face, medicine as we find and experience it remains an artifact of a fallen world, a world at least partly in rebellion against God. Thus medicine's benefits, while considerable, are not absolute. Christians must therefore use them judiciously.

Who, though, is prepared to confront, rather than acquiesce to, the power of medicine? Where should one begin? To be sure, access to modern medicine is mediated by a vast, complex bureaucracy and an esoteric language that makes medical knowledge mystical to most of us. Demystifying these might go a long way toward revealing the ambivalent nature of medicine as it is typically practiced. Others have shouldered this task, and we do not wish to discourage them from their important work.[30] We, however, think Christians would do well to address something more fundamental and perhaps less obvious. Medicine primarily functions among the powers, we contend, by occupying a revered social position through which it appears to wield nearly sovereign control over life and death. One thing contemporary North American culture—and we suspect this may be true of every culture—has in common with Christianity is its regard for death as an enemy. In contemporary North American culture, medicine aspires, if not to defeat, then at least to forestall the inevitability of death. Most people living in contemporary North American culture understand that there are ways in which they or people they know and love literally owe their lives to modern medicine. It is perfectly appropriate, moreover, to be grateful for this fact. Gratefulness, however, is not the same thing as worship or allegiance, which are perhaps better ways to describe our society's general disposition toward medicine. There is no apparent limit to medicine's ambition to control the circumstances of human life and death by bringing them under human control. Billions of dollars are invested each year in research that has as its ultimate aim the elimination of contingency from the biological circumstances of human existence, and few people seem interested in asking whether or to what extent such an aim is appropriate for creatures of a providential God.

We must reiterate here one important point: the fundamental interconnectedness of the powers and the desires of those the powers hold subject. The medical project of controlling life and defeating death is attractive to us not simply—not even largely—because medicine compels our acceptance, but because a denial of our own mortalities and a desire

35

to be in control is very near the center of our own disordered desires. It is certainly the case that the medical industry wants us to believe it wields this kind of power for our good. Think, for example, of how we are bombarded by advertisements for products designed to treat the effects of growing older, conditions like baldness, impotence, and anxiety, advertisements whose message is clearly "you *need* this in order to be happy." Yet it is also the case that such advertisements succeed because they are so completely consonant with the spirit of our culture, a spirit produced and reproduced by our unchallenged avoidance of our own fragilities. Arthur McGill suggests that the "most crucial task" for this culture is to "create a living world where death seems abnormal and accidental." In such a world,

> life is so full, so secure, and so rich with possibilities that it gives no hint of death and deprivation. Here we have the first ethical duty imposed by the conviction that death is outside of life and that life is the only good for which we should live. According to this duty, a person must try to live in such a way that he or she does not carry the marks of death, does not exhibit any hint of the failure of life. A person must try to prove by his or her own existence that failure does not belong essentially to life. Failure is an accident, a remediable breakdown of the system.[31]

The project by which medicine becomes the chief mediator of the power of death is clearly in some respects a religious one, if by *religious* we mean pertaining to the particular objects of affection around which our lives revolve. In this sense, insists Nicholas Lash, all persons are religious, for all "have their hearts set somewhere, hold something sacred, worship at some shrine."[32] Lash goes on to suggest that although the heart seldom settles on a single object, contemporary objects of "religious" devotion could include "beliefs and practices protective of . . . things we are too terrified to mention, or of instincts, prejudices and convictions lying at the very heart of who and how we take ourselves and other things to be."[33] In this culture, surely, one such object is the integrity and vigor of our individual bodies. Just so, concludes Arthur McGill,

> If we ask about religion in America, you can see the conclusion which I must draw. The God whom Americans worship as the final and absolute reality is the power of death. Here I do not use the term "god" to designate the divinity revealed in Jesus Christ. I use the word in a more open way, to name what a people believe to be the final, the ultimate reality which controls their lives. Many Americans (notwithstanding their dedicated commitments to the ethics of success and resistance) still believe that death is the ultimate reality that will finally and permanently determine their existence.[34]

36

It is important to acknowledge, on this side of the grave at least, that death remains a fearsome, indeed an awesome, thing. Few are prepared to welcome "our sister, bodily death," as St. Francis of Assisi sang on his deathbed. Even Francis required a lifetime of prayer and practice to add "sister death" to his canticle praising God for and through *all* creation, not just the warm and fuzzy bits. Jesus himself wept at the reality of death (before the tomb of Lazarus) as well as the prospect of death (in the Garden of Gethsemane). Christians cannot loathe the body, which is, as we have already noted, God's good creation, nor can they welcome death as merely the soul's liberation from its fleshy prison.[35] Paul, echoing the prophet Isaiah, concludes his extended discussion of the ultimate fate of the body—resurrection—with the cry: "Death is swallowed up in victory / Where, O death, is your victory / Where, O death, is your sting?" (1 Cor. 15:54–55 NRSV). Yet the Christian victory over death is a victory won *through* death, and death seldom is unaccompanied by suffering, and the prospect of suffering—far more than its present reality—inspires fear.

The twentieth-century Jewish theologian Abraham Joshua Heschel is often quoted as saying, "Just to be is a blessing; just to live is holy." Yet, the psalmist responds, across the centuries, that God's "steadfast love is better than life" (Ps. 63:3). The contradiction is only apparent; to make sense of it, we appeal again to Augustine, who reminds us that the right ordering of loves, the *Ordo Amorum,* is essential to our living faithfully: life is good, death is fearsome, yet God's steadfast love—and our lives, conducted in response to that love—must be our first and highest concern. Only among God's gathered people, only by God's grace, can we make this a real part of our lives. Margaret Mohrmann, herself a physician, hints at the significance of this ordering in the context of medical practice:

> First, we can bring to our work a balance and a perspective that come only from knowing that health can never be anything other than a secondary good. God is our absolute good; health is an instrumental, subordinate good, important only insofar as it enables us to be the joyful, whole persons God has created us to be and to perform the service to our neighbors God calls us to perform. . . . Second, we must be aware of the extent to which the idolatry of health represents a failure of trust: trust, for example, in our own bodies to get us through a life given a reasonable amount of care, trust in the food God provides and in those who supply it to us.[36]

In contrast, the world in which we live at once "worships" death as ultimate reality and at the same time treats it as practically alien to this life. Because the modern world, in practice if not in word, refuses to trust the God revealed in Christ to save us from death, those sanctioned with the power to preserve life and vigor and to forestall or control death are understood within modern culture to represent, if not to possess, godlike power.[37] This is not because these people think of themselves more highly than they ought, but because of the social significance we give to the power they represent. This is how the fallen powers function; they cooperate with the disordered appetites of those who use and depend upon them, allowing us to see them not as God's instruments, but as gods, period. To a significant extent, they are successful because they promise to deliver us (while God appears unwilling or incapable) from the evil of certain contingencies.[38]

Of course, death is not the only contingency from which we seek deliverance. Generally speaking, we are unwilling to tolerate anything unpleasant *happening to* us. One of us is an adoptive father, and I see in my pediatric practice a number of families who, for various reasons, have adopted children, many arriving from countries other than the United States. One of the services I and others in the young field of "adoption medicine" provide is a review of medical information on a child before the prospective parent or parents decide to accept that particular referral. Depending on the country of origin, details about family, birth, and medical history range from adequate to nonexistent, although even in the former case the information received is often contradictory and worrisomely inconclusive. As long as the child remains abroad, there are many questions about his or her health that simply cannot be answered. Matching parents with the needs of particular children is an important task, for not every parent, however willing and loving, is prepared to care for a severely handicapped child.

Most of the prospective parents who express such concerns do so because they have legitimate concerns about their own abilities to care for a child with known, complex medical problems. A few, however (judging from e-mails I receive from physicians across the country), insist on ruling out every defect before saying yes to a particular child. In doing so, they give expression to our society's unwillingness to abide with contingency and imperfection, especially in our children. Although medicine cannot yet provide that degree of certainty, it seems to be moving in that direction, as witnessed by the thrust of modern "reproductive medicine" toward planned pregnancy, prenatal diagnosis (with the implicit assumption of selective abortion as an appropriate response to discovered imperfection), and ultimately "designer offspring." However much I and my colleagues dislike this attitude, we are complicit in it just to the extent our many tools in the struggle against illness create the impression that we can overcome, given enough time and technology, even contingency itself. All the parents I have met have wanted to be proud of their children. Some are proud of the way a child has overcome the limitations of birth defects or illness, some of their child's desire to learn or to help others. A few, however, find it possible to be proud only of achievements consistent with the expectations of a consumerist culture, a disposition that allows scant room for unexpected medical problems.[39]

Such an outlook makes parenting something other than the dangerous practice of welcoming the stranger, a notion with little practice in our culture. In counseling new parents—adoptive or otherwise—I often tell them the first law of parenthood is, "You are not in control." Christians, we think, ought already to have learned this lesson from the stories we share; however, parenthood—rather like the realization one is to be hanged in the morning, which concentrates the mind wonderfully—offers a helpful reminder. In every sense of the word, parenthood renders all who are blessed with its responsibilities *painfully* aware of—and subject to—contingency. Children become ill and even face death while we, their parents, still live. Frequently we face such situations helplessly, unable to do anything to change them. In the face of that kind of contingency, who wouldn't be tempted to grasp even at the illusion of control?

Bearing Contingency in Hope

In his seminal work on the powers and principalities, G. B. Caird notes within the biblical narrative, in Judaism and then Christianity, a gradual shift concerning how to think about the relationship of God to the contingent, especially as the contingent appears in what we call the "natural" world. Remaining constant over the course of this shift is the basic conviction that the God of Abraham and Moses is also "Lord of history."[40] As Lord of history, God is depicted in the narrative as generally sovereign over the contingent, both in human nature and in the natural world as such. At the same time, however, "There were always recalcitrant elements which refused to be brought within the scope of the divine sovereignty" (*P&P*, 57). These "recalcitrant elements" are understood and eventually explicitly articulated in terms of sin, and give rise to the notion in Judaism and Christianity of both a distinction in kind and a breach in relationship between a holy Creator and a good, but nonetheless fallen, creation (*P&P*, 59).

In the New Testament this incongruity comes to be depicted increasingly as an eschatological problem, which is to say that there is a deep sense that the unruly remainder, both in human life and the natural world, will be perfected and so fully made subject to God only in the Age to come, the consummated Kingdom of God. As Caird notes:

> It is worthwhile to notice in passing that the Creation myth plays a large part in the symbolism of Revelation. The crystal sea in heaven represents all that bars man from access to the throne of God. Out of the sea rises the beast, which is both the parody and the usurper of God's authority. Like the Red Sea before the Israelites, the heavenly sea parts to allow the martyr throng to pass into the security of the promised land, and having passed they sing

the song of Moses and the Lamb. . . . And when the victory of God is complete the heavenly city is revealed, in which there is no more sea. (*P&P*, 62)

In the writings of Paul, Jewish (and Christian) apocalyptic concerns about the eschatological redemption of creation are brought into conversation with popular Greco-Roman culture, which had been heavily influenced by the concerns of Greek philosophy. The great philosophical concern of the Greeks, Caird explains, was to "discover a unity within the manifold facts of experience," a concern that derived from "the realism with which they regarded the phenomena of change and decay" (*P&P*, 73)—which is simply to say that they were deeply concerned to find meaning in a world where every living thing ultimately grew old and sick and died. The mystery religions, which Caird believes Paul counts among the powers, flourished precisely because they professed to offer such meaning.

It is as a voice in this conversation, insists Caird, that we should read Paul's ruminations about human fragility, and especially those dealing with his own weakness and frailty. In his second epistle to the Corinthian church, Paul speaks at some length about such matters and at one point says that he had been given "a thorn . . . in the flesh, a messenger of Satan to harass me, to keep me from being too elated" (2 Cor. 12:7). Caird believes that Paul is referring here to a chronic illness, a condition that the apostle strangely regards at once as incompatible with the ultimate intentions of God and at the same time as a gift from God (75). "Three times," says Paul, "I besought the Lord about this, that it should leave me, but he said to me, 'My grace is sufficient for you, for my power is made perfect in weakness'" (2 Cor. 12:8–9). Paul was able to hold together seemingly incommensurable conclusions about his illness, not because he had some perverse sense that illness was good for him, but because he was convinced that some of the unhappy contingencies that happen to our bodies may have to be borne patiently while we wait for the consummation of God's redemptive work, a work achieved in the cross and resurrection of Jesus of Nazareth (*P&P*, 77–78).

Such patient waiting is far from passive. It entails neither an abandonment of hope nor a simplistic projection of hope into the life to come. It is difficult to say *in principle* which contingencies must be borne patiently and which attacked and overcome by the resources God has given to us, but we can say that medicine remains among those instruments for which we may be thankful. Yet to see medicine as an instrument for the promotion of Christian (and so of human) flourishing requires that we learn to see our bodies and the health we enjoy as gifts from God. In the next two chapters we will talk about what this means, arguing that the life of the body is made to follow a natural trajectory from conception to death, [41] and that to see our bodies as gifts from God is to respect and embrace that trajectory.

3

Life as a Body

■ What does theology have to do with medicine?[1] As we hope the last two chapters demonstrate, medicine as power would like us to believe the answer to that question is "Precious little!" The specialized language of medicine and its promises of control persuade many Christians that this is the case, leading them to allow narrations of the body and human relationships in ways that serve medicine's ends. Yet there's more than one way to tell—or read—a story.

One of us once heard an acquaintance describing the celebrated film *Babette's Feast,*[2] and, for her, the story was all about food. More specifically, it was about the triumph, through good food and drink, of life-affirming sensuality over the body-denying ways of a dying, ultraconservative Protestant sect. Being postmodern enough to accept that hers was, per-haps, a plausible interpretation, I didn't object at the time. She seemed to enjoy the telling almost as much as the glass of white Zinfandel she topped off repeatedly as she spoke.

As it happens, I disagreed, not only with her choice in wine, but also with her interpretation. The movie is about food, to be sure,[3] but in the same way *Romeo and Juliet* is about adolescent sexual attraction. It is there, to be sure, but so is a great deal else.[4]

In Isak Dinesen's story, Babette Hersant is the French cook and house-keeper for a pair of aging sisters, daughters of the long-deceased founder of an ascetic Lutheran congregation in Berlevaag, a village in coastal Norway

41

(the film places the town in Denmark). Once a famous chef at the Café Anglais in Paris, she fled France after the death of her husband and son in a Paris uprising. After twelve years of quiet, faithful service, preparing split cod and ale-and-bread soup for recipients of the sisters' charity, Babette wins 10,000 francs in a lottery. The sisters expect Babette to return to France with her newfound wealth, but, surprisingly, she asks—her first request in twelve years—to cook a meal for the upcoming hundredth anniversary of the birth of the community's former leader, the deceased father of the two sisters. Babette actually makes three requests: to cook the dinner, that it be a French dinner, and that Babette alone pays for it. The sisters agree, but watch with mounting alarm as strange bottles, crates of birds, and a live turtle arrive in advance of the meal. Fearing they've agreed to some papist-inspired satanic ritual, the sisters ask the eight remaining parishioners for advice. The decision is to go ahead with the meal, but, in keeping with the spiritually focused and flesh-denying practices of the sect, they will say nothing about the food or drink. They will eat but will refuse to taste and certainly will not enjoy.

The plan doesn't work. General Lowenhielm, who unsuccessfully courted one of the sisters years before and is now back in the region, receives a last-minute invitation to the meal. He is astonished to find simple country folk dining on fine French food and wine as if they had done so every week of their lives, while the locals find their tongues loosened, their memories of good and holy moments restored, the sting of old losses and still festering wounds healed. Inspired by "the noblest wine of the world," the general makes a brief speech about, of all things, grace:

> We tremble before making our choice in life, and after having made it again tremble in fear of having chosen wrong. But the moment comes when our eyes are opened, and we see and realize that grace is infinite. Grace, my friends, demands nothing from us but that we shall await it with confidence and acknowledge it in gratitude.[5]

When the meal ends, the diners leave for their homes, transformed and rather disoriented:

> The guests from the yellow house wavered on their feet, staggered, sat down abruptly or fell forward on their hands and were covered with snow, as if they had indeed had their sins washed white as wool, and in this regained innocent attire were gamboling like little lambs. . . .They stumbled and got up, walked on or stood still, *bodily as well as spiritually hand in hand* . . ."[6]

Alone at last, the sisters ask Babette when she will return to France. "I am not going back to Paris," she tells them, explaining she has used all her ten thousand francs to pay for the just-concluded meal. Stunned by their housekeeper's largesse, one of the sisters admonishes, "You ought not to have given away all you had for our sake."

"For your sake?" she answers. "No. For my own."[7] She explains to the sisters that, as an artist, she will never be poor. Despite her many losses, she has been given, through this strange relationship with the sisters and their community, the opportunity to "do her utmost." For Babette, the feast was no act of self-denying charity, but an outpouring of love and talent, done not as a duty, but as a joy.

There is, as we've already noted, much more to the story. Perhaps unbeknownst to our rosé-sipping friend, a deliciously subtle Eucharistic imagery pervades *Babette's Feast*. To take one frequently overlooked instance, the feast's main course features Babette Hersant's famous—at least among high society—*Cailles en Sarcophage,* which the movie version portrays as a whole roasted quail elegantly served in a pastry ring. *"Cailles en Sarcophage,"* translates as "quails in coffins." Alert readers will recall God fed the people of Israel, as they wandered in the desert, not only with manna, but with flocks of quail (Exod. 16:13). *Sarcophage,* the equivalent of the English "sarcophagus," combines two Greek words, meaning "flesh eater." The grave devours our flesh after death, of course, but—as we shall see—we discern, eat, and become the flesh of Christ in the Eucharist. The general is astonished at what he finds served at this simple table:

> General Lowenhielm turned to his neighbor on the left and said to him: "But this is Cailles en Sarcophage!" The neighbor, who had been listening to the description of a miracle, looked at him absent-mindedly, then nodded his head and answered: "Yes, yes, certainly. What else would it be?"[8]

The story, for all its spare elegance, is too dense to reduce to allegory, but the carefully crafted eucharistic references invite theological observations crucial to a proper Christian understanding and use of medicine. What concerns us here is the staggering gratuity of Babette's joyful gift, and the general's understanding that so gracious a gesture requires nothing in response but our confidence and gratitude. If Babette's artistry somehow points toward God, and the general's gratitude suggests a particular human response, perhaps the story can teach us how to respond to God's grace in all aspects of our lives, meals and medicine included.

So what's to learn? Insofar as God is Creator, God is an artist.[9] The God Christians worship as Trinity had no need to make a universe, for God already existed in and as perfect relationship—three persons in one God. God nonetheless creates, for some of the same reasons Babette cooks: as an act of pure and gratuitous artistry, a work of pleasure. Furthermore, the Christian mystery of the Trinity makes clear that God's very nature is relationship.[10] As humans are created male and female in God's image (Gen. 1:27), Christians understand all humanity as necessarily related, first to God as creature to Creator, then to each other as fellow creatures, and finally to the remainder of the creation, in which we delight and upon which we depend for our very lives. That human pretensions deface God's gift is, we think, amply demonstrable. That God still calls us into proper relationship is an article of Christian faith.

We use the adjective *proper* here, instead of *right,* to describe our relationship with God. *Proper* comes from the Latin *proprius,* meaning "one's own," hinting at the uniqueness of each person's relationship to God, but also that it must never be abstracted from the person. Vague and airy "spiritual" language has no place in such a particular embodied exchange. *Proprius* also provides the root for our word *propriety,* suggesting that our uniqueness and particularity is always found in relation and accord to others, and tempered by behaviors that recognize the uniqueness and dignity of others. Part of what makes any relationship with God "proper" is acknowledging that we ourselves are creatures, that we owe our very existence to God, and that there's nothing so special about us that we needed to exist in the first place. We live at and for God's pleasure—not that any of us does our job especially well.

So learning to be a Christian is, in a sense, learning to see all of life as gift. To say, "In the beginning God created the heavens and the earth" (Gen. 1:1) is to acknowledge the universe as God's gift.[11] Even when humanity alienates itself from God, the gifts continue. As Francis of Assisi instructed the friars: "Go humbly begging alms. Don't be ashamed, because after sin everything comes to us as an alms, and the Great Almsgiver gives generously and kindly to all, to the worthy and unworthy."[12]

Living as fallen members of a creation alienated from God, we may wonder what sort of gifts HIV, cancer, or tsunamis might be, and we join Dostoyevsky's Ivan Karamazov in asking how God can be good when children suffer.[13] The suffering of innocents presents a serious challenge for those who claim to worship a loving God. These days, however, such questions increasingly serve not as an invitation to mature faith, but rather as an excuse, a welcome amnesty from divine demand. At the risk of oversimplification, the demand we allude to here is that of living in proper relationship to God and all creation, however flawed that creation might now be, and of undergoing the very painful transformation required of us to live that way. That some Christians—physicians, nurses, and therapists included—struggle against natural and human-made suffering, not in spite of their faith in a loving God but precisely because of it, suggests Ivan Karamazov's challenge has serious limitations. For some, participating in the life of a loving God in the face of suffering is not a simple matter of either accepting suffering as inevitable or striving to eradicate it, but a complex challenge to do both, and in a very particular way.

For worshippers of a crucified Lord, embracing God requires embracing innocent suffering: the child dying on Peed Onk, the Alzheimer patient abandoned by his adult children, the Sudanese mother unable to feed her family. A visible reminder of this Christian reality can be found in the cathedral in Würzburg, Germany, where a large crucifix stands in a recessed arch to the side of the nave. The battered body of Christ has gaunt, Gothic features, his eyes fixed upon the viewer, his hands, pulled from the arms of the cross, extended outward in a gesture of embrace, inviting the viewer to enter. In pulling his arms from the arms of the cross, however, this carved Jesus still carries the spikes that nailed him there, embedded in his hands. There is no way to enter that embrace without feeling the iron instruments of Jesus's torture. The loving embrace of God in the flesh necessarily involves entering the pain of that flesh. For Christians, this is how we become what God intends us to be.[14]

Embracing a wounded world is not a form of religious masochism. The attentive Christian knows the world has more than enough pain already. Embracing pain through embodied care is a grace-led response to the world as it is, an active acknowledgment that, even in our own wounded-ness, we must bind the wounds of others. Our response is itself a way of giving thanks and glorifying God. Recall how, in John's Gospel, the disciples ask Jesus if the man born blind is suffering from his sin or that of his parents. Jesus answers: "It was not that this man sinned, or his parents, but that the works of God might be manifest in him" (John 9:3). In Matthew 25, we learn that Christ is encountered in the least of suffering humanity, and those who respond are blessed by God.

Jesus, who knew the Psalms well, understood how often the psalmist turned to lament—even demand—when addressing God. The Psalms reveal a palpable familiarity with suffering and show how imploring, beg-ging, and arguing with God can be forms of praise. Israel, which won its name wrestling with the Creator, held both God's goodness and the world's wounds in its prayer at the same time. Christians, grafted by God's grace onto that good tree, do well to cry to heaven while acknowledging everything as gift.

Even our capacity to accept these gifts is a gift, a capacity dependent upon first receiving God's gift of life. But the "gift of life" is never purely abstract, nor is it something we can bestow on another by donating blood or signing the organ donor portion of a driver's license application. Life is God's gift, always given in particular, discrete, but necessarily depen-dent forms, for humans live in, through, and as bodies.[15] Embodied, we participate in God's good creation: touching and being touched, loving and receiving love. Bodies, when they suffer and fail, cause us to pause, to rest, and sometimes to visit doctors. The body itself is a gift to be accepted with confidence and gratitude, with all its limits and failings. If we are to understand anything about proper relationship before the powers of medicine, we must begin to understand what our tradition says about bodies, first by considering the Jewish and Christian understanding of the physical body in scripture and the writings of the early church, and second, by recovering an understanding of the gathered church as Christ's body.

Good Is the Body?

Good Is the Flesh

Good is the flesh that the Word has become,
  good is the birthing, the milk in the breast,
  good is the feeding, caressing and rest,
  good is the body for knowing the world,
Good is the flesh that the Word has become.

Good is the body for knowing the world,
  sensing the sunlight, the tug of the ground,
  feeling, perceiving, within and around,
  good is the body, from cradle to grave,
Good is the flesh that the Word has become.

Good is the body, from cradle to grave,
  growing and aging, arousing, impaired;
  happy in clothing, or lovingly bared,
  good is the pleasure of God in our flesh,
Good is the flesh that the Word has become.

Good is the pleasure of God in our flesh,
  longing in all, as in Jesus, to dwell,
  glad of embracing, and tasting, and smell,
  good is the body, for good and for God,
Good is the flesh that the Word has become.[16]

Brian Wren's hymn is at once profoundly orthodox and, at least to the modern Christian ear, unsettling and perhaps even offensive. Contemporary composer J. A. C. Redford included a setting of Wren's hymn in his Christmas oratorio, *Welcome All Wonders.* Upon its premiere, some self-described Christians were baffled by this selection and asked Redford, "What were you thinking?"[17] Who can blame them? "Good is the flesh?" Isn't "the flesh" what Saint Paul says we are struggling against?

46

"Only," we might tentatively respond, "if you misread Paul." Paul, especially in Romans and Galatians, sharply contrasts *sarx* (flesh) with *pneuma* (spirit), associating the former with law, sin, and death and the latter with life in the new creation of God's reign. So, it looks at first glance like Paul *is* suggesting that the Christian life—real life, if you will—includes a rejection, or at least a deprecation, of the life we live in and through our bodies. Yet Paul, for all his concern about the flesh and its mortality, continued to think and behave as a first-century Mediterranean Jew who understood Jesus to be the fulfillment of the Jewish messianic promise. He was not, in other words, a proto-Cartesian dualist policing the philosophical boundary between flesh and spirit or, as Descartes puts it, between body and mind.[18] For Paul, the body remains as part of God's good creation and the theater of God's redemptive activity. It is the *way* the body is lived that leads him to speak critically of the flesh.

A detailed account of Paul's use of the word *flesh* is a project for another time. Yet it is worth mentioning that Kittel's *Theological Dictionary of the New Testament* affirms that Paul, by associating "flesh" with law, sin, and death, is not suggesting that the material body is of no consequence, or that faithfulness entails a flight from the realm of "body." Kittel summarizes Paul's use of the word *sarx* in five brief sentences:

a. Humanity is qualified by the relation to God.
b. *Salvation does not lie in a retreat from the physical* to the spiritual.
c. *Flesh is not a separate and intrinsically bad sphere* but becomes bad only with orientation to it in either licentiousness or legalism.
d. The flesh as a wrong disposition away from God seems to become a controlling power.
e. Salvation through Christ means liberation from earthly goals in a life that is lived as God's gift.[19]

As the fourth assertion suggests, even the flesh can act as one of the powers and principalities, and we have seen in the previous chapter that this implies the threefold story of having been created good, having fallen, and being in need of redemption. Thus, the flesh of our bodies is, at least since the "fall," another "alloyed" good, "groaning inwardly," as Paul tells the Romans, "while we wait for adoption, the redemption of our bodies" (Rom. 8:19 NRSV).

While ever the faithful Jew, Paul, like the majority of his Eastern Mediterranean contemporaries, wrote in Greek, which presented him with a linguistic difficulty. Ancient Greek uses two different words to refer to human flesh: *sarx,* usually translated "flesh," and *soma,* rendered as "body." Biblical Hebrew makes no linguistic distinction between these concepts, while Greek does. Once again, we turn to Kittel for a summary of the difference:

> Hebrew had no special term for the body, and Greek-speaking Jews must choose between *sarx* and *soma*. Paul adopts *soma* as a term for our creatureliness, for the place where we live, believe, and serve. For Paul, however, *soma* also means relationship with God and others rather than a self-contained individuality. If the community as Christ's body is a self-contained unit, it is so only in mutual service as the body of the crucified Lord.[20]

In fact, Paul thought highly enough of the body to use it as a primary metaphor for the gathered Christian community, the church (Rom. 12; 1 Cor. 12). Indeed, Paul's first letter to the very confused and fractured church in Corinth includes a sustained reflection upon the body, beginning in chapter 11 with a consideration of the Lord's Supper unworthily celebrated by those who do not "discern the body," and continuing through chapter 15, with a discussion of the body glorified in resurrection.[21]

Paul had been taught by the Torah that God's basic disposition to the creation, including the human bodies made in God's image, was to say that it was very good (Gen. 1:31). Furthermore, Paul read Torah thoroughly enough to know that flesh can never be viewed as a palace of autonomy or prison of the soul. In a single, theologically dense and poetically brilliant verse, he (and we) read: "Then the Lord God formed man of the dust from the ground, and breathed into his nostrils the breath of life; and man became a living being" (Gen. 2:7). *Man* in this RSV translation reads in Hebrew *ha-adam* (the human being), punning on "dust from the ground," which in Hebrew is *ha-adamah.* The Lord God breathes into the dust, transforming the earth creature into a living being. *Breath* in Hebrew is *ruach,* which like the Greek *pneuma* also means "wind" and "spirit." "Living being" is *nephesh,* as much "soul" as "being," though far earthier than the Greek word for "soul," *psyche.* Poet, novelist, and farmer Wendell Berry—a down-to-earth person himself—summarizes the theological insight:

> The formula given in Genesis 2:7 is not man = body + soul; the formula there is soul = dust + breath. According to this verse, God did not make a body and put a soul into it, like a letter into an envelope. He formed man of dust; then, by breathing His breath into it, He made the dust live. The dust, formed as man and made to live, did not *embody* a soul; it *became* a soul. "Soul" here refers to the whole creature. Humanity is thus presented to us, in Adam, not as a creature of two discrete parts temporarily glued together but as a single mystery.[22]

The point of this linguistic exercise is to dispel the mistaken assumption that Christian tradition teaches we are souls trapped in bodies, longing to break free. Folks still speak of "keeping body and soul together" or whisper of an aging relative whose "body is failing him." Imagine if Christians reclaimed their Jewish roots, understanding the soul as union of dust and divine breath. Medicine's long-standing mind-body distinctions might finally collapse, and Christians would rightly ask which self is being failed by the failing body.

For Paul, both *body* and *flesh,* like the Hebrew *soul,* signify relationship. Paul understood and taught, in other words, that bodies do not live except in relationship to other bodies. While an awareness of the ways we get these relationships wrong is important, far more important is realizing that our bodies are meant for relationship. Not long after the Genesis passage examined above comes another account of creation, in which the man first encounters the woman and exclaims, "This at last is bone of my bones / and flesh of my flesh" (Gen. 2:23). To the dismay of the modern mind, the Bible shows little regard for individual autonomy. If skin marks a boundary between "me" and "the rest of creation," it is a highly permeable one, with brisk two-way traffic.[23] In Christ, the body is no prison, but the sign of our connection to humanity, to all creation.

What Jesus Does for the Body

Christian understanding of the body is most fully informed by the person of Jesus, whom John refers to as "Word made flesh" (John 1:14). God becoming man, what Christians call the mystery of the Incarnation, is far too scandalous, far too offensive to reasonable categories for even Christians to accept without at least some struggle. That Jesus was born a child who nursed at his mother's breast, lived among the poor, ate and spoke with sinners, preached a gospel of liberation, and died a miserable, humiliating death at the hands of Roman authorities makes for an interesting—perhaps inspiring—biography of a "good man." It does not, however, fit with most conventional views of how God should behave, including those held by many Christians. Other religious traditions include fascinating tales of gods taking human form, but the sheer earthiness and mind-numbing indignity of Jesus's life is unique.[24] For Christians, God became fully human—not just assumed a human appearance—and transformed creation in the process. Realizing this is a mystery, we should explore why we follow the tradition in making so preposterous a claim.

All four Gospels stress the embodiment of Jesus. As we noted in the first chapter, many of Jesus's cures explicitly involve physical touch. Matthew and Luke dwell on the physical realities of Jesus's birth. A recurrent theme in Luke is Jesus's use of eating, in the social context of meals, to invite, include, and heal the poor, separated, or socially outcast.

Luke, who surely had a wealth of "Jesus stories" to choose from as he composed his Gospel, showed uncanny sensitivity to embodied human need in emphasizing these particular episodes.[25]

The ways in which touch and "breaking bread together" can heal were brought home to us recently in the form of a teenage girl, hospitalized for months following an accident that left her paralyzed from the waist down. Understandably depressed about the disastrous turn her life had taken, and finding scant support from a mother whose own life was too chaotic to provide the emotional support her daughter needed, she had little patience for the medical staff trying, however clumsily, to care for her. She grew increasingly sullen and uncooperative, until one day when an intern, on a whim, brought his lunch into her room and ate with her. He did most of the talking that first day, occasionally repositioning her in bed so she could better reach her largely untouched lunch tray, but he returned the next several days, and by the end of the week, they were friends, talking together as long as he could stay. We don't know if this doctor in training learned his approach from reading the Gospels, but he demonstrated the embodied action that the Gospels recurrently stress in Jesus's healing action.[26]

All four Gospels describe Jesus's passion and death in powerfully physical terms. The bodily resurrection of the dead, so troubling to the Sadducees and Greeks—the former because they based all doctrine on a strict reading of Torah, which makes no mention of a resurrection, the latter because nothing could be more offensive than a soul returning to the very same body from which it had finally escaped—is similarly emphasized.[27] Particularly in the Gospel of John—often described as the most "spiritual" Gospel or the one with the "highest Christology"[28]—the first and most lasting of Christian heresies, Gnosticism, is anticipated and challenged.[29]

Gnosticism, loosely construed, names the bewildering variety of alternate interpretations of Jesus's identity, running counter to the orthodox understanding developed over time and definitively expressed in the Nicene Creed, that Jesus Christ is true God and true man. Neither Gnosticism nor orthodoxy were monolithic. Not only are there many Gnostic accounts of spirit's descent into the ugliness of matter, but lumpers and splitters argue whether to call certain groups—such as the Marcionites—Gnostics. Nor can anyone familiar with the fights within early Christianity claim that orthodoxy was a self-consistent, singular entity. For much of the first millennium, however, "orthodox" ("right worship") and "catholic" ("according to the whole") were nearly synonymous, since heresy ("to choose") was to select only a part of Christian teaching, which inevitably led one to worship God poorly.[30]

For many in the first centuries after Christ, Gnostic theology and practice was very attractive, as it offered a certain superiority, often through serial initiation rites, to "spiritual" or "pneumatic" souls in contrast to lesser, "psychic" folk.[31] As a group, they were called Gnostics because they generally stressed the importance of specially imparted knowledge, or *gnosis,* unavailable to the merely "psychic," which permitted the "pneumatic" access to a higher, spiritual realm. For Gnostics, the notion that God would sully himself with gross flesh was laughable, since the airy, spiritual reality was blessedly free of the limitations of solid matter.[32] In response to what they regarded as the sheer, offensive implausibility of the story of Jesus told in the Gospels, the Gnostics erected "checkpoints" to assure that spirit remained separate from and unsullied by matter,[33] or they denied the bodily nature of the historical Jesus, rendering him an apparition.[34] A modified Gnosticism lives on in medicine, influenced by René Descartes's fateful split of mind from body and reinforced by the technological power to alter, augment, and reshape the body as medicine—and its consumers—wish.

In contrast to the Gnostic ideal, John's Jesus, while consistently serene and in control, is repeatedly shown to be material. In the prologue to the fourth Gospel, we read: "The Word became flesh and dwelt among us" (John 1:14). *Dwelt* here is translated from a form of the Greek verb *skenoo,* which literally means to pitch or inhabit a tent. The eternal Word's encampment is moveable, an earthy dwelling. John's Jesus makes a whip of cords (2:15), asks for a drink of water (4:7), spits on the ground (9:6), weeps (11:35), and permits his feet to be anointed (12:3). John 13 includes a detailed description of Jesus washing the apostles' feet, and John's passion account includes scourging (19:1), crucifixion (19:18), the piercing of Jesus's body with a spear (19:34), and burial (19:42). John stops his narrative to emphasize the treatment of Jesus's crucified, dead body, citing two scripture verses (Exod. 12:46, et al.; Zech. 12:10) to "explain" why Jesus was pierced but did not have his legs broken, which was a common practice used to hasten the victim's death through suffocation (19:36).

Whatever else the flowing of blood and water from the side of Jesus may mean, it is a very messy, very embodied event, and anyone who has ever attended a delivery knows at what other, more common, time blood and water flow from a body. The death of Jesus is a birth, restoring creation to its proper relationship with God through Jesus's human body. But John is not finished with the body with Jesus's death. He goes on to cite the corporeality of Jesus's post-resurrection, glorified body, such that Thomas can place his hands in Jesus's wounds (20:27), while Jesus himself can cook and eat fish with his friends (21:9–13). Even after his death, Jesus's body is the sign and source of relationship.

Surprisingly, John's Gospel leaves out a central scene of the three Synoptic Gospels: the so-called words of institution, where Jesus takes, blesses, and shares bread and wine, calling them his body and blood. Instead, John places the "Bread of Life Discourse" (chap. 6) in the account of Jesus's public ministry. There, Jesus says:

> Truly, truly I say to you, unless you eat the flesh of the Son of man and drink his blood, you have no life in you; he who eats my flesh and drinks my blood has eternal life, and I will raise him up at the last day. For my flesh is food indeed, and my blood is drink indeed. He who eats my flesh and drinks my blood abides in me, and I in him. (John 6:53–56)

Theologized through various Christian traditions, these words have lost most of their power to shock. John, however, details the disturbed reaction of those who heard Jesus's words. It horrified those Jews faithful to God's commands against ritual uncleanness, and it explains how later Roman pagans would accuse Christians of cannibalism. It should disturb us, too, at least enough to awaken us from our Gnostic slumbers.

Narrating the Body after the Apostles

In the early patristic period, well after the texts forming the New Testament had been written and circulated among local Christian communities, the foremost defender of orthodoxy against Gnosticism was Irenaeus of Lyons, born in Asia Minor around 130 CE and martyred in France early in the third century.[35] One of Irenaeus's favorite themes was recapitulation (in Greek, *anakephalaiosis,* which, like our Latin-derived English word, means "return to the head"). Paul is the first Christian writer to use this word, when he tells the Ephesians that God has planned from the beginning to gather all things in Christ (Eph. 1:9–10). For Paul, Christ is the "head" of creation. Taking Paul's cue, Irenaeus spins tropes on this theme: through Christ all things were made, and through Christ all creation is restored; Jesus is the second Adam, repairing the damage done by the first; the history of salvation told in the Old Testament is re-imaged and brought to fullness in the New. The key to this recapitulation and restoration is Incarnation, the Word of God taking flesh in a fully human body. Irenaeus summarizes his central theme succinctly: "In his immeasurable love, He became what we are in order to make us what He is."[36]

For Irenaeus, the history of the universe turns on an embodied human life: Jesus Christ, born of a woman, who lived among the poor, who willingly bore humanity's sins and suffered in the flesh, and who is raised in a glorified body, bringing us to eternal life by subjecting all creation to him.

To those who doubt the goodness of the body, Irenaeus responds that the body is doubly good: first because God made it so in creation, and second because, even after the body's corruption through human sinfulness, all is restored through the Incarnation.[37] Humanity is so transformed by God made man that, in Irenaeus's most famous phrase, "the glory of God is the human, fully alive!" *(Gloria Dei, vivens homo!)*.

We would have preferred that the theological discussion, which we have immensely simplified for our purposes, ended here. If it had, this book might be unnecessary. Gnosticism, however, was and is the perennial heresy —not from some secret, lingering conspiracy within or beyond the church to denigrate the body, but rather because subordinating body to spirit or mind is so powerfully attractive. If this claim seems strange, we invite you to observe the mixed blessings of online chat rooms, in which physicality is electronically obliterated, flesh is disguised, for good or ill, through pseudonyms and avatars, and harsh words one would never speak face to face flow like poison from the keyboard. The Internet is, like all technology—indeed, like all powers—a wonderfully mixed thing, full of gifts and traps, spanning immense chasms in some places while burning well-traveled bridges elsewhere.[38] We could use the warning Harry Potter received from Albus Dumbledore, who found the boy staring for days into the Mirror of Erised: "It does not do to dwell on dreams and forget to live, remember that."[39]

The body remains suspect today, even among so-called orthodox Christians.[40] As Christianity moved from a small Jewish group to a large, increasingly Gentile movement eventually encompassing an empire, much of the gospel's sharp edges dulled against other habits of thought. In particular, the Stoic emphasis on the male ideal of self-control, a function of mind, of the passions forever springing from the body overwhelmed the more integrated Jewish ethic. The consequences for embodied relationships were massive, as Catherine Wallace summarizes:

> Christianity comes under massive pressure to assimilate and thereby mute its traditional norms of compassionate wholeheartedness and radical egalitarianism. . . . As Peter Brown documents in *The Body and Society: Sexual Renunciation in Early Christianity,* Christian sexual asceticism and sexual renunciation complemented the *severitas* of the virtuous Roman man into a universal principle of holiness based upon denial of the body.[41]

Some of Irenaeus's near-contemporary orthodox admirers, such as Tertullian, turned against him later. With the establishment of Christianity in the Roman Empire and the advent of forceful threats against heretics, Gnosticism covered itself in orthodox language. In reciting the creed, Christians could mouth phrases like "resurrection of the body," yet still look forward to a time when the soul would shuck off the flesh like a useless, withered husk.[42] Bodies might be honored with water and oil at baptism or fed with the Eucharist, yet still be thought inferior to the alleged perfection of spirit. Like us, those living in a suddenly "Christian" empire found it far easier to accommodate the gospel to their own assumptions and desires than to undergo the always difficult, sometimes painful transformation discipleship entails. In time, some Gnostic tendencies found their way into the Christian mainstream. By the Middle Ages, Christians like Abbot Joachim of Fiore could propose that the present Age of the Incarnation would soon pass into a far more advanced age of "pure spirit." From this notion of spiritual progress, propagated through the Renaissance and the Enlightenment, spring a dizzying array of modern challenges to the orthodox emphasis on Incarnation: the dualism of René Descartes, the Kantian preference for pure reason over traditional practice, the appeal of Romantic excess, and Hegel's historical deification of *Geist,* or spirit. Hegel's intellectual heir Karl Marx, while no friend of Christianity, called for a renewed emphasis on the material. But Marx is, practically speaking, dead as an intellectual force in the world, and Gnosticism appears to have won the day, as "spiritualized," albeit profoundly secular, theories of progress abound, whether in neoconservative free-market ideologies of unlimited economic growth, liberal projects of democratic expansion, or medicine's technological promise of a posthuman future free from the limitations of a failing body.

As we shall see in chapter 7, contemporary medical Gnosticism seemingly idolizes the body, but primarily as an expression of the mind's (or the will's) quest for perfection or permanence. The body is altered almost at whim, reinforcing its role as the malleable—and someday, perhaps, fully replaceable—envelope for something far more real and pure. Some reshape the body to fit a desired image, while others seek endless fixes to keep themselves alive. Even the resistance among some Christians to withdraw futile mechanical support from a dying relative can be a form of Gnosticism, valuing the ability to control and manipulate the body over the mysterious gift of an embodied life—a gift that was never actually ours to keep.

The church need look no further than itself if it seeks someone to blame for all this. Not only did so-called orthodox Christianity retain, through Platonism and other sources, a higher opinion of spirit than body, but the established churches, when openly challenged on "approved interpretations" of these and other points, reacted violently, suppressing and killing theological opponents rather than witnessing the fullness of the Christian life as they understood it. Nonetheless, it is from this sorry history that we must recover the orthodox understanding of the body, created good, fallen through our sinfulness, and restored by Christ. As we shall see, the first and most important place for us to recover such an understanding is in the same flawed entity to which we are called by God: namely, the church.

The Gathered Body

Paul, as we noted above, used the body as a metaphor for the people God gathered as the church (Rom. 12; 1 Cor. 12). As we noted before, the famous passage in 1 Corinthians is part of a much longer treatment of the body, encompassing chapters 11–15. For our purposes—and, we think, for Paul's—it is most significant that this discourse on the body begins with worship.

In chapter 11, Paul takes the Corinthians to task for permitting divisions and factions (1 Cor. 11:17ff.). Specifically, Paul is furious that in eating what should be the Lord's Supper, some are well fed while others go hungry. Paul recounts the "words of institution" by which Jesus commanded the disciples to share the Eucharist ("the body" and "the blood") in his memory, stressing "For as often as you eat this bread and drink this cup, you proclaim the Lord's death until he comes" (11:26). He continues:

> Whoever, therefore, eats the bread or drinks the cup of the Lord in an unworthy manner will be guilty of profaning the body and blood of the Lord. Let a man examine himself, and so eat of the bread and drink of the cup. For any one who eats and drinks without discerning the body eats and drinks judgment upon himself. . . . So then, my brethren, when you come together to eat, wait for one another. (11:27–29, 33)

For Paul, then, proper worship of God requires "discerning the body," an understanding and response to the bodily needs of those with whom one worships. The neediness of one's fellow creatures is not an issue separate from the worship of God. There is no "individual self" in Christian worship, as all are gathered into one body by the very act of sharing Christ's body and blood.

Moderns are at a distinct disadvantage here, since we inherit two hundred years or so of intellectual baggage in that troubling metaphysical notion the "individual self."[43] Being a psychologically informed, post-Enlightenment people, we imagine the existence of the self to be self-evident, but "it ain't necessarily so." As Bruce Malina notes, "The first-century Mediterranean person did not share or comprehend our idea of an 'individual' at all . . . (but) would perceive himself as a distinctive whole *set in relation* to other such wholes and *set within* a given social and natural background."[44]

What distinguished the early Christians from their non-Christian contemporaries, however, was an emphasis on communal worship and communal moral practice. Wayne Meeks explains:

> Even those practices which are urged upon individuals in the privacy of their homes . . . are extensions of the community's practice—indeed they are means of reminding individuals even when they are alone that they are not merely devotees of the Christians' God, they are members of Christ's body, the people of God. That is how the Christian movement differed most visibly from the other cults that fit more easily into the normal expectations of "religion" in the Roman world. The Christians' practices were not confined to sacred occasions and sacred locations—shrines, sacrifices, processions—but were integral to the formation of communities with a distinctive self-awareness.[45]

Liturgy (from the Greek *leitourgia,* or "people's work," in contrast to the private *ourgia,* from which we derive the word "orgy") is, in Alexander Schmemann's words, "an action by which a group of people become something corporately which they had not been as a mere collection of individuals—a whole greater than the sum of its parts."[46]

As with the physical body, the gathered body—as well as any ability to discern that body—comes to us a gift from God. We once heard a visiting priest speak to a parish about the importance of good liturgy. He stressed the need for prayerful preparation but reminded his listeners that God alone is source of the liturgy and everything in it. "Christians often claim the role of host at liturgy, but they have to remember, they're never the host. Jesus is the host. If you have any doubts about that, look around you next Sunday and remember that, were you the host, half these people wouldn't have been invited."

One can learn a great deal about the gathered community by watching who comes forward to be fed. A woman with cerebral palsy places the Eucharist in the hands of a man using a walker. Behind him, another waits with his working dog, trained to recognize his human companion's "spells." Farther back, the white adoptive parents of two Korean boys join the queue. For churches that embody the gospel, there's nothing new about this. Christians' Sunday gatherings merely continue the gathering God began with the people of Israel. Gerhard Lohfink reminds us:

> The one who gathers the people is always God. It is never said that Israel will gather itself. In most cases the background image is that of the shepherd who gathers the flock and leads it home. . . . Just as the liberation from the house of slavery in Egypt was the work of God, so is the bringing back of the people from exile God's work, and God's alone.[47]

Thus, the gathering for liturgy is a reenactment of Exodus. An Orthodox priest once gave us another way of seeing this: "Every Sunday is a little Pascha [Easter]." The body is not only called together, it is called *out*, out of the alienated ways of the world. That's what the Greek word for church, *ek-klesia,* means: to be called out. Lohfink adds:

> In Greek the *ekklesia* is the assembly of the people, the coming together of all those with citizen rights in a given city. When the community in Jerusalem adopted this term of civil law from the life of the *polis,* the city-state, for themselves they asserted an extraordinary claim. Thus they indicated that they did not see themselves as a group of like-minded friends and also not as a group of people who had joined together because of particular interests; they were a gathering created by God, one that was "public" and had an interest in all things.[48]

The Body Sent Forth

Christians claim that, through God's gathering them together in liturgy, they encounter the way all things really are, the way God has made them, redeemed by Jesus, whose life we share in the form of gathering, praising, eating, and drinking. We are meant to see in liturgy the way God desires us to live our entire lives, not just the "religious parts." Liturgy, in other words, schools us in the proper way to work or make love, to raise children or respond to social injustice, to argue or visit the doctor. Most of us arrive "at church" rather like the aging community in *Babette's Feast,* perhaps not consciously refusing to taste and see the goodness of the Lord, but acting as if we've come together for a comforting, if rather colorless, ritual of duty, a memorial for something no longer real. Rarely, we are joined by someone like General Lowenhielm, who knows the food and wine we share for what it is and is astonished at our nonchalance.[49]

Here, the old proverb works: "You are what you eat."[50] As Paul's language to the Corinthians stresses, there is a reality joining the body and blood of Christ in the meal and the body of Christ we become. And we become this body, not to escape the prison of the earthly body, not to find some individual bliss, and certainly not to escape the world God made. Through God's grace we become Christ's body, in Alexander Schmemann's phrase, "for the life of the world."

What the Orthodox call "Divine Liturgy," Roman Catholics call "Mass," from the Latin phrase concluding the liturgy: *Ite missa est*—"It is dismissal," or "You are sent." For many Christians today, that "sending forth" is something like a reentry into the "real world," leaving behind the comforting poetry of Christian worship and returning to "the way things really are." While we may be back in a week for another helping of sentiment, except for an occasional mealtime prayer done mostly to edify our children, we live Sunday afternoon through Saturday night as the world demands. Religion, as "pie in the sky," quickly loses out to the earthly realities of making a living, the dismal science and politics, "the art of the possible." Most presume that Christians who wish to make the world a better place will do well to spend less time in church than in schools of social work, law, medicine, or public health. That "making the world a better place" may not be what Christians are necessarily about, especially if "better" is defined by the powers of this world, is examined by Stanley Hauerwas as he describes an introductory Christian ethics course he teaches in which the context for understanding ethics is always Christian worship:

> Students might then begin to get a hint that worship is not something Christians do to make them "moral" and that worship and the holiness of life intrinsic to worship cannot be related as cause and effect. Rather, the activities of worship are not intended to effect a direct consequence exactly because they are purposefully directed to God. Because worship puts all that we do before God, we are made part of God's praise and joy. That is why the first task of the church is not to make the world more just, but to make the world the world. For the world can only know that it is the world through its contrast with the church that rightly knows the joy of worshipping the true God.[51]

As we read Hauerwas, the importance of emphasizing worship over "making the world better" is that the latter, if done entirely by our own effort and according to the world's vision, will never come close to the transformation God wishes. Whatever service we render the world in all its suffering, we do so first and always because it is a form of worship. This may come as a surprise to Christians working in medicine—or anywhere else for that matter—who imagined they were pursuing a career or doing whatever it took to feed and clothe themselves or the family. Such service is neither optional nor the price we pay to get God to love us and the world, but rather the embodied continuation of the proper worship of God we first learn in liturgy. For many, the notion that God may transform the world through lives of Christian discipleship learned and rooted in liturgy is bizarre—perhaps as bizarre as the notion that a pinch of yeast can leaven three measures of flour (Matt. 13:33; Luke 13:20–21), an enormous amount, sufficient to feed a hundred people.

We are not arguing that Christians shouldn't learn as much as necessary about law, medicine, farming, or water purification, but rather that Christians should first learn what end such powers should serve. The proper place to do so is in the community gathered to worship God. Left to their own devices, the powers will demand we follow ends other than the service of God and God's creation, and the powers will expect us to consider such "ways of the world" as normal. In this way, the powers keep us from imagining that things could be anything other than the way they already are—or are becoming through the "glorious march of progress," a promise held out to us like a carrot before a donkey, a promise we never quite reach as long as the driver needs us to pull the cart.

Here at last, we may begin to see what all this liturgical theology has to do with medicine. We noted in the previous chapter that one of the gods of this world, absent Jesus, is death, a fetish we simultaneously fear and worship in many of our strange activities. Medicine is but one power among many used by humanity to impose its will (and thus its anxieties, fears, and fetishes) upon the world. While the powers are delighted to welcome us into their projects through persuasive cooption, they will use coercion when required. When creation, including our bodies, ceases to be understood as God's good gift to be used for God's glory, there are inevitably parts of creation we encounter that must be altered or eliminated by any means necessary. One of the disorders of medicine we will soon explore is how medicine, like all powers, sometimes achieves desirable ends through coercion or violence, and calls such behavior, however regrettable, good. Another is the way in which medicine often demands we act as autonomous selves, separate agents seeking our own, individual good as if health were a treasure to be hoarded rather than a gift to be celebrated in community. Aidan Kavanaugh, after reflecting on the church's lamentable history of abandoning its early commitments against unnecessary possession and against violence in general, speculates what full attention to right worship ("orthodoxia") might reveal to modern Christians:

> That secular societies and attitudes attend far more to violence and the amassing of riches in no way renders abnormal orthodoxy's traditional insistence on nonviolence and evangelical poverty for the baptized. Disciples of Jesus Christ have every right, given the historical record of secular society's demonstrable march of folly, to regard the regularization of violence and the lust for wealth as fatal abnormalities which go against the grain of reality itself. Orthodoxia has every reason to regard a child dead of war or starved by poverty as anything but normal. It also has every right to expect this world will not be able to abolish such horrors if left to its own resources, and that such a world will not accept gladly the resources of God's grace in the effort. The orthodox are justified on the evidence to regard the world's rejection of such help as the greatest abnormality of all.[52]

That medicine as power will reject the body of Christ's help is just as much to be expected. But, welcome or not, we are compelled to act through the saving grace of God. How we act is learned first in liturgy, changing us into Christ's body in the world, so we can act properly within the community even as we are dismissed from the physical gathering place. One of the most important acts of the liturgically gathered and dispersed community is to live out what it has learned (i.e., what "normal" really looks like) and, through its way of living more than through its words, to show that the world is not normal, that the world's ways of doing things are seriously out of touch with deepest reality.

The "way of living" mentioned here is perhaps best illustrated in a scene in John's Gospel, when Jesus and the twelve are gathered "before the feast of the Passover" (John 13:1–20). Jesus rises from the meal (the setting is absolutely crucial), ties a towel around his waist, and washes the disciples' feet. Peter—whose inability to get the point the first time around should be a sign of hope for all of us—says he won't let Jesus wash his feet, acquiescing only after Jesus warns him, "If I do not wash you, you have no part in me" (John 13:8b). This passage might remain a nice image of baptism except for what follows:

> When he had washed their feet, and taken his garments, and resumed his place, he said to them, "Do you know what I have done to you? You call me Teacher and Lord; and you are right, for so I am. If I then, your Lord and Teacher, have washed your feet, you also ought to wash one another's feet. For I have given you an example, that you should do as I have done to you. Truly, truly, I say to you, a servant is not greater than his master; nor is he who is sent greater than he who sent him. If you know these things, blessed are you if you do them. . . . Truly, truly, I say to you, he who receives any one whom I send receives me; and he who receives me receives him who sent me." (John 13:12–17, 20)

The model Jesus provides is service, and thoroughly embodied service at that. One of us participated in a field clinic in a Honduran mountain village, a one-day visit of North American doctors that the locals had learned of only a week before, and which attracted patients from a wide area. Some set out on foot from their homes hours before sunrise in order to arrive before the clinic closed in the afternoon. How they planned to return home before nightfall, I never knew. One woman made the journey to have her swollen, aching feet cared for, and we were pleased one of our physicians had some training in podiatry. I translated in halting Spanish while the doctor carefully examined, washed, and treated the woman's feet as if this were the greatest privilege a physician could enjoy. The Honduran woman beamed, delighted as much with the attention as the opportunity to sit down at last, and she began inquiring about our families, our homes, our reasons for coming to Honduras. For a moment, humble service crossed chasms of culture, language, education, and class, and I witnessed something very much like communion.

Anyone who has washed another's dirty, sweaty, calloused feet needs no reminder of what sensory assaults are involved in the process. Still more humbling, however, is permitting another to wash your own feet. Putting together Jesus's admonition here with Matthew 25, we begin to grasp how service to one another in the body of Christ is service to Jesus—indeed, it is properly understood as worship. This service, then, is near the heart of what we should experience in liturgy, and if this picture doesn't quite fit with your own experience of liturgy, perhaps you and your pastor need to talk.

The experience we are describing here can be seen as fourfold, although we caution readers from inferring that this fully describes the experience of Eucharistic liturgy or implies a necessary sequence. First, having been gathered by God to worship, we *discern* the gathered body. We *discern* ourselves as sinners crying out, "Lord, I am unworthy to receive you, but say the word and I shall be healed." We *discern* the immense neediness of each person present, the hungers—literal and metaphorical—and suffering in each life, none of which we may have noticed had we not been physically gathered in one place. We see how each one of us is the embodied gift of God, created good but fallen and in need of redemption.

Second, we *eat* the body, given to us as God's astounding gift. While various denominations debate whether the blessed bread and wine commemorate, signify, or are the actual body of Christ, all understand this action as gratuitous, a sign of God's undying love. Like the villagers of Berlevaag, our nonchalance belies the preciousness of what we eat.

Third, we *become* the body, having been transformed by Christ into a new people, God's people. As Paul's extended metaphor in 1 Corinthians 12 shows, we each have different, important roles within the body, but we are truly joined together, so that the talents and needs of one involve all the others.

Fourth, we *serve* the body, as Jesus himself commissioned us to do. Having discerned our common neediness, having eaten the gift of God in the Eucharist, and having become an organic body of united lives, how could we do otherwise? Sharing each other's burdens, washing each other's feet, binding each other's wounds is a way of life learned in liturgy, not in medical school.

Once again, many readers may be wondering what this dynamic and transformative description of liturgy has to do with their own, perhaps lifeless experience of Sunday worship. That disconnect, we suspect, is a significant reason for the acquiescence of Christians, who should know and do better, to medicine and the other powers. That many churches are now experimenting with or wholeheartedly adopting user-friendly, contemporary "worship experiences," complete with multimedia spectacles and espresso bars suggests how far we have strayed from the Eucharistic experience that transformed the lives of early Christians. If our worship has no substance, we hope people still come for the style. Once again, Hauerwas pointedly observes:

> The Eucharist is usually not considered an essential aspect of Christian worship by those concerned with church growth. Evangelism means getting people to church, because unless we go to church, it is assumed, our lives are without moral compass. Thus the assumption that lack of attendance at church and our society's "moral decay" go hand in hand. What such people fail to see is that such decay begins with the assumption that worship is about "my" finding meaning for my life rather than the glorification of God. Such evangelism is but another name for narcissism. Christian worship requires that our bodies submit to training otherwise unavailable so that we can become capable of discerning those who use the name of Jesus to tempt us to worship foreign gods. Without the Eucharist we lose the resource to discover how those gods rule our lives.[53]

While we trust the Holy Spirit's power to transform lives even in non-eucharistic settings, there is, we think, a better way—a Christian reclaiming of the body. If this "reclamation" is merely a change in intellectual categories, no one will be transformed. Instead, we must reclaim not only the image of the body, but the communal, embodied practices that serve and sustain it. How Christians understand the body—physical and gathered—is not "theory" in distinction to some set of "practices" to which we now turn. Rather, the practices of Christian community are further ways of embodying what we already do in the liturgies of Word and Eucharist. What those practices have to say about the gifts of the body is our next subject.

4

The Shape of What's Given

■ In T. S. Eliot's poem "The Journey of the Magi," the speaker recalls, after many years, his difficult passage to pay homage to a newborn king. In the end, he wonders if he traveled so far to witness a birth or a death. He knows he saw a baby, of course, but this birth, he says, felt like death, his own death. Upon returning to his old kingdom, he finds himself unhappily transformed, estranged from a people "clutching their gods," and wishing for another death.[1] Eliot's unhappy wise man lives in a disrupted landscape, alien to a country he was born to command.[2] He no longer fits, too distorted by his encounter with the newborn king to complete the cultural puzzle.

Encounters with God do that. It is, after all, "a fearful thing to fall into the hands of the living God" (Heb. 10:31). Falling into God's hands disrupts not just our thinking, but the entirety of our lives, including our bodies. To the extent our encounters with God awaken us to the complex and subtle ways our bodies are members—of God and each other—we recognize ourselves as aliens among a people who worship many strange powers and gods: self, death, and medicine, to name three. Awakened, we at last see these idols for what they are, not as "the old dispensation" tells us to see them. Yet, apart from our membership in a sustaining community, any real dissonance with the old dispensation cannot last. Christians who hope to live as members of Christ's body need more than ideas, they need *practices*—repeated communal actions—important less for what they get us than for what sort of people we become by doing them.[3] In Christian tradition, such actions have often been called *sacraments:* outward signs of an inward grace, to be sure, but also bodily gestures, good in themselves because God makes them so, done in community, and learned from a long line of sisters and brothers in faith who preceded us.

We've already suggested how eucharistic practice reshapes a Christian understanding of relationship and connectedness, but before a Christian is brought to the table, she or he enters the community through baptism. Baptism, according to Saint Paul, is the Christian's sacramental death to the life of the old dispensation. The neophyte Christian is told to live at odds with the world's ways, and that oddness is reinforced with every Eucharist.[4] Like Eliot's wise man, the Christian should find even birth and death—as well as the power of medicine claiming control over them—marked by baptismal and eucharistic encounters with the incarnate God. Sadly, many Christians have permitted the sacraments to become acculturated formal rites without cost or demand.[5] One of us had a very old-school history professor who, lamenting the modern aversion to sustained intellectual work, claimed that universities were the only place people spend huge sums of money and expect nothing in return. If anything, the domestication of baptism is worse. Many Christians drown in the waters of baptism, hoping that nothing in their lives will have to change.

Early Christians understood baptism as a liminal experience, a movement from one world to another by drowning the old body and its sin-scarred life and taking on the new. The Gospels link baptism and death in Jesus's words (Mark 10:38; Luke 12:50), and Paul makes this linkage (and the expected transformation) explicit:

> How can we who died to sin still live in it? Do you not know that all of us who have been baptized into Christ Jesus were baptized into his death? We were buried therefore with him by baptism into death, so that as Christ was raised from the dead by the glory of the Father, we too might walk in newness of life. (Rom. 6:2–4)

In his Letter to the Colossians, Paul extends his argument, showing how our baptism into Christ's death challenges the powers attempting to rule our lives:

> You were buried with him in baptism, in which you were also raised with him through faith in the working of God, who raised him from the dead. And you, who were dead in trespasses and the uncircumcision of your flesh, God made alive together with him, having forgiven us all our trespasses, having cancelled the bond which stood against us with its legal demands; this he set aside, nailing it to the cross. He disarmed the principalities and powers and made a public example of them, triumphing over them in him. (Col. 2:12–15)

Christians are baptized into Christ's death by being baptized into his body (1 Cor. 12:12–13), in which all the baptized are bodily united (Eph.

4:4–6, Gal. 3:27–29). A hallmark of this embodiment into new life is the giving up of old ways (1 Cor. 6:9–11; Rom. 6:10–14; 2 Cor. 5:16–6:2; and Eph. 4:17–5:20) in order to worship God and love and serve one another (1 Cor. 12:27–13:13; Rom. 15:1–6).

By being joined through baptism to Jesus's death, burial, and resurrection, we are freed from death's bondage: "Death is swallowed up in victory" (1 Cor. 15:54; cf. Isa. 25:8; Hos. 13:14). In chapter 2, we described how the powers gain control over us by portraying death as a god to be appeased. Because death challenges our claims of control, we make it a fetish, clutching talismans in pill bottles and seeking the help of shamans (who sign their names with an "M.D.") to keep the angry god at bay. Even for Christians, a sting lingers in the prospect of our own deaths, but baptism into Christ's death offers an alternative to death-worship. We can live our lives trusting that God, through the gift that is the life, death, and resurrection of Jesus, has freed us from this idolatry.

One reason Christians can live this way is that being joined to Christ grants our lives a peculiar shape. Physical birth and death still mark discernible passages, though far less important than our baptismal passage into Christ's body and the hope of our own bodily resurrection. Through Christian practices, we learn that life has previously unimagined contours, rather like the visitor from "Flatland" in Edwin Abbott's nineteenth-century mathematical fantasy, who is astonished to find that, for those of us in "Spaceland," things have *three* dimensions.[6] To the culture surrounding us, this new shape will seem an unnecessary and alienating distortion, but this is the shape God grants our bodies and lives through the grace of baptism. In a reshaped life no longer dominated by skirmishes and bargains with death, we are liberated to receive God's gifts with confidence and gratitude.[7] Rather than ignoring or attempting to control death, we learn to see death rightly: not as a god, nor even as "the next stage of life," but rather as a mysterious passage to be undergone now as members of the body of Christ.

None of this happens by magic; its realization is part of the work of discipleship. Orthodox theologian Vigen Guroian concurs that "baptism is the symbolic beginning of the Christian's remembrance of death and a point of reference for it throughout the rest of life,"[8] but he warns that a life freed from the domination of death isn't an automatic consequence of baptism. Christians must struggle to remember the mystery into which they are plunged:

> Christians dare not fail to practice the pedagogy of death. Forgetfulness of the dying and crucified Son of God leads to forgetfulness of the Father's infinite and all-forgiving love for his creatures. Forgetfulness of the dead whom we have loved is bound to grow into forgetfulness of the dying among us. And

forgetfulness of the dead and the dying is a sure step toward forgetfulness of Christ and eternal life.[9]

One vision of what such forgetfulness can lead to is John Cheever's short story "The Death of Justina."[10] An advertising writer we know only as "Moses" learns while at work that his wife's elderly cousin, Justina, has unexpectedly died on their living room sofa after a lunch party. Moses's boss shows no sympathy, demanding he write a commercial script before attending to his wife and the late Justina. The commercial is for "Elixircol," a medicine peddled on television by an actress "who was neither young nor beautiful but who had the appearance of ready abandon and who was anyhow the mistress of one of the sponsor's uncles."[11]

Worse still, Moses finds he can't bury poor cousin Justina, much less have her pronounced dead. A zoning regulation, passed hurriedly some years before to keep a funeral parlor from opening in the neighborhood, has made it illegal for anyone to die in his subdivision. While pleading his case to the mayor, he's told the townsfolk find the thought of death depressing: "People don't like to live in a neighborhood where this sort of thing goes on all the time."[12] When the mayor finally issues a death certificate on the condition that Moses will "keep it a secret," Justina is buried at last. But as Moses reflects on the rainy funeral afternoon:

> Justina's life had been exemplary, but by ending it she seemed to have disgraced us all. The priest was a friend and a cheerful sight, but the undertaker and his helpers, hiding behind their limousines, were not; and aren't they at the root of most of our troubles, with the claim that death is a violet-flavored kiss? *How can a people who do not mean to understand death hope to understand love, and who will sound the alarm?*[13]

Who indeed? The witness of Christian discipleship should be the "alarm" Moses looks for, and our action or inaction, far more than our words or beliefs, shows the world which god we finally worship. Powers like medicine are strong, and we are tempted to embrace them uncritically or resist them individually. Christians are called in baptism to understand death in the light of Christ, and to share with one another that understanding, in Guroian's terms, as a "point of reference." We do that—and thereby continually reshape our lives—through practices that make us more alien to the world around us.

Practices Mark People

Learned and judged through tradition, practices are inherently social, even when carried on in solitude. Communal practices give identity and purpose to a group, uniting those who observe the practice and differentiating them from those who do not. Before religious dietary practices faded into a homogeneous American consumer culture in the late twentieth century, one could know the scent of frying bacon didn't come from an observant Jewish household, or from a Catholic one if it happened to be a Friday. From its inception, the Christian church has stressed certain practices that distinguish its community from others. Written in the second or third century, the anonymous *Epistle to Diognetus* observes of Christians:

> They live in their own countries, but only as aliens; they participate in everything as citizens, and endure everything as foreigners. Every foreign country is their fatherland, and every fatherland is foreign. They marry like everyone else, and have children, but they do not expose their offspring. They share their food but not their wives.[14]

Among the practices that Christians adopted and passed on were those that reflected the particular emphases they placed upon the body, namely (as we explored in the previous chapter): that (1) the body is God's good gift; (2) the body has been rendered imperfect because of sin; and (3) while this imperfection remains in all embodied life, Christians are gathered together in Christ's body to praise God and serve one another. Christians recognize that bodies inevitably fall ill and die. One response to such inevitability is to accuse God of making the world badly, a variation on Ivan Karamazov's complaint that a good God would not allow children to suffer. The modern response to such questions has been the development of a philosophical problem called "theodicy" (from the Greek for "God's justice"), a parade of theories to help God fit into our ideas of how things ought to be. Premodern Christians rarely bothered with such head games and asked instead, "How do we respond to suffering, sickness, and death, given what we know of God as revealed in the person of Jesus?"[15]

Such responses then and now should always reflect our peculiarly Christian understanding of the body, as gift and gathering. In the rest of this chapter, we will consider three Christian practices that embody this understanding and enable us to use medicine's power rightly. The first will be the practice of hospitality, the second the liturgical rite of anointing the sick, and finally, we will consider the practice—some would say the virtue—of patience.

Hospitality Is More Than Entertaining

The New Testament enjoins care of the sick upon all who would claim to follow Jesus. This is most famously the case in Matthew 25, but also in the many stories of healing mentioned above in chapter 1. Hospitality, not just to the ill, but to anyone in need, is a preeminent mark of the early church. The Letter to the Hebrews is quite explicit:

> Let brotherly love continue. Do not neglect to show hospitality to strangers, for thereby some have entertained angels unawares. Remember those who are in prison, as though in prison with them; and those who are ill-treated, since you also are in the body. (Heb. 13:1–3)[16]

Those who followed the apostolic generation took such enjoinders very seriously, and a wide range of practices of hospitality became associated with the Christian minority in the empire. While some Roman writers, such as Lucian, ridiculed the Christian example, others were drawn toward the practice, as Rowan Greer notes in an essay on early Christian hospitality:

> The example of Christian community life was probably more persuasive to unbelievers than the proclamation of the Christian message. It is impossible to resist the conclusion that at one level the Church grew rapidly more because its common life acted as a magnet attracting people than because the Christians were effective in their public preaching.[17]

Furthermore, hospitality to the sick was essential to the health of the body of Christ, as Gregory of Nyssa described in a fourth-century homily:

> Do you not see that in addition to persons in good health, there are other sound persons who often suffer affliction. . . . What should we do? Do we not combat illness which afflicts a bodily member? On the other hand, we turn our attention to cure a diseased member by using the health of the entire body.[18]

Over time, hospitality to the sick within the gathered body became institutionalized through various church-supported entities and was particularly associated with monastic life, as described in the Rule of St. Benedict:

> Before all things and above all things, care must be taken of the sick, so that they will be served as if they were Christ in person; for He Himself said, "I was sick and you visited me," and "What you did to the least of these ones, you did to Me."[19]

Why is this important today? Nothing trains us more to value the gift of the body than to care for it even as it suffers, fails, and ultimately dies.

The great temptation for us today is to turn the care of our bodies over to "experts." Such persons, who clearly know a great deal, typically assure us they will only provide what's best—that is, what we want. But Christians come to know "what's best" only through a shared life in Christ. Medicine knows a great deal. What it doesn't know, as an institution, is Christ. Our reaching out to others in need and our refusal to consign the sick solely to the power of medical "experts" witnesses to our faith in God's goodness, while further transforming us through the virtue of hospitality.

We are not telling Christians to stop seeing doctors. Among other things, that would put one of us out of a job and make it very difficult for the other to teach classes in bioethics. What we are saying is that Christians should never consider a doctor's care sufficient for the needs of the ill. We must be present bodily to the sick in our midst, even—and perhaps especially—those we do not know or are not related to. Why? Because it is precisely here we embody the constellation of relationships that make up the body of Christ. We care for the sick in part because they need care, but also because such care transforms us as we provide it—helping us see our own connectedness, our own vulnerability, our own utter dependence upon the gifts of God.

Of course, it's possible and even likely that by visiting the sick, by participating in their care, by providing food, rest, comfort, and medicine, we may secretly think, "There but for the grace of God go I." Nietzsche always suspected this was the real motivation behind Christian charity: magnanimous and ultimately self-serving gestures from the merely fortunate who enjoy gloating over the troubles of their betters. The Christian understanding of the gathered body, however, compels us instead to say, "There *by* the grace of God go I." Sufferer and caregiver share a body in which there are no absolute distinctions. Yes, the caregiver reaps benefits from performing "charity" but is mistaken if he or she sees these as including justification before God or a way to feel good about oneself. We offer hospitality because, in so doing, we participate in the life of Christ, building up the very body through which we live.

One of us, while on a medical mission to Central America, met Roberto, an eight-year-old boy who was severely malnourished. Roberto is developmentally delayed, and his impoverished family, living in a mountain hut, lacked many the resources necessary to care for and feed him. When he arrived at the clinic, he weighed no more than his two-year-old brother, Santos. Roberto's body hurt from hunger, from infection, from the harshness of his circumstances, and he made no polite efforts to hide his anguish. The North American medical professionals were heartbroken by his appearance, but the Honduran clinic workers and members of the Catholic and evangelical churches understood Roberto's condition as a failure of communal hospitality. "How," they asked themselves, "could we permit such a thing to happen among us?"

Their response was equally dramatic, showing nothing of the paralyzing guilt for which "compassionate" North Americans are justly famous. As the doctors rehydrated, deloused, and disinfected the boy, the real community began to plan and act for the long term. Food and clothing were collected, the family's water supply was evaluated, and neighbors were recruited to assist the family once Roberto returned home. The doctors could have done this, too, but the locals had several advantages over the visiting "experts." First, Roberto was one of their own, and they knew the larger community in all its riches and needs. Not only familiarity, but actual identification with the local community trumped our claims to expertise. The Hondurans intuited which actions were necessary, sustainable, and acceptable to the family and community as a whole. Related to this was the keen awareness that Roberto was theirs, part of a communal body that suffered as long as Roberto suffered. We would soon return to our comfortable houses and well-stocked supermarkets in the land of endless choice, but Roberto would remain with his people. Finally, the Hondurans embodied the practices of hospitality far better than any of the visiting North Americans. Perhaps we were in greater need of hospitality's transforming power, but for them, hospitality is a lifelong habit.

Subsequent medical "brigades" have paid Roberto's family a visit, looking for signs of medical progress, of which there are some. Roberto is better fed and cleaner, and he has learned to walk with assistance. To his community, though, the work is ongoing, a sustained practice of hospitality resistant to standard medical "outcome measures."

This way of living collides headlong with at least one widely held North American sentiment, namely that of "not wanting to be a burden." Even non-Christians should understand that those who hold such a sentiment are far too late. Having been carried by our mothers, raised from infancy, eaten food grown by other people, lived on land others sweated and bled over, learned from the work of countless humans with whom we have had the unacknowledged honor of sharing the planet, all of us, sick or well, are always already burdens. What we suspect people mean by not wanting to be a burden is that they wish not to lose their illusions of autonomy. It's difficult to know if our lust for autonomy and our phobia for "being a burden" are symptoms of or the root causes of the present age's lack of trust. Are we terrified of losing control because there's no one left to trust, or do we lack trust because we assume everyone (even our children) will exercise their control at our expense? Either way, the hole at the center of our lives is at once community-shaped and God-shaped. Like refugees pushed to the edge of starvation, we lunge for anything that resembles food, clawing even at our neighbor's unfinished plate, though the food we seek is something like comfort, a sense of place, a respite from the desperate sense that we are abandoned, alone in the universe without companionship.

Medicine, as practiced in North America, has an array of technological fixes to make control—or at least comfort—look possible, at least for awhile. Yet we've already noted how parents—at least those not fully indoctrinated by the culture to ignore their own experience—quickly learn the illusory nature of any alleged control. At its best, the church (and the church is rarely at its best) embodies the alternate vision, providing not so much comfort, if by comfort we mean soothing illusion or stoic resignation, but a confidence that we are always in relationship, and a quiet trust that we are never alone. Christians shaped by baptism and the practice of hospitality learn to receive everything as a gift, and simply don't have time for nonsense like "not wanting to be a burden." For the people Jesus gathers to love and serve the Lord and each other, there's too much to be done.[20]

Suffering and Anointing

Elaine Scarry entitled her powerful meditation on human suffering *The Body in Pain: The Making and Unmaking of a World*.[21] Few things call into question the goodness of the world and its Maker as do pain and suffering. Beyond the modern philosophical problems of theodicy, however, physical pain challenges our solidarity with others. For the one who suffers, notes Scarry, nothing in the world is more certain than his or her pain. But for the one who attempts to understand and empathize with the sufferer, there is nothing less certain, for pain cannot be measured, nor can it be experienced or expressed by anyone but the sufferer.[22]

Suffering shrinks the world of the sufferer, first by limiting one's ability to act purposefully in the world, but ultimately by shrinking the world to the dimensions of one's individual body: "Intense pain . . . destroys a person's self and world, a destruction experienced spatially as either a contraction of the universe down to the immediate vicinity of the body or as the body swelling to fill the entire universe."[23] Furthermore, pain destroys language. Even the hope of communicating one's pain is lost in the disintegration of self and words: "Physical pain does not simply resist language but actively destroys it, bringing about an immediate reversion to a state anterior to language, to the sounds and cries a human being makes before language is learned."[24]

Pain even calls into question the power of medicine. Medicine claims to be a scientific discipline, altering the measurable and verifiable things of the world for human good. Pain, as we have noted, is uniquely immeasurable, despite appeals to physiologic correlates of pain (such as heart rate, sweating, grimacing, etc.) and clinical pain scales, which, for all their pretense of quantification, still rely on the unquantifiable report of the one who suffers. Worse still, medical language and behavior further alienate the sufferer through jargon unfamiliar to the patient, and the objectification of illness (and often the ill themselves).[25] Taught in medical school and residency to privilege the objective, quantifiable, and isolatable over the irremediably subjective, qualitative, and integral, physicians attend to certain parts of the medical history while systematically ignoring others. Doctors do so in order to properly diagnose and treat illness, judiciously choosing among possible treatments. Along the way to this desirable end, however, the patient is objectified into a consumer of health-care resources. What is lost to medicine is the patient's *embodied experience.*[26]

When pastors and hospital chaplains abandon the language of religious connectedness for the individualistic language of medicine and psychotherapy, insisting, for example, that the suffering patient move expeditiously through the accepted "steps of dying," they intensify the alienating effects of medicine's power. Such pastoral advice reinforces the helplessness of patients, reducing their suffering to a set of largely private tasks that others, however much they try to help, can never truly share or understand. The Christian practice of hospitality points to an entirely different approach, aiming to reincorporate sufferers into the body, if not by curing—which is to say, eliminating the cause of their suffering—then at least through healing, by making their suffering a real part of the life of the body. The task for the sufferer, then, is communal rather than private. She or he gives the community something it would otherwise lack. As M. Therese Lysaught observes in considering the healing mission of Jesus, those who were healed were enjoined to carry on the message of God's saving power, an evangelizing and transformative practice "embodied in the contemporary Church in the Eucharist and in the practice of ministry to the sick."[27]

In these sacramental embodiments of Jesus's healing ministry, the sufferer is not only physically touched by the community, but assured that he or she still actively contributes to its life. Sacraments are *never only about* the "individual recipient," because all sacraments are inherently communal; the "recipient" of the sacramental grace is Christ's gathered people and ultimately the whole world.[28]

Particularly in the liturgical practice of anointing, biblically derived from the New Testament Letter of James (5:14) and found in the Roman Catholic rite of Anointing of the Sick and the Orthodox *Evchelaion,* the sick and suffering are understood to have special duties:

The sick in return offer a sign to the community: In the celebration of the sacrament they give witness to their promises at baptism to die and be buried in Christ. They tell the community that in their present suffering they are prepared to fill up in their flesh what is lacking . . . for the salvation of the world. . . . And the sick are believed to be and seen as productive members of the community, contributing to the welfare of all by associating themselves freely with Christ's passion and death.[29]

One of us recalls a particularly moving example of this in his local church. John, a longtime parishioner recently diagnosed with a brain tumor, asked to receive sacramental anointing at the liturgy his family regularly attended. After we had shared the Eucharist, the priest called the family forward. John's wife supported her ailing husband, with their son alongside, struggling to contain his emotion until he finally began crying silently, arms around his father. The priest anointed him while the entire community prayed for healing. This was powerful in itself, but when John's neurosurgeon, also a parishioner, came forward to embrace the family and to receive the blessing of the community, most of us cried, too. More importantly, we were blessed as a community that John's illness did not separate us but united us in liturgy.

Now, some years later, John is doing well after his surgery and a course of chemotherapy. Some observers might infer a causal relationship, however tenuous, between the "spiritual moment" and John's recovery. As we suggested earlier, this uncritically assumes medicine's view that illness is a problem to be eliminated so the patient and those caring for him can return to more "productive" activities.[30] "Healing" is thus defined medically and economically rather than theologically, and spiritual practice is reduced to little more than a therapeutic tool, one more weapon in the medical arsenal. Others might see the anointing as primarily an emotional experience, hardly the thing one expects in a Catholic church. Theologically, though, this was a community reclaiming one of its own, while the one who was ill gave witness to the gathered people that even illness and death do not cut us off from one another. Not despite his infirmity, but rather through and because of it, he ministered to the assembly.

Through the liturgy (understood as the "people's work") of anointing, the sick serve the community, parrying the threat illness poses to the integrity of the so-called autonomous self by providing the gathered body with an alternate vision of the world.[31] This practice and the alternate vision it embodies makes us, like Eliot's wise man, alien to the world we thought was ours to manipulate:

Christian understandings of suffering, illness and healing embodied in the rites and liturgies of common worship challenge contemporary cultural understandings. The Church's "discourses" challenge those of secular soci-

73

ety. They refuse to locate a creature's value solely in its rationality, refusing to accept the designation "enemy" for the realities of suffering and death, refusing to validate a posture that is closed to the world and fearful and ostracizing of those who are "other." Those physicians and patients formed by ecclesial practices of Christian communities will find themselves navigating the world of medicine and biomedical ethics along a different path. For what they see as "persons," "threats," "dilemmas," and even "the world," may differ significantly from their colleagues.[32]

To the extent that we serve Christ and his people through reshaped lives, *vive la différence!*

Patients and Patience

Each spring, a local garden shop puts up a large sign proclaiming, "*Impatiens* is a virtue." They're right, of course. Few flowers brighten sun-starved corners of the garden as well as this familiar annual. But the pun aims at the clichéd image of gray-haired matrons advising impetuous offspring to wait, since good things are soon to come. In our day, even the term *patience* has given way to psychologically tinted phrases like *delayed gratification.* Whether we choose to "delay gratification" or follow another bumper sticker's advice—"Don't Postpone Joy"—we understand that, sooner or later, we'll get what we want. Grandmother's nattering on about "virtue" simply doesn't cut it in a consumer society.[33]

When we are ill, most of us want to get better immediately, or at least as soon as possible. Talk about "the virtue of patience" makes sense to us only as a therapeutic technique, a bit of wisdom used in grudging acceptance of the present and hopefully temporary limitations of medicine. Future generations, who presumably will exercise complete control over every evil befalling the body, will have little use for such rough learning. For now, though, if we apply the "techniques of patience," we may appreciate our health that much more when we are, at last, rightfully restored to the top of our game. The trouble here, however, is that "techniques of patience" is as much an oxymoron as "jumbo shrimp."

Techniques, whether used in medicine, engineering, or cake baking, are instrumental procedures by which we bring about a desired outcome. They are, in short, ways of imposing our will upon objects in the world. Patience, which is rarely passive, cooperates with the way things are, with the shape of the gifts we are given. Patience is often very hard work, requiring us to labor with the grain of the universe.[34]

The National Park Service spends a great deal of time and money repairing the damage done by hikers who leave marked trails. Particularly in the canyons of the American Southwest, a shortcut between two parts of a long switchback can take years to revegetate, and the complex micro-enviroments destroyed by boot prints in fragile soil may never recover. Those hikers wishing to enjoy but not harm the canyon learn how to walk *with* the slope, along the meandering switchbacks, and not rush headlong to the river below, leaving a swath of destruction. They also recognize that particularly fragile places in the canyon are best left unvisited, since human traffic will only mar what treasures remain there. Canyon hiking is no walk in the park. Done well, though, it teaches the hiker another way of seeing the world's beauty. Patience is something like that.[35]

The practice of patience requires knowing not only when something should be done, but what particular things should or should not be done. Roberto's Honduran neighbors knew which social conditions could be changed and which were intractable. They also understood how to provide liberating care without encouraging learned helplessness.[36] Moreover, they were in a better position, both by habit and location, to accept the demands of patience regarding Roberto. We North Americans were making one of our regular two-week visits and would be returning to the States very soon. The locals had to remind us how to slow down, to look for improvements in small but real increments, and to accept that immediate results, even if they were possible, might not be desirable.

All of which is to say simply that being patient when we are ill is hard work. As Stanley Hauerwas and Charles Pinches warn, "If the first time we are called on to exercise patience is as patients, we will surely be unable, since there is no worse time to learn patience than when one is sick."[37] Illness assaults our sense of order, interrupting the seamless chain of command from mind through body to the manipulable objects of the "outside world." Christians, as we suggested earlier, should be suspicious of such distinctions, but even in a gathered body, it's hard to shake all the assumptions of a society. As in the song by the band Little Feat, we suspect we're ". . . over the hill / When your mind makes a promise that your body can't fill."[38] In order to act properly when ill, we must practice patience throughout our Christian life, which means recovering a practice close to the heart of the gathered body.

Patience is not resignation. Nor is it shouting, as one of us heard an elderly woman cry repeatedly from her bed at the far end of a hospital wing, "O Jesus, I am waiting for you to bring me breakfast," until the nurses finally learned to serve her first. Practicing patience is part of the virtue of hope and springs from our confidence that God's gracious gifts come to us not only during our life's prime, but also at its end. Through Jesus's death and resurrection, our most fearsome enemies, death and frailty, have already been overcome. Patience does not mean singing, "Always look on the bright side of life," while we die in agony.[39] Rather than biting their lips in resignation before "God's perfect plan," some of God's best friends trust God enough to lament bitterly. The Jews, elder sisters and brothers in faith, know this far better than Christians. The Jews, of course, guided by the Spirit, composed the Psalms, most of which are anything but portraits of contentment.[40] Patience requires us to properly grieve the failing body—ours and our neighbors'—while we wait in joyful hope for the coming of the Lord.

But what shape would such hope possibly take? Hauerwas and Pinches suggest three signs of Christian patience. First, it is embodied. Our bodies inevitably grow weak and die, but practicing patience requires us to love "the good things our bodies make possible without hating our bodies," confident in God's saving power, and always remembering that "we are not our own creations."[41] Second, it is communal. "To learn to live with the unavoidability of the other is to learn to be patient. Such patience comes not just from our inability to have the other do our will; more profoundly, it arises from the love that the presence of the other can and does create in us."[42] Third, it will be lived out over a lifetime, not quickly adopted as a self-help technique for the suddenly ill. The practices through which we learn patience include "worthy activities such as growing food, building shelters, spinning cloth, writing poems, playing baseball, and having children. Such activities not only take time but they create it by forcing us to take first one step and then another."[43] "Put simply," they conclude, "our ability to take the time to enjoy God's world, when we are well as well as when we are sick, depends on our recognition that it is indeed God's world."[44] That enjoyment requires a great deal of trust—trust in God and trust in the people God gathers us into, hard to come by in a world marked more by terrorism and hatred than trust.

One of us knew a woman whose later years were plagued by a series of medical setbacks involving Parkinson's disease, heart problems, and crippling back pain. She was steeped in the Catholic practices and attitudes of her generation, including the Jansenist-tinged habit of "offering up" suffering as reparation for one's sins. For all that, she had no fondness for her pain and constantly prayed for it to pass. Her eldest son, with whom relations were sometimes strained, interpreted this and other remarks as a desire on her part for something like physician-assisted suicide, a permanent technological release from pain, with only piety preventing her from acting. Most others found this dubious at best, inconsistent with the way she had lived her life in patient service as a mother and a teacher. Those who knew her best noted how, despite her suffering, she loved to tell jokes and was particularly fond of sharing them with her grandchildren. It joined her to them in a story-telling community, and if today you ask these children where they learned how to tell jokes, they'll launch into tales of their grandmother. When she died—of natural causes—the visitation, funeral mass, and subsequent family gathering were punctuated with laughter, as favorite stories and jokes were exchanged. Her grandchildren still recall her suffering and are noticeably sensitive to other people's pain, perhaps because of this familiarity, but they mostly remember their grandmother as the woman who loved jokes. That was her bequest, a gift that outlasts her earthly life. She died without hurrying things along, living until the end—and past the end—in community.

Medicine as Service and Calling

As a people who have been and are being reshaped by peculiar practices, how should Christians engage the power of medicine? In the next several chapters, we intend to explore this question in the context of particular moments in our lives, providing concrete, lived examples of Christian practice. For now, however, we will briefly consider the shape medicine itself might take if brought into proper relationship with the Creator.

Jean-Claude Larchet, an Orthodox layman and professor of philosophy, writes insightfully on this subject, and we rely on his work in what follows. Our treatment of medicine as one of the powers is similar to Larchet's concession that medicine "is generally seen as a very special way of putting charity into practice," but that it is at least as imperfect as any other human endeavor and is capable of causing as much evil as good.[45] What Christians cannot do, Larchet argues, is treat medicine as a good *independent* of God's goodness: "Christians, while they rely on physicians, see them simply as mediators. They call on them in the name of God, and it is through them, but from God, that they ask for healing."[46] Christian physicians, then, must cultivate a proper humility, understanding, in the terms we've used above, that they are called to work with the grain of the universe, patiently following the shape of what is given in God's good creation. The Christian physician may not divorce knowledge of physiologic phenomena from the person before him or her: "an ailing body is always that of a person; its condition is always connected to the soul, the psychological as well as the spiritual state of that person."[47]

Christian patients, as well, must understand that they are never *merely* a body, but—again in the terms we used above—breath and dust united in an embodied soul. "By invoking God in times of illness, a Christian makes these an occasion for the salvation of his body, but also, and more importantly, of his soul. . . . The important thing is to experience both healing and the illness in God, whatever the means of healing may be."[48] For physician and patient, then,

Every medical intervention becomes both a symbol and a calling. In turning to the sick, the physicians invite them to consider God's mercy and to turn to Him. As they heal their bodies, they invite the sick to invite healing for their souls. As they change illness to health, they encourage a conversion of their hearts. Thus, they reveal within the medical arts a symbolic meaning that transcends its primary function without ever denying it.[49]

This vision of medicine as a symbol of God's saving power isn't a major part of the modern medical curriculum, not even in religiously affiliated universities. If medicine is seen as anything more than a profession (though it has very little to profess these days beyond the gospel of consumer choice), it is construed as a service or even, on rare occasion, as a work of justice. Christians can and should embrace this, though never losing sight of the One we ultimately serve and whose justice we seek.[50] Such vigilance isn't easily sustained, which is again why God gathers us together into one body—a body that may look quite peculiar, occasionally backward, and sometimes utterly nonsensical to a watching world. The powers of the world will claim, as always, that they have a better way, and one of those ways, as we have seen, turns health into a fetish and death into a ravenous god. Once again, Stanley Hauerwas:

> The reason Christian and non-Christian find ourselves dominated by our "concern for health" is that in the absence of the church, medicine cannot help but dominate our lives. For medicine has become a powerful practice without end, without context, without any wider community to give it purpose. Accordingly nothing could be more important today than for Christians to recover a Christian practice of medicine shaped by the practice of the church, and in particular baptism. . . . For lives determined by that reality—that is, the reality of life with God—how sickness is understood and cared for cannot help but look quite different from how the world understands what it means to be sick.[51]

In the following chapters, we will see precisely how different Christians, reshaped by practices such as baptism, look.

5

What Are Children For?

■ Were this a conventional book on medical ethics, we might spend a few paragraphs on the matter of "normal" childbearing before moving on to "real issues" like abortion, assisted reproduction, or cloning. Medical ethicists are no different from the rest of us in assuming that, after a million years of practice, humans know all about making babies, why we do it, and what it's for. Having never planned to write a conventional book, we want to pause a moment to consider these apparently settled questions.

One way the powers and principalities maintain control is to limit our imagination, to stifle impertinent questions like, "Why do things this way?" If we already know why children are desired, our imaginations and energies can remain fixed on obtaining them. Yet the technological power of medicine also changes the ways in which we think about things, gradually altering our expectations by promising to provide "what we want."[1] Technological medicine, always good at providing what we want, is increasingly able to deliver not just any children, but made-to-order ones. This is something quite new. Can the advent of in vitro fertilization (IVF), surrogate pregnancy, and pre-implantation genetic diagnosis (PGD) to screen for and eliminate embryos with unwanted traits possibly leave our understanding of "normal childbearing" unaffected?

New technologies bring more and more of the particulars of our children within the control of those who can afford such "treatments," which, in turn, alters the way we see our children. Jackson Lears, reflecting on the nineteenth century's nearly idolatrous image of childhood, remarked that Victorians transformed children from miniature adults to superior pets.[2] The subsequent hundred years has further transformed children into something more like a consumer item. Ethicist Amy Laura Hall notes how contemporary sentimental images of children differ from those only a few decades earlier:

> Look at the Ann Geddes pictures, an image of a child as pumpkin, or a child as flower: the baby as the commodity you get to consume or pluck and put in your vase, versus the kind of images you have with Norman Rockwell. Almost all of his images of children are children with skinned knees, are of the chaos of kids—I think about the one with the boys running and trying to pull up their pants, they've been swimming in the water hole with their dog. The images of children that he depicts are children with other children, who are showing signs of mess, which children inevitably are. . . . [Anne Geddes's images are] . . . a kind of really dangerous idolatry . . . a kind of purely platonic form of "baby," the "baby" one can fashion according to one's own desires, the "baby" as consumable. And notice that those babies never have a sign of food on themselves; if you know anything about toddlers they are constantly covered in food. These pictures are children that do not consume; *these are babies that we consume*. And those icons of childhood are indicative of a dominant culture in America that sees children as a way to accessorize and fulfill one's own life, rather than as interruptions into our own hopes, dreams and goals.[3]

The power of our technologies and the images they generate turn children from people to pets to consumable accessories, and each step is taken with our consent and approval. Christians ought not fall for this. Our lives are reshaped in Christ through baptism and Eucharist, making us misfits in a world still under the yoke of powers and principalities. If Christ transforms all creation, surely among the transformed is our answer to the question, "What are children for?"[4]

That's a rude question to ask in public. If we ask anyway, after the sputtering and uneasy laughter quiet down we may be told something like, "Children aren't *for* anything; they're ends in themselves." This may be true, but there's scant evidence we believe it. In oral presentations on pediatric hospital rounds, for instance, a child is often described as a "product of a planned pregnancy," with the implicit understanding that "unplanned" pregnancies are problematic. What matters in this view are the adult intentions behind the child's existence. In this and other ways, children are subjected to unspoken tests of value, both to the parents and to "society." In contemporary North American society, children—at least the children of the materially comfortable—are technologically spaced and provisionally accepted pending the results of prenatal diagnostic tests.

Such calculations of value are shot through with tacit assumptions and myths. To begin with, it's unclear what "society" might be under consideration here—the world, North America and its economy, the "consuming public," or the medical-industrial complex. There is also broad room for interpretation in calculating "cost" and "value" in human life. One medical article proposing the "triple screen" as standard of care in pregnancy (the triple screen is a group of prenatal tests used to diagnose Down syndrome and other conditions, providing prospective parents with information with which they can decide whether or not to abort a fetus) included in its analysis a dollar amount as the "cost to society for raising a child with Down Syndrome."[5] Two obstetrician/gynecologists, both parents of children with Down syndrome, offered a rebuttal that cleverly included a proposed "cost to . . . society of a 'normal' person who becomes a physician."[6] While there is yet no reliable prenatal diagnostic test to determine whether a fetus will become a physician, the "triple screen" and other such prenatal quality assurance tests are used widely and often. In the United States, it is estimated that 90 percent of all Down syndrome fetuses diagnosed in utero are aborted.[7] So much for children as "ends in themselves."

Planned Parenthood claims its goal is to ensure every child born is a wanted child,[8] which still begs the question of why we might want children in the first place. Stanley Hauerwas asked his students in a Notre Dame course on marriage, "What reason would you give for you or someone else wanting a child?":

> I would get answers like, "Well, children are fun." In that case, I ask them to think about their brothers and sisters. Another answer was, "Children are a hedge against loneliness." Then I recommended getting a dog. Also I would note that if they really wanted to feel lonely, they should think about someone they had raised turning out to be a stranger. Another student reply was, "Kids are a manifestation of our love." "Well," I responded, "what happens when your love changes and you are still stuck with them?" . . . It happened three or four times that someone in class, usually a young woman, would raise her hand and say, "I don't want to talk about this anymore," . . . they know that they are going to have children, and yet they do not have the slightest idea why. And they do not want it examined. You can talk in your classes about whether God exists all semester and no one cares, because it does not seem to make any difference. But having children makes a difference and the students are frightened that they do not know about these matters.[9]

As Christians, then, we must push into frightening territory, trusting that even here, when we seem most confused, we will discover the God who calls us together into the body of Christ. For Christians, life must first and always be seen as God's gift, incomprehensible outside of relationship with God. Life itself, though deserving the utmost respect, is not "sacred." Only God, who gives each one of us life, is sacred. Christians must, therefore, respect life but not worship it. "Life" is never encountered in disembodied abstraction, but always and everywhere in particular bodies.[10] If a particular life can be called "sacred," it is only in the awareness that this particular body is God's unique, irreplaceable gift.

Likewise, if we asked God what children are for, the answer may well be, "Which child do you have in mind?" Fashionable idolatries of children and childhood have no place in Christian life. Children—who will, in time, die just like us—are not "our hope for the future," since our hope is in the Lord (1 Tim. 1:1; Ps. 39:7, 146:5). Thus, even biological imperatives to reproduce and "perpetuate the species" wither under theological inspection. Karl Barth spells this out:

> It is one of the consolations of the coming kingdom and expiring time that this anxiety about posterity, . . . that we should and must bear children, heirs of our blood and name and honor and wealth . . . is removed from us by the fact that the Son on whose birth alone everything seriously and ultimately depended has now become our Brother. *No one now has to be conceived and born.* We need not expect any other than the One of whose coming we are certain because He is already come. *Parenthood is now only to be understood as a free and in some sense optional gift of the goodness of God.*[11]

Here, after clearing away thickets of sentimentality and cliché, we are at last able to see children properly: extravagant gifts, yet subordinate to the greatest gift of salvation through Christ: "No one has to be conceived or born . . . because He has already come." With Jesus as Brother, we have all the kinship we shall ever need. The early Christians, who sustained hope in Christ while living in a hostile empire, understood this far better than we. In a society where women produced children useful to the emperor, the refusal to bear children was a threat to imperial "family values." Incorporated into the body of Christ, early Christians saw the church as their family and rejected the traditional, imperial model. Rowan Greer observes:

> The rejection of the family that often characterized Christianity in the age of martyrs often carried with it the notion of the Church as a new and true family. In one respect the Church was a family not only in theory but in practice. . . . The New Testament shows us that from the earliest times the Church took under its protection widows and orphans, and there seems also to have developed an institutionalization of virgins, single women who found their family in the Church.[12]

It is in this confidence that Christ, our Brother, has made the bearing of children unnecessary for the survival of our new family, that we may best understand the earliest practice of Christian vowed virginity.[13] Yet early Christians, in contrast to some Gnostics, did not insist upon virginity or view the birth of children as the tragic imprisonment of spirit within gross matter. Rather, they saw the gift of children in the light of the God who is their source. Again, Rowan Greer:

> Only God is the proper object of love; all other loves are of value only to the degree that they are ordered under the love of him. This means that the family, and indeed any human relationship, can never be regarded as an end in itself. At the same time, human loves receive their meaning and value when ordered by the love of God. They are transfigured by him and are vehicles through which we may find him. And so we find a warrant in Augustine for the notion that the Christian ideal can transform the meaning of the family.[14]

As we have learned, all gifts—including the gift of children—are to be received in confidence and gratitude. That's easy enough to say, much harder to embody. How, though, can we foster this response? Through what communal practices can we school one another in gratitude?

Children as Strangers

The Christian practice most applicable to the daunting tasks of child-raising is, once again, hospitality toward strangers. If children are God's unnecessary gift, then they are never "ours" in any real sense.[15] Our care of and responsibility for them does not translate into ownership, and any parent of teenagers can confirm that children—even "biological" children[16]—are strange creatures. Given the North American fetish for independence and "autonomy," these strangers occupy space in a family's life very briefly, temporary boarders on the road to another country. But children are always already strangers to us, springing from the womb with characters and callings beyond our control. The first lesson of parenthood, we've noted before, is: "You are not in control." Sitting with parents whose children are dying, knowing there are no words to "make it better," will convince even the most skeptical person this is true. To welcome a child into one's home makes one vulnerable.

It's a lonely practice, even for those who aren't single parents, and such loneliness can grow unbearable. Yet, if the church acts as it is called to, there should be no "single parents," since raising children is thoroughly communal. That is, it takes a church to raise a (Christian) child. The *Catechism of the Catholic Church* states that the godparents' task is "a truly ecclesial function. . . . The whole ecclesial community bears . . . responsibility for the development and safeguarding of the grace given at Baptism."[17]

This statement contains the kernel of an important Christian truth: the body of Christ does not grow through sexual reproduction, but through lifelong practices of conversion. Conversion is itself a gift, one which demands much hard work from the recipient. Seen this way, childraising becomes an opportunity for conversion, presenting opportunities to love when one prefers independence, to practice gentleness before efficiency, mercy rather than control. In time, we may learn to be grateful for these interruptions. Such work must be shared by the entire body. Part of what the gathered body remembers is the body itself, in precisely the ways we discussed in chapter 3. Children, remember, come to us not as ideas or emotions, but as bodies, and it may be hard to see them as a gift from God when they disrupt our ideas of what "the good life" might look like. Furthermore, they enter with us into the Body of Christ, becoming part of a story reaching back past David, Moses, and Abraham to the very creation of the universe and forward to the gathering of all things in Christ.

Discerning the Body: Two Very Different Stories

If the destiny of Christ's body is to gather all things within it, then Christians must discern the body past boundaries of genetic kinship. That reminds us of a story, namely Flannery O'Connor's "A Good Man Is Hard to Find." A tale in which an entire family is brutally murdered by a psychopathic killer named The Misfit seems an unlikely place to learn about recognizing children in the stranger, but O'Connor was never one to pretty up the facts of Christian life with sentimentalities. Near the end of the story, the grandmother—an entirely unsympathetic character—and The Misfit engage in an unlikely theological discussion, engendered by her plea: "I know you come from nice people! Pray! Jesus, you ought not to shoot a lady."[18] The Misfit blames his sorry life on punishment for things he can't remember doing. When told to pray, he says, "I don't want no hep. . . . I'm doing all right by myself."[19] He particularly blames Jesus for raising the dead, which "thown everything off balance." He continues, "If He did what He said, then it's nothing for you to do but thow away everything and follow Him, and if He didn't, then it's nothing for you to do but enjoy the few minutes you got left the best way you can . . ."[20]

In the end, just as The Misfit's buddies return from killing the last of the grandmother's family, her head "cleared for an instant":

> She saw the man's twisted face close to her own as if he were going to cry and she murmured, "Why you're one of my babies. You're one of my own children!" She reached out and touched him on the shoulder.[21]

In the unlikeliest of circumstances, the grandmother, perhaps for the first time in her life, sees the stranger—The Misfit—as her own child. In some parts of the Old South, shoulder blades were referred to as "wing buds," the spot where one's heavenly wings might eventually sprout.[22] The Misfit will have none of it. He shoots the woman three times through the chest.

When his small gang returns, the eerily calm Misfit tells them, "She would of been a good woman . . . if it had been somebody there to shoot her every minute of her life."[23] Most of us would prefer a subtler reminder of our kinship with the stranger, but can something other than a loaded gun to the head call us to our senses? For Christians who have forgotten the terrifying scandal of the cross, maybe not. Still, there are signs of hope.

Friends of ours shared with us the story of their own struggle to recognize who their children were. They recall their frustrated desire to have children while in graduate school, and their initial, awkward encounters with "infertility specialists." When the couple

> visited a local hospital twice to see an older guy at an infertility practice, we were intrigued with the range of possible strategies and open to learning more about them. . . . [T]his fellow seemed to have acquired some wisdom over the years and noticed our hesitancy. The high tech methods at which we balked seemed to begin at pouring a semen sample onto a single ovum on a Petri dish and stirring it up, or something like that, which must have been no more complex to him than putting Miracle-Gro on his tomatoes. He calmly asked, "Are you Catholic?" in a tone of voice that indicated he doubted our willingness to do whatever needed to be done to solve this problem. He assured us that he had participated in IRBs [institutional review boards] with priests who approved of these methods. [24] We so wanted a happy ending and found ourselves already on the border of this brave new world, thinking about it and looking across but not actually . . . plung[ing] in. The next likely steps seemed morally manageable and were tempting indeed.[25]

Unable to afford expensive technological solutions, they held off awhile, consulting a priest, who referred them to a number of articles by contemporary theologians, which suggested that

> anything short of (technologies involving) abortion seemed to be in play and to some degree even morally good. If you wanted kids, technology, or at least some approvable technologies, could provide them, and that was that. Why not put some Miracle-Gro on those tomatoes? . . . The flip-side of this freedom . . was that we were on our own. It was a lonely place to be. There wasn't much in the way of tradition here—after all, who needed Aquinas or Augustine on GIFT when we have those clerically approved IRB decisions? [26] No scripture either, except perhaps the thought that at least we wouldn't be roping any Hagar . . . into the process.[27]

Then the couple did some very strange things. They read, among other things, the *Catechism of the Catholic Church,* surprised and "grateful for its severely skeptical stance on these applications of biotechnology." They also prayed. They talked. They went to church and joined in the liturgy. They began to ask where God fit into this world technological medicine was inviting them to enter:

> At our last appointment the older physician used the term "selective reduction" to describe the abortion of technologically-induced multiple conceptions. We both knew then that we were well into the dystopia that right wing Catholic moral theologians had warned everyone about all along. We did not want to take part in any further dehumanization of family life, and mutually agreed to end our consideration of technological solutions to our infertility.
>
> As strong as our desire to beget a child had been, that was how firmly sealed this issue was. I was really kind of surprised that my wife and I came to the same conclusion at the same time with the same strength of conviction. And for the same reasons. I began to see what faith in God was—not just a belief that, "Sure, He's out there somewhere," but a characteristic of a continuing relationship. . . . That took me a long time to understand. Eventually, when we adopted our twin girls I could see at least a little of what I had been blind to during our fertility misadventures: God's love for us, our helplessness to force His grace to come our way the way we want it when we want it, and His inescapable presence among us all the same.[28]

There is much here worth exploring, but we will limit ourselves to these brief comments. First, this couple didn't peer into the display case of assisted reproduction because they were self-absorbed or greedy. They wanted the good that childbearing is. What they learned along the way, though, was how to properly order such gifts in the light of God. They came to this understanding in large part through the practices of the church: prayer, shared and private reflection, reading, and the sacraments.

Second, the older doctor who wanted to "solve this problem" sniffed them out as odd. The couple is, in fact, Catholic, and their allegiance to a people gathered by God qualified any allegiance to technological medicine. Would that more Catholics were sufficiently odd to be found out, not to mention more Episcopalians, Lutherans, Methodists, Baptists, and Presbyterians.

Third, when they acknowledged their inability to fit into a world determined by medicine (having been shaped by the practices of the church into misfits), they recognized their children in the stranger: they adopted twin girls. Their children were waiting for them in a place they hadn't been looking. For those who know the proper stories, this should not be at all surprising: God's people have always been built up through extraordinary and surprising means.

Reclaiming the Body in Unexpected Ways

The "genealogy of Jesus Christ," with which Matthew begins his Gospel (Matt. 1:1–17), includes four unusual women: Tamar, Rahab, Ruth, and "the wife of Uriah" (i.e., Bathsheba). As scripture scholar Raymond Brown notes,

> there is something extraordinary or irregular in their union with their part-
> ners—a union which, though it may have been scandalous to outsiders,
> continued the blessed lineage of the Messiah, . . . (and) the women showed
> initiative or played an important role in God's plan and so came to be con-
> sidered the instrument of God's providence or of His Holy Spirit.[29]

Joseph, Mary's husband, understands the "extraordinary and irregu-lar" nature of Jesus's begetting and chooses to stand with his betrothed, welcome the child, and protect him from Herod's murderous power. The salvation of the world is effected outside of what we've come to consider "normal circumstances."

One of the most powerful temptations offered by the power that is medicine is the illusion that, through medical technology, we can restore unpleasant situations to "normal circumstances."[30] The couple who in other times might have been considered "barren" can now have the baby they've always dreamed of, free of genetic diseases and even undesirable "normal variants," while still looking like Mama or Papa. "Problematic" and "unwanted pregnancies"—some from situations so horrific any reasonable individual would understandably seek an escape—can be "terminated." Fetuses and now embryos can be examined for defects that might require more attention and resources than the parents believe they are able to give, the undesirables being aborted or discarded.

By appealing to our desires for certain qualities in children—we want our children to be happy, successful, attractive, independent, and smart—technology has redefined the sad, the unpromising, the imperfect, the dependent, and the slow as abnormal. While the rhetoric of choice sug-gests an explosion of options, increased control often brings a narrower range of publicly acceptable outcomes, and our understanding of what constitutes normal is diminished. A line is drawn, the human circle is shrunken, and technology offers to dispose of those who don't make the cut. By framing the use of technology in individual terms, the powers distract us from communal resources that might help us welcome the less than optimal child. Arguments for enhancing "human flourishing" over "needless suffering" often rely on this seductive narrowing of imagina-tion.[31] Even some Christians have argued that all means available should be used to eliminate suffering, including the unasked-for elimination of the sufferer. The powers encourage us to reframe this destruction as "collateral damage" or a "tragic choice," keeping us focused on the desired ends of individuals. The Christian story does not claim that all temporal suffering should end with the Christ's victory but rather that, as we wait in hope for the eschatological fullness of that victory, all suffering is shared in Christ's body.[32]

Naming abortion as an "individual choice" or even an "individual sin" fails to discern the body. Each abortion is a negation of community, a failure of the gathered body to find room for even the most unpromising of children. It is a communal failure to say clearly to the pregnant mother and her growing child, "You are welcome here." The principal way in which the church can reduce abortions—a goal even "pro-choice" organizations claim to favor—is less by becoming an organized voting bloc championing certain individual rights than by reclaiming the body in all its forms. The pregnant woman, frightened and battered by the powers, is not an individual who simply needs to behave in a morally upright fashion. She is part of *our* body. The child she carries is not any child—he or she is *our* child.

William Willimon describes hearing an African-American pastor's response to the grim realities of teen pregnancy:

> "We have young girls who have this happen to them. I have a fourteen-year-old in my congregation who had a baby last month. We're going to baptize the child next Sunday," he added.
>
> "Do you really think that she is capable of raising a little baby?" another minister asked.
>
> "Of course not," he replied. 'No fourteen-year-old is capable of raising a baby. For that matter, not many thirty-year-olds are qualified. A baby's too difficult for any one person to raise by herself."
>
> "So what do you do with babies?" they asked.
>
> "Well, we baptize them so that we all raise them together. In the case of that fourteen-year-old, we have given her baby to a retired couple who have enough time and enough wisdom to raise children. They can raise the mama along with her baby. That's the way we do it."[33]

What this church has done is not merely discerned the body, but reclaimed it from the individualistic, technological solutions medicine as power offers. Heeding the warning of James, they have become doers of the word rather than merely hearers.[34] This may not be the ideal American nuclear family, but, as Matthew's genealogy recalls, salvation often is carried out in irregular circumstances.

Baptizing one fourteen-year-old's child doesn't eliminate the perceived need for more than a million abortions in the United States every year. Nor does it respond to the heartbreaking circumstance of a child born with severe, even lethal, abnormalities. Welcoming such children, and in such numbers, would require an even stronger sense of gathering in Christ, a much deeper network of support empowered by the Holy Spirit. Welcoming the fourteen-year-old's child is, however, a start—one which the church might grow accustomed to. Such a practice of hospitality to the stranger may well lead to the situation Bill Tilbert imagines: "What if there were abortion clinics but nobody went in? What if abortion was a legal choice, but it was a choice nobody took?"[35]

Christians should not fool themselves into believing that reclaiming the body will drive abortion clinics out of business. Abortion, like war, is a human invention of great antiquity, arising from the deepest brokenness within humanity. Like any other violent rupture of community, abortion requires sustained, patient, and nonviolent communal witness to women and men across generations.[36] While less gratifying than angry condemnation and less flashy than political power plays, such quiet resistance to the powers shows—instead of merely telling—those contemplating abortion, "There are other ways."

Which Children Are Ours?

Welcoming children is a good thing. Wanting one's own children is part of the human experience. What if having "one's own" children is difficult, not because of financial or social reasons, but—as in the case of the couple who eventually adopted—for medical reasons?

Medicine answers this challenge through the new technologies of assisted reproduction: IVF, PGD, GIFT, ZIFT: an entire alphabet soup of techniques. The United States Centers for Disease Control and Prevention documented in one recent year 107,587 "procedures," resulting in 29,344 deliveries and 40,687 live births.[37] No calculations of monetary cost were included in the report. We realize many Christians welcome and baptize children born following assisted reproduction technologies each year. We agree such children should be baptized, but how is the body being discerned in their begetting? Are Christians properly ordering goods in this respect?

Perhaps a place to begin is to place the number of assisted reproduction procedures side by side with three other statistics. First, in the year 2000, there were 1.31 million abortions in the United States, making induced abortion one of the most commonly performed surgical procedures in the United States.[38] Second, as of September 30, 2001, there were 542,000 children in foster care in the United States, with 290,000 entering the system and 263,000 leaving in the previous twelve months.[39] Third, the estimated number of children less than five years of age who died in the year 2000 worldwide was 10.8 million.[40] The British journal *Lancet* asked, "Where and why are 10 million children dying every year?"[41] The short answer is in mostly poor, so-called developing countries, and for entirely preventable reasons, such as diarrhea, malnutrition, and measles.

In this context, the welcoming of children through assisted reproduction techniques becomes much more problematic. Without even considering the ethical concerns raised by the techniques themselves, can Christian communities justify the pursuit of children through such costly means when millions conceived naturally die by "choice" or from causes most North Americans consider ancient history? And what of the thousands in foster care, waiting for a home?

We will consider the church's response to medical disparities between rich and poor nations in the following chapter, but it is worth noting here that if, in Christ, there is neither male nor female, Jew nor Greek, slave nor free, then surely there is also neither white nor black, American nor Sudanese, able-bodied nor handicapped. Furthermore, if all children are gifts from God, and never truly our possessions, then pondering the ethical complexities of embryo disposal and selective reduction while ignoring the gift of children already present but strangely invisible to us seems a luxury we can neither afford nor justify.

Given this incredible worldwide death toll, how might Christians properly welcome children? The struggling graduate-school couple whose story we shared above found one: adoption. Full of moral complexity and potential for abuse itself, adoption nonetheless provides a home for tens of thousands of children each year. Many of these children do not meet North America's changing standards for ability or promise, but some brave women and men adopt them anyway. Most arrive at a decision to adopt as isolated couples, often after meeting another adoptive family. Churches generally endorse the practice, but it is harder to find a church that actively encourages and supports these families. How many churches consider adoption integral to its communal witness to the world? How many churches support birth mothers in their heartbreaking courage, as they witness to the life we share? Or, as happens all too often in the churches of the rich and materially comfortable, is the subject mentioned only when convenient, as part of the parish "outreach report," or on "Respect Life Sunday"? The church's failure to witness communally this response surely implicates Christians in the ten million child deaths around the world and more than a million abortions in the United States each year.

One small church that has taken up this calling is Bennett Chapel Missionary Baptist Church in the wonderfully named town of Possum Trot, Texas. Pastor William C. Martin and his wife, Donna, led the congregation by example, adopting several children themselves.[42] Susan Ramsey, a caseworker for the Texas Department of Protective Services, was then contacted by Pastor Martin:

"I told him I would come to teach the training classes for prospective adoptive and foster parents if he could get 10 potential families to attend," Ramsey explained. "When I arrived there were 24 families at the first meeting. It was incredible. And Reverend Martin let us hold the meetings in the church, which is the center of the community."

The small church has since surpassed one hundred total adoptions and foster care placements, including abused, special needs, and other "hard-to-place" children. In reflecting on the Bennett Chapel witness, Ramsey noted:

The people in the Bennett community are comfortable with who they are . . . They are good, honest, hardworking people who aren't threatened by the idea of bringing children into their homes. They don't view themselves as a blessing for the child. They view the child as their blessing.

Adopting a child will not solve the world's problems, and the world might well do without more North Americans, whose aggressive consumption of God's gifts severely taxes the earth's material bounty. Yet adoption can be a first step beyond the comfortable boundaries of biological and even national kinship, toward a fuller understanding of our kinship in Christ. For example, one of us is the adoptive father of a girl from Guatemala. Part of our family for over eight years now, she still calls us to deeper conversion and reminds us of undeserved privileges in an unfair world. One of those privileges, the freedom to choose when and if to challenge racism and poverty, was lost the moment we stepped into the Houston airport with her. There, everyone who looked like her new parents was hurrying to catch a flight, while everyone who looked like her was pushing a broom. Whenever we encounter racism—in institutions, in others, in ourselves—we know silence hurts her, and that hurts us as well.

But what about the many millions more who are not being adopted, and whose parents might well wish for some less drastic solution? The adoption experience connects us, in a surprisingly visceral, embodied way, to the needs of our daughter's people. We sponsor another Guatemalan child, so her family can feed her and send her to school without leaving her parents or her village. For several years now, one of us has worked with a medical team in rural Honduras, in what has become a permanent, Honduran-staffed and -run medical-dental clinic with locally designed nutrition and education projects. We also work to educate medical students and residents how to bridge the cultural, linguistic, and economic divides immigrants encounter upon entering the American medical-industrial system. We have not done enough. We can't do it alone.

Parenting When One Has No Children

The enormity of this cosmic woundedness overwhelms us. How do we answer the world's need if every child is our responsibility? If we are dazzled by "global problems" and only ponder individual responses, there is no hope. Yet the world's woundedness, like life, is never encountered in the abstract, but in particular, embodied manifestations—some of them very close to home. We best not engage in "telescopic philanthropy," as did Mrs. Jellyby, in Charles Dickens's *Bleak House,* who devoted her energies to assisting natives of "Borrioboola-Gha, on the left bank of the Niger," while her own neglected children picked their way through her crumbling house. Knowing where and with whom to begin requires wisdom, discernment, and ultimately a choice, recognizing that faithful Christians may be called to different, particular needs. What is important is to ground each response in the community while acknowledging the diversity of the body.

The parish with whom one of us worships sponsored an Afghan family that arrived in our town after the American invasion of their country. In getting to know them, we learned the children were forced to watch as the Taliban assassinated their father outside their home in Afghanistan. We assisted them in finding an apartment, schools for the children, and a job for the mother. We helped them move twice, once to a larger house and again when they experienced repeated acts of prejudice and intolerance in that neighborhood, which sadly did not welcome "foreigners." We took the family to local parks, giving the children a change of scenery and their mother a break. Our kids and theirs played soccer and flew kites together, overcoming barriers of language, nation-state, and religion. After a few years, they no longer needed help from us, having established their own networks of support and care—and that was as it should be. The kids were doing reasonably well in school, made friends, and embraced—for good or ill—American tastes. Once again, we wonder how many North American consumers the world can survive, yet a mother and her children were materially and spiritually supported in time of great need.

During this time, the parish sustained its other witnesses—some local, some distant—each connected to the church by one or more bodies seeing a need and responding to it. In reclaiming the body wherever and however it manifests itself, we reclaim the essential practice of hospitality and recover the meaning of sanctuary so all can find safety and support in the house of the church. The possibilities are limited only by the boundaries of Christian imagination.

Some may insist that hospitality as "mere charity" prolongs suffering without eliminating its cause. Indeed, a crude form of this argument was used by American progressives to justify the eugenics campaigns of the twentieth century. Christians, we contend, should embrace efforts to reform structural evils to the extent that such actions are nonviolent and respect each life as God's gracious gift. But the Christian practice of hospitality can never be "mere charity," a bureaucratic warehouse of undesirables into which the affluent toss occasional offerings to salve their conscience. Hospitality, like the medical buildings named for the practice, involves bodies. Real bodies are harder to face than the idea of the poor. Real encounters leave people changed—unpredictably so—but rarely in ways the powers encourage. The messy reality of bodies is a powerful antidote to the dehumanizing dreaminess that makes it easier to love the poor in the abstract than to be present to the poor person in the flesh. As Dostoyevsky warns, "Love in action is a harsh and dreadful thing compared to love in dreams."[43] Without direct encounter, hospitality grows Gnostic, as indeed much of the contemporary church's "social action" has already done.

What the church proclaims is Christ crucified for the salvation of the entire world. What it exemplifies is often quite different. Though we are gathered into one body in Christ, our history as sinners does not permit dividing humanity into "us" and "them." If we do, then only too late and to our infinite regret will we realize, like Joe Keller in Arthur Miller's *All My Sons,* that they—all sons and daughters—really are ours. Most parents learn—and often to their embarrassment or regret—that their children are forever watching them. Adolescents, in particular, are vigilant for signs of hypocrisy and, like *The Catcher in the Rye*'s Holden Caulfield, they quickly sniff out phonies. Rather than take this as a threat, Christians might welcome another call to conversion. In welcoming children into our families, into our churches, and into the families we support and nourish, we become more than vulnerable, we become *accountable to them.* Children's powers of observation are incentives to live up to our call, to embody the life we say we live. In turn, we witness back to those who watch us.

Becoming doers of the word and embodying the way of life we call Christian has never been easy. Where once there were violent threats from a hostile empire, now Christians are surrounded by the temptations of a culture and economy in bondage to the powers. We, too, are at least partially enthralled by these same powers, and only by living as the body can we begin to resist them. We will, at times, fail—that much is certain this side of the grave—but God forever calls us back to the gathered body, where we hope to be supported, hope to gather strength, hope to be witnessed to and to witness. For our innumerable children, even our repentance, our returning to reclaim the body we lost and denied, can be a witness, an invitation to their conversion as well as our own.

6

A Body without Borders

■ In a culture bedazzled by electronic entertainment, "good old stories, plainly told" get little hearing. Jesus told plain stories in his lifetime, some of which the evangelists found important enough to record.[1] But Jesus was no stand-up comic headlining nightly shows with two performances on Saturday.[2] He told stories to instruct, and for a first-century Palestinian audience as stuck in their ways as we are in ours, he told them both to intrigue and discomfort. Unfortunately, like the theatergoer who complained Shakespeare was only a patchwork of clichés, Christians have heard Jesus's stories too often truly to listen. Through overuse, Jesus's stories have lost much of their power to disturb and convict.

Consider the familiar tale that Jesus, in good rabbinical tradition, tells in the middle of an edgy debate over the essence and fulfillment of the law (Luke 10:25–37). A man lies half dead at the side of the road.[3] A priest happens by but quickly crosses to the other side of the road and heads on. We have no window into his head—Jesus is more interested in the social than the psychological—though we can infer that the priest is connected to the cultic life of the temple. Touching a body which may be Gentile, dead, or both, would render this honored man defiled under the law.

A Levite, a student of the law, passes along as well and, perhaps for similar reasons, does the same. A third traveler—a Samaritan—sees the injured man and provides medical assistance, takes him to shelter on his own beast, and pays for the injured man's care. Anyone who knows how to tell a joke knows the "rule of threes": three situations, three tries, three people, with the punch line held out until the end. For his first hearers, Jesus pushes this joke to the border of poor taste, and our pious modern habit of calling it "the Good Samaritan" ruins the punch line.[4] Samaritans were despised by first-century Palestinian Jews as enemies, outside the law and alien to God's people, but this Samaritan goes beyond what might be expected even for a friend. Jesus's verbal sparring partner, a lawyer who came to test Jesus and justify himself (vv. 25–29), can't even bring himself to say the word *Samaritan* when prompted. To his first hearers, a "Good Samaritan" was an oxymoron, which of course was Jesus's point: the God of Israel is Lord of all creation, Samaria included, and the demands of the Torah are universal. That a Samaritan can observe the law better than those who constantly study it reinforces the universal validity of the law—the love of neighbor (Lev. 19:18) in particular—while extending its obligations past boundaries Jesus's hearers thought uncrossable.

Luke's Gospel is also full of stories *about* Jesus, often taking the following form: a person is separated from the life of the community by some socially defined mark: foreignness, gender, disease, or sinful activity.[5] Jesus encounters this person, frequently touching him or her or permitting himself to be touched, and welcomes him or her back into full relationship. The marginalized and excluded are, through an embodied encounter, reunited with the people of God. These reclamation stories are far more social than individual and generally occur in one of two settings: healings and meals.[6] Both serve the life and health of the community, addressing physical needs and spiritual distress in the same embodied action. We know no better summation of reclaiming of the body than this sequence of aphorisms by Wendell Berry:

> The grace that is the health of creatures can only be held in common. In healing the scattered members come together. In health the flesh is graced, the holy enters the world.[7]

These gospel themes should prod us into greater discernment, finding the body—both gift and gathering—in unexpected places, especially among the marginalized, those cut off from the whole. This requires recognizing the bodily needs of the marginalized: healing, of course, but also the physical and spiritual nourishment shared in community. In traditional Mediterranean cultures, meals were about much more than just food. They were also social markers, declaring openly with whom one associated, and with whom one did not. In his First Letter to the Corinthians, which we examined in chapter 3, Paul makes explicit the intimate connection between meals, the gathered body, and bodily health: "For any one who eats and drinks without discerning the body eats and drinks judgment upon himself. That is why many of you are weak and ill, and some have died" (1 Cor. 11:29–30). As Luke Timothy Johnson explains, Christians of the New Testament and succeeding generations understood the eucharistic meal as dining together in the presence of Christ and sharing in the power of the risen Lord.[8] Jesus's invitation to the table always includes a demand for painful and complete transformation, but his invitation is nonetheless radically inclusive.[9] If we share in the power of that risen Lord, how can we not wish to properly discern the body and reach out to those separated from us by social barriers?

Rival Visions

What keeps us from seeing and touching our own world's "lepers," the marginalized whom our economy and culture prefer to keep invisible, flailing about among the tombs? One obstacle, curiously enough, is the power of medicine, which, echoing the thrust of Western liberal political and economic thought, speaks an almost uninterrupted language of individualism. To be sure, there are university departments of social medicine and entire schools of public health, but these are hardly central to the medical-industrial complex in North America, even though much of what we consider the "blessings of modern medicine"—significantly decreased infectious disease mortality, longer lives, etc.—come more directly from public health efforts (clean water, improved sanitation and nutrition, and immunizations, among others) than from technologically enhanced individual care. Nonetheless, the "developed nations," the United States in particular, show increasing disregard for the health of populations as opposed to individual selves.[10]

In medical ethics, there is a flourishing strain of utilitarian thought, with its maxim concerning "the greatest good for the greatest number," though that "number" is understood as a summation of individual selves, particularly those with the resources necessary for "agency," that is, the power to make choices. Arguments are typically framed, often under the cloak of "cost-effectiveness," to value some people (able-bodied "contributors to society") over others (the severely impaired).[11] Within the "deontological" strain of medical ethics (i.e., the study of moral obligations or rules), the two most commonly used principles are beneficence (doing or at least intending good) and autonomy.[12] Doctors are supposed to direct their efforts toward a patient's "good"—a conspicuously vague term—while the patient exercises her autonomy largely by choosing among various options in a process called "informed consent." Through such mysteries and rituals, we—or at least the fortunate—are left to pursue our individual lives in freedom.[13]

Thus, when most of us hear the phrase "medical ethics," we think of difficult *individual* cases, often at life's margins: the terminal cancer patient, sick both from her tumor and chemotherapy, asking her physician to help her die; the pregnant woman pondering late-term abortion versus fetal surgery for her deformed child; or the dizzying technological manipulations aimed at the human zygote. Those who have worked in so-called developing countries or the inner-city slums and rural backwaters of the United States know these issues rarely arise there. Such highly individualized questions are almost exclusively the concern of the well-off, since ethical dilemmas at life's margins usually involve uncommon material and financial resources. An enormous chasm gapes between the topics explored in most medical ethics curricula and the realities and health and disease endured by most of the world's population. Physician Paul Farmer notes:

> Conventional medical ethics, mired as they are in the "quandary ethics of the individual," do not often speak to these issues, because the bulk of their attention is focused on individual cases where massive resources are invested in delivering services unlikely to ever benefit most patients."[14]

Consider only a few of the immensities about which "quandary ethics of the individual" has nothing to say. We noted in the previous chapter that 10 million children die globally each year, mostly from preventable or easily treatable causes no longer considered problems in the "developed world."[15] In 2004, there were 3.1 million AIDS deaths, half a million of which were children.[16] The vast majority of these deaths were once again in "developing countries," since in the "developed world" Highly Active Antiretroviral Therapy (HAART) turns HIV from a death sentence into a manageable, if life-threatening, chronic disease. Nor are health disparities limited to "developing nations." In 1990, mortality rates for persons between the ages of five and sixty-five years were higher in Harlem than in Bangladesh, one of the poorest countries in the world.[17] In 2003, 15.6 percent of the United States population—45 million people!—had no health insurance coverage, making even the most basic medical services financially burdensome.[18] Most considerations of the health effects of such disparities treat them as social or political problems in search of "cost-effective" solutions, entering the territory of modern medicine only through the neglected hinterlands of public health. As to any moral obligations of the medical-industrial complex to rectify these inequities, standard medical ethics is largely silent.[19]

The Christian understanding of the body should—though often fails to—shatter this silence. For starters, every body on the planet is a gift. Peter tells Cornelius and his household, "Truly I perceive that God shows no partiality" (Acts 10:34). Christians worldwide eat at the same table, are served by the same Lord, and live as neighbor to non-Christians, whom we are called to love as self. As with the Samaritan in Luke's Gospel, faithfulness leaves no choice but to reach across boundaries of human design. Discerning the body Christ gathers, while recalling how Jesus explicitly identifies with "the least of these" (Matt. 25:40), makes denying our responsibility to the world's poor a rejection of Christ himself. Certainly Christians have cultivated such denial over the centuries, often blaming God for the misfortunes of others and engineering calamities in God's name, but to pin the suffering of millions of God's children on "God's will"—rather than on human deafness to God's call—makes God a capricious sadist.

Compared to the quandary structure of standard medical ethics—the beneficent or maleficent aims of medical technology brought against the individual patient's sacred autonomy—Christian "body ethics" is vastly more complicated. For the Christian, all things are seen first in the light of God, the maker of all gifts. Furthermore, the patient cannot be understood as an isolated individual, but as a person within a larger whole, defined by family, friendships, and various interpenetrating communities.[20] "Health" is similarly redefined within such communities to include far more than pharmaceutical needs: food—remember the social importance of meals in Luke's Gospel—as well as water, housing, jobs, and a reasonable amount of safety. Understood in this way, no medical interaction concerns a single autonomous patient, nor does it place moral obligations only on medical personnel. An entire web of relationships must be considered and constantly reevaluated.

What might standard medical ethics say about the health inequities we mentioned above, if they were to speak of them at all? Using the bourgeois liberal categories of contemporary ethical thought, that which can't be reduced to the private world of contractual interaction or voluntary association typically falls to the nation-state and its governmental apparatus. Alternatively, one might employ alternate bureaucracies, such as the International Red Cross and the World Health Organization. Such nongovernmental organizations (NGOs)—a category name that makes explicit the normative place of nation-state governments in the secular world —often act more effectively than states, though they sometimes are less publicly accountable. Unfortunately, such NGOs grow into bureaucratic mirror images of the governments they are supposed to be so unlike. Thus, the chasms separating the health care of rich and poor are turned over to bureaucratically administered policies and programs, acting as much or more in their own interests than in the interests of those they claim to serve. By adopting the state model, medicine also adopts the logic of envy, rivalry, and competition characterizing the state when the tactics of co-option fail and those of coercion become "necessary." Not only did "progressive medical science," allied with the state, forcibly sterilize over 60,000 in the United States and purposely export eugenicist theory and practice to the rest of the world—including pre-Nazi Germany[21]—it also conducted the Tuskegee Syphilis Study, following but not treating syphilis-infected African American males in Alabama from 1932 to 1972, even though effective treatment for syphilis became available in 1947.[22] While various governmental entities have apologized for such mistakes, similarly troubling research continues in resource-poor, often disease-rich countries, invariably among the people least able to say no.[23]

In emulating the state, medicine further adopts the utilitarian, zero-sum calculus of scarcity that decides some people are worth saving while others are too costly to bother about, and there is little comfort in the knowledge that such exclusionary decisions are now being made individually—at least in "developed" countries. What little we seem to have learned from American and Nazi eugenics amounts to this: quality control of human "stock" ought to rest in the hands of the individual consumer, not in the bureaucratic state. Marketing itself as a supplier of technological options, medicine claims the messianic role of savior, softening the harsher edges of the state in a false promised land of individual choice, never mentioning the extent to which individual choice has been formed by available options and prevailing fashions.

Bridging the divides of care between rich and poor will surely require the power that is the nation-state as much as the power that is medicine, but Christians must not be content with merely voting persons or parties with the best policy into power. Our responsibility to the body can never be delegated. We are personally and corporately responsible to the marginalized, and the shape of that obligation is embodied in the life of Jesus: we are required to reach out to the marginalized and reincorporate them into the community, the body that Christ gathers.

Solidarity with the Poor

What shape might medicine take if lived according to gospel demands? To begin with, such medical practice would look odd enough to annoy medicine's entrenched Pharisees. One group doing precisely this is Partners in Health (PIH), led by its cofounder Paul Farmer, the physician whose observations on "quandary ethics" we noted above. Farmer is best known to the general public as the subject of Tracy Kidder's compelling biographical study, *Mountains beyond Mountains*.[24] Dr. Paul Farmer, internist, infectious disease specialist, and professor of medicine and medical anthropology at Harvard Medical School, spends the majority of each year living and working in Cange, Haiti, located in the heartbreakingly poor central plateau region of the poorest country in the western hemisphere. In a world of health disparities, Haiti is an extreme:

Haiti has the highest infant and maternal mortality, the worst malnutrition and the worst AIDS situation in the Americas. The general mortality rate . . . (is) also the highest in the Americas. A quarter of children suffer from chronic malnutrition, 3 to 6 percent from acute malnutrition. . . . Acute respiratory infections and diarrhea cause half of the deaths in children under five years of age. There are complications in a quarter of deliveries. . . . 40% of the population has no real access to basic health care, 76% of deliveries are made by non-qualified personnel, and only half the children are vaccinated."[25]

In such an unpromising place, Farmer's organization, Zanmi Lasante (Haitian Creole for "Partners in Health"), has built a general hospital with ambulatory and women's clinics, a tuberculosis treatment center, a school, and a kitchen serving 2,000 meals a day, all in the immediate vicinity of an Anglican church. While the clinics and hospital charge nominal fees, no one is refused service for inability to pay, which means many patients receive much-needed care for free. What makes Zanmi Lasante work, however, is less the incredible drive of Paul Farmer than the solidarity and community ownership embodied in its many activities and institutions. Money, medicines, and supplies come from donors in the United States and elsewhere, but it is the people of Cange who make them count. As just one example, locally trained community health workers carry out regular home visits to the many tuberculosis and HIV patients, identifying along the way those who need food, transportation, housing, or access to clean water. The health shared in common here transcends individual therapeutic intervention: there is as much meal as medicine at Zanmi Lasante.

The results are clear: mother-child transmission of HIV has been reduced to 4 percent, significantly lower than the current U.S. rate. More than 700 area patients receive HAART, the antiretroviral drug regimens most HIV patients in the United States now receive but that is largely unavailable in impoverished Haiti. Infant mortality and malnutrition have been drastically reduced. Tuberculosis is treated in systematic, communally based fashion at a fraction of U.S. costs, with no TB deaths in the Cange region since 1988.

Farmer and his colleagues work in other impoverished areas of the world, taking on similarly "impossible" projects. One of Farmer's early supporters was Father Jack Roussin, pastor at St. Mary of the Angels in an impoverished neighborhood of Boston. After Father Jack succumbed to multidrug-resistant tuberculosis (MDR-TB), contracted during his work in the slums of Lima, Peru, Farmer and fellow PIH-er Dr. Jim Yong Kim demonstrated to the World Health Organization that WHO's deliberate neglect of MDR-TB was based on faulty assumptions and false economies. Using expensive "second-line" medications—those typically reserved for patients in wealthier "developed" countries and used only when first choices fail—in a carefully monitored approach, Farmer and Kim were able to achieve an astounding 85 percent cure rate among people most TB experts had written off as "beyond hope." WHO has since changed its MDR-TB guidelines to incorporate this newer approach and—for those focused on the bottom line—reduced treatment costs by 90 percent in five years.[26]

What we find so interesting about Farmer is that this baptized Roman Catholic who never considered the religion of his birth very compelling, lacked suitable language to describe his vision for health care until, following the assassination of Salvadoran Archbishop Oscar Romero, he discovered liberation theology. Through his reading and growing familiarity with the struggles of the poor, he increasingly made common cause with impoverished Haitians as well as the nuns and "church ladies" who championed their cause. Kidder describes Farmer's process:

> He was already attracted to liberation theology. "A powerful rebuke to the hiding away of poverty," he called it. "A rebuke that transcends scholarly analysis." In Haiti, the essence of the doctrine came alive for him. Almost all the peasants he was meeting shared a belief that seemed like a distillation of liberation theology: "Everybody else hates us," they'd tell him, "but God loves the poor more. And our cause is just.". . . (Farmer) felt drawn back to his Catholicism now, not by his own belief but in sympathy with theirs, as an act of what he'd call "solidarity."[27]

It would be easy to construe Farmer's work as that of a secular physician-anthropologist who merely exploits "church connections" or employs religious language to do "mercenary work" for his causes. On the contrary, Farmer uses explicitly theological language to describe the reality he sees, opposing that vision to the one embraced by the powerful, who, if they responded to the poor at all, did so with cast-off materials and substandard "cost-effective" therapies:

> The fact that any sort of religious faith was so disdained at Harvard and so important to the poor—not just in Haiti but elsewhere, too—made me even more convinced that faith must be something good. . . . I know it sounds shallow, the opiate thing, needing to believe, palliating pain, but it didn't feel shallow. It was more profound than other sentiments I'd known, and I was taken with the idea that in an ostensibly godless world that worshiped money and power and, more seductively, a sense of personal efficacy and advancement, like at Duke and Harvard, there was still a place to look for God, and that was in the suffering of the poor.[28]

Farmer, who speaks French, Haitian Creole, and Spanish, is also multilingual when it comes to social thought. He seems comfortable using the language of liberation theology or that of human rights, depending on his audience.[29] Even so, in his book *Pathologies of Power: Health, Human*

Rights, and the New War on the Poor, he characterizes his descriptive narratives as "bearing witness," and he begins his more theoretical second half with chapters entitled "Health, Healing, and Social Justice: Insights from Liberation Theology" and "Listening for Prophetic Voices: A Critique of Market-Based Medicine."

The unofficial but incessantly used motto of Partners in Health is "O for the P," "Option for the Poor," a phrase brought into the theological lexicon at the 1979 Latin American Bishops conference in Puebla, Mexico, after much social, biblical, and ecclesial reflection.[30] Partners in Health claims this option not because the poor are better or more loved by God, but rather because the powers preferentially serve the powerful, rendering the poor and powerless invisible. The poor are where we find Christ (per Matthew 25), who demands far more than donations from our cash surplus or obsolete equipment and cast-off medicines sent abroad to salve guilty consciences. As Farmer puts it:

> Many of us . . . have heard a motto such as . . . : "the homeless poor are every bit as deserving of good medical care as the rest of us." The notion of a preferential option of the poor challenges us by reframing the motto: the homeless poor are *more* deserving of good medical care than the rest of us. Whenever medicine seeks to reserve its finest services for the destitute sick, you can be sure that it is option-for-the-poor medicine.[31]

Farmer directly takes on the alliance of medicine and state by reminding the reader how much medical "scarcity" is an invention of the nation-state. Global health resources are in fact not scarce at all, but inequitably distributed with national borders often acting as barriers to access. In *Pathologies of Power,* Farmer makes explicit the connection between the structural violence that the powers encourage us to accept as necessary and the immensity of human suffering across the globe. The zero-sum logic of scarcity leads to highly predictable patterns of violence, deprivation, and illness. In contrast, Farmer calls his readers to engage in "pragmatic solidarity," reaching beyond borders to recognize a larger community to which we are responsible.

Getting Out of the Way

Partners in Health, while using Christian language and theory, is nonetheless not a Christian organization. What it does provide Christians, however, is a model for healing outside the powers that rule the world. Those seeking a more ecclesial approach might consider the remarkable history of the San Lucas Toliman Mission along the shore of Lake Atitlan in Guatemala.

102

For forty years, the people of San Lucas Toliman, with the assistance of Father Greg Schaffer and the support of the Diocese of New Ulm, Minnesota, have answered the needs of many by simply being the church. When most Americans hear the word *mission,* the image conjured is of well-intentioned white Middle-Americans invading the jungle to convert naked heathens. Having been schooled by his Guatemalan colleagues, Father Schaffer describes this proselytizing model as "the struggle to fill the tent," contrasting that with evangelism, which he understands as "bringing what the Creator wants to God's creation."[32] "What we've learned to do," he admits, "is give the people a chance and then get out of the way."[33] After forty years in one place, "getting out of the way" clearly means something other than offering a handout and walking away. Perhaps it is better understood as being present without hindering. If anything, it serves as a reminder to all involved that each person is a channel of grace, serving the others as called upon, but never unnecessarily encumbering the other with an ego-driven need to be "helpful."

Since 1964, "La Parroquia" in San Lucas Toliman has moved from distributing relief aid in the form of food to building a communal farm to cultivating beehives, growing and selling "fairly traded" coffee, securing farmland for families, and engaging in reforestation and conservation projects.[34] Health care was first provided in a small room in the parish office, while the new two-story clinic provides modern inpatient and outpatient care, including pediatric, adult, obstetric, and eye and dental clinics, as well as a nutrition center, emergency room, and operating room. Primary and secondary schools have been built and staffed, land has been more equitably distributed, and houses and farms have been constructed with access to reliable drinking water. Every step in this process has come about because of the expressed needs of the people, with the church acting both as catalyst and the embodiment of the people. Perhaps most amazing is that all these things were accomplished despite a thirty-six-year civil war, which, while sparing San Lucas Toliman from the most horrific atrocities, nonetheless did not leave it untouched.[35]

Like Partners in Health, the San Lucas Toliman Mission cannot survive without patrons from the "developed nations," busy people who have many worthy causes from which to choose. Father Greg is in Guatemala because his religious superior asked him to go, but as he now admits, the Christian understanding of the body of Christ emphasizes that we have no actual choice with whom we associate. Rather like family, we are all brothers and sisters, dependent upon the same God. What his work teaches him, he says, is the prophets' continual reminder to the people of Israel: we are all abjectly dependent upon God, and this primary relationship to God defines our relation to everyone else. When we lose sight of this, we stray from the kingdom of God.

Father Greg shared with us the story of Celestino, a once witty and jesting neighbor in San Lucas Toliman who grew discouraged with his overbearing employer, his poor housing, and the many things he could not afford for his family.[36] In medical terms, Celestino looked clinically depressed. When Father Greg asked why he looked so downtrodden, Celestino replied: "(I) found out something today, Padre. I am an animal." Whatever had made him so resilient through years of bitter poverty was at last buckling under the weight of the powers. Soon after, at a meeting of potential parish catechists, Father Greg asked who could help turn out hand-sawn lumber for the local building projects. To Father Greg's surprise, Celestino tentatively raised his hand, saying, "Don't know if I can, Padre, but I sure will try." Celestino sought out an old craftsman who knew how to use the seven-foot pit saw, with which he soon grew skilled enough to begin training others. About the same time, he and his wife learned how to read and write through evening classes offered at the mission. Their oldest daughter was one of the first Maya-Cakchiquel girls to attend the church-sponsored school, which she later returned to as an auxiliary teacher to encourage other girls in their education. One of her brothers is also a teacher, and another went on to study medicine and now serves his people as a physician. A sister helps with the fair-trade coffee program.

Celestino helped friends and neighbors build houses before finally building one for his family—one he could at last be proud of. He also received three acres from the parish "Land for the Landless" program, from which he feeds his family and raises a small crop of coffee. Now he jokingly shows how much better his hand-sawn boards are than the milled lumber available elsewhere. In relating Celestino's story, Father Greg concludes: "A proud man, and rightly so! He had his chance, made the most of it, and we just had to get out of his way!"

This is no standard American rags-to-riches story, an individual rising above circumstances to achieve material success. Celestino's story is communal—growing out of the people's shared needs—in this case, not only lumber for building, but land to farm, schools to attend, and work to be proud of. And it started because someone (in this case, Father Greg, but it could have been anyone) saw, wondered, and asked what was wrong.[37] Celestino's material and spiritual poverty ceased to be invisible, and he was reclaimed by the community. As in Luke, there is no bright line between physical disease, material want, and spiritual distress: all must be addressed within community for any true healing to occur.

Not everyone can devote a lifetime's work to the people of Haiti or Guatemala, but every year, hundreds work short-term in these and similar endeavors, while thousands offer monetary and material support. Christians never satisfy their obligation to the body merely by writing checks, but recognizing the shared body across national borders may at least begin here.

Not Just for Saints

Not everyone can travel to developing countries. Not everyone is Mother Teresa. Many well-intentioned Christians write off such service as "saintly," by which we mean, "for other people who don't have to live in the real world." But the honor Christians have shown the saints becomes theologically incoherent if they are placed in a superhuman category. The saints are honored because, through each of them, God reveals yet another way to share the life of Christ. Through them, we get a glimpse of what God can do through our own lives if we only open ourselves to God's power. By putting saints "over there," we effortlessly escape their disturbing demand upon the way we live. Dorothy Day, no pushover herself, shot down claims that she was a living saint by insisting, "I don't want to be dismissed so easily."

The chasms in medical care we tacitly encourage through our excessive concern with the individual and his or her sacred autonomy are easily found within the borders of a country such as the United States. What makes matters worse, the invisible proximity of the indigent to the exorbitantly wealthy, as is the case in most American cities, is only exacerbated by media portrayals of what constitutes "normal": large vehicles, jewelry, the leisure time necessary to engage in self-help regimens. David Hilfiker, a family physician who left rural Minnesota to work in inner-city Washington, D.C., observes that poverty can be cruelly internalized in such circumstances.[38] Among many of the "dirt poor" here and abroad, simply lifting the yoke of economic and political oppression is sufficient—do that, and the poor will do well. For others, even the tools for sustenance have been lost, and creative economic and educational assistance is necessary. For a third group, however, even the hope of escape from poverty has been lost—they no longer believe things can be any different.[39] Drugs, alcohol, abusive relationships, and indiscriminate violence only cement this despair. Simply "getting out of the way" no longer works when people are possessed by something very much like demons.

In the capital city of the United States, Hilfiker practiced something very different from the medicine that generally worked well in Minnesota. In D.C., Hilfiker was practicing a new specialty: "poverty medicine," in which "the 'strictly medical' is not the most crucial factor in most healing."[40] By his own admission, Hilfiker's practice and writing are less about medicine than they are about race, culture, and "medical helplessness before drugs lodged . . . deeply in our society" (*NAUAS,* 13). They are less about

bold prescriptions for political or societal change than about what it's like to find oneself suddenly enmeshed in the crumbling relationship between government and the poor. It's about the grim consequences of two decades of governmental withdrawal and the deliberate underfunding of social agencies, about the helplessness of helpers running into closed doors and cul-de-sacs of social policy. It is about the wholesale abandonment of the poor. (*NAUAS,* 13)[41]

But, like Paul Farmer and the missionaries of San Lucas Toliman, Hilfiker sees the violence done to the poor in theological terms:

> If one dismisses spiritual (or even explicitly religious) motivation for medical work with the inner-city poor—in Washington, at least—there's not much left to talk about in the 1990s except the leaching of all care from the ever-growing worlds of poverty and homelessness. . . . Often all that was left were church groups and other parareligious organizations trying against overwhelming odds to address even the barest, most basic needs of the poor. . . . The "liberal" inclination to see in economic and political oppression the causes of poverty must not blind us to the fact that an unjust society produces a kind of brokenness that cannot always be addressed by removing the injustice. (*NAUAS,* 21–22)

What Hilfiker, strengthened by his church community, finds himself called to do is live with the poor to whom he provides medical care, in their own neighborhood, in a residence just above the inpatient facilities for "Christ House." He reclaims the poor into community less by healing wounds than by being present, by entering, in the limited ways available to him, into the community of the poor. Hilfiker may not be as accomplished a writer as Paul Farmer's biographer, but his story is compelling nonetheless, in part because of his unsettling honesty: Hilfiker picks apart the bourgeois defenses most of us employ whenever responsibility to the poor is mentioned. He unflinchingly examines the divides of race, class, and life experience that inevitably distance him from those he serves. He devotes as much attention to his failures as to his successes:

> Perhaps the deepest pain involved in living among the poor is the juxtaposition of my own limitations and woundedness with theirs. . . . The demands of justice, at least in this city, are endless. And it is precisely in trying to respond in some small way that I find my own damaged heart, my own limits. (*NAUAS,* 168)

But the limits he embraces in practicing "poverty medicine" are not only personal. The power of medicine imposes many of its own: urban hospitals creaking under the weight of patients unable to pay a fraction of what their care actually costs, a system of medical education that uses the urban poor for training purposes, and doctors who applaud Hilfiker's work even as they question his decision to "waste your professional education" on something better suited for "a social worker or nurse practitioner" (213). We are all broken people working under the influence of the powers. Only by God's grace and strengthened by the community into which we are gathered can any of us hope to persevere.

Practices of Presence

Hilfiker ultimately left Christ House to establish a similar residential facility for HIV-infected patients. What remains unchanged in his new setting is the uncomfortable bodily closeness to the poor, the direct encounter resisting the power of medicine to dissolve the poor into abstraction—a patient who goes home (if he has a home) to a place most of us, in more comfortable surroundings, choose not to think about. Others, both in and outside the medical professions, are called to be present in their own way. If we can't move to the inner city and practice "poverty medicine," we can be present through other practices of hospitality: soup kitchens, food banks, housing assistance, drug treatment programs, and halfway houses. We can also witness, as Christians, to secular powers, encouraging them to consider the needs of the poor to be at least as important as the needs of the fortunate.

Within the systems of medical education, a greater awareness of the needs of the poor is essential. Christian Community Health Fellowship encourages such awareness and calls students, nurses, therapists, and physicians to pay attention.[42] Many sustained endeavors, such as Crossroad Health Center, located in one of the most poverty-stricken neighborhoods of Cincinnati, have been inspired by the work of John Perkins. Perkins's reflections on his work with impoverished and oppressed communities stresses the responsibility for Christians to relocate, reconcile, and redistribute: living and working among the people we serve, loving God and neighbor properly, and putting our lives, education, and talent in the service of the community. The goal is, with God's grace, to address the universal needs so often unmet in poor and oppressed communities: the need to belong, the need to be significant and important, and the need for a reasonable amount of security.[43]

The goal for Christians is not a world where everyone can afford cosmetic surgery or use medical technology in purely individual terms, but rather a community where our webs of connection are recognized and nurtured in faithfulness to God. Such communities require bodily presence, not "telescopic philanthropy" or acts of drive-by charity. Bodily presence opens mind and spirit to the senses, enabling us to truly see the poor, hear the suffering, touch the sick—and for them to see, hear, and touch us. What Paul Farmer, Father Greg, David Hilfiker, and countless others have undergone is no less than a conversion, guided by the very people the powers encourage us not to see, hear, or touch. By being present to the poor, we learn how to inhabit our own bodies, recognizing ourselves in places we did not expect, across borders we once imagined uncrossable.

107

7

Perfection Money Can't Buy

■ Imagine yourself a movie director filming the Gospel of Matthew using a script that emphasizes "word-for-word fidelity to the text."[1] You've tried to clear your mind of images from DeMille, Zeffirelli, Scorsese, and perhaps even Monty Python, but, to your annoyance, these depictions keep creeping into your work. Today you're shooting the Sermon on the Mount,[2] and you hope to bring something fresh, even startling to the scene. You seek authenticity.

From the perspective of his listeners, you film Jesus, sitting (as was the custom of the Jewish teachers of his day) on a hilltop, surrounded by his disciples. You've asked makeup and wardrobe to make your Jesus look like an unkempt first-century Palestinian prophet: tired, scruffy, dust-covered; anything but the statuesque, Nordic, and vaguely effeminate Jesus of popular North American imagination. Jesus is teaching—not an inherently interesting visual—challenging the disciples to follow in the way of the kingdom of God, interpreting for them the "Law and Prophets,"[3] exhorting them to live peaceably with each other, to love their enemies, to care for those in need, and to lay up for themselves treasures in heaven. The Sermon on the Mount is full of difficult, disturbing sayings, but, for dramatic effect, you emphasize the shocker at the center of Jesus's discourse: "Be perfect, therefore, as your heavenly Father is perfect."[4] The music swells; the camera closes in until nothing is visible but Jesus's considerably less than perfect face.

To modern ears, Jesus's often-rehearsed exhortation to moral perfection sounds at best quaint and at worst offensive. Nobody, after all, is perfect. To the extent we can even imagine what it might mean, most inhabitants of contemporary North American culture have long since given up on perfection where our own behavior is concerned, pragmatically regarding it variously as impractical, impossible, unimaginable, or even dangerous. Even most contemporary Christians, it seems, have little interest in being perfect; after all, as the bumper sticker says, "Christians aren't perfect, just forgiven." In this sense, we have become unknowing followers of the twentieth century's best-known "public" theologian, Reinhold Niebuhr, who famously regarded the teachings of Jesus as an "impossible ethical ideal,"[5] something to be admired, but certainly not aspired to. The way of life taught by Jesus, Niebuhr claimed, "transcends the possibilities of human life in its final pinnacle as God transcends the world."[6] Niebuhr must be right. Surely Jesus didn't mean those words to be taken literally, did he? Well, that depends . . .

Perfection of a Different Sort

Imagine now a different scenario, one probably more familiar than the Sermon on the Mount by virtue of its being broadcast weekly via cable television into millions of American homes. It might take the form of any one of a variety of television genres: a salacious serial drama, a "reality television" game show, or a documentary, albeit one designed to entertain as much as to inform. Regardless of the type, the spatial hub around which the show turns is a physician's office, almost always in an upscale, predominantly white suburb. The physicians are often young, usually male, and invariably charismatic and attractive. They offer not instruction, but service; they sit, confronted not by disciples, but by clients. They are cosmetic plastic surgeons,[7] and they, like Jesus, are advocates and purveyors of a kind of perfection.

One of the more popular of these shows, a serial drama, recurrently features one nearly identical scene. Sitting across the table in their well-appointed office from a prospective client, two cosmetic surgeons inquire: "Tell us what you don't like about yourself." The responses, given the context, are unsurprising: "My ass," says one client; "my breasts," says another; "my knees," intones a third. And of course, the young doctors are nearly always willing to use their expertise and the technology at their disposal to give—or rather, to sell—these patients the things they desire, be it a better ass, better breasts, or better knees.

109

Better Bodies? Better Selves?

Our culture's present obsession with cosmetic surgery in particular and more generally with so-called enhancement technologies is fascinating, if not incredible. According to the American Society of Plastic Surgeons, physicians performed nearly nine million procedures in 2003 alone, ostensibly freely chosen by patients in order "to proactively manage signs of aging or enhance their appearance."[8] And this is to say nothing of the millions who now use drugs like Viagra™ for sexual enhancement, who take selective serotonin reuptake inhibitors (SSRIs) like Prozac™ to elevate their mood, or who eagerly anticipate the time when developments in medical genetics will make them or their yet-to-be-conceived progeny smarter, more athletic, or better looking. Enhancement via medicine has gone mainstream.

In light of the previous chapter, and given that the enhancement industry tends frequently to caricature itself, it would be easy enough to condemn all these procedures and technologies as nonsense or worse, to say that Christians should never use them, and be done with it. Yet we wonder if a blanket condemnation of all those practices and technologies that may be described as enhancement—whether cosmetic surgery or SSRIs or medical genetics—might not be a subtle variety of body-denying Gnosticism.[9] For surely there are valid places in our lives for at least some of the therapeutic benefits these things afford. Moreover, an appreciation of the physical beauty of another person, the pleasure of lovemaking, the capacity to take pleasure in confronting a new day, or the possibility of a future free from certain genetically borne illnesses are in themselves not wholly inconsistent with how Christians have understood the good gift of God's creation. And if this is the case, why not use the technology at our disposal to enhance our appreciation of these gifts?

We have to concede that this is a good question without a simple answer. We readily admit that reconstructive plastic surgery, antidepressants, and medications designed to treat sexual dysfunction are all potentially significant goods. Yet we believe that there are compelling theological reasons for Christians to reject these technologies in many circumstances. Like all features of this contingent creation, goods like physical beauty, sexual pleasure, or relative freedom from melancholy or physical restrictions are at best subordinate goods. The desire for such goods is legitimate only insofar as it is placed in the service of that vision of human flourishing that counts as its greatest good friendship with God, and it seems to us that enhancement technologies are for the most part used without much thought of God. Just so, we think it important to ask about the sources of our desire for the goods these technologies offer, as well as the origins of the account of human perfection those goods imply.

Buying a Better Body, Making a Better Me

What we are suggesting is that it might be helpful to interrogate a couple of fairly common presumptions about these matters. One of these is that the desire for a youthful, vigorous appearance and a cheerful, energetic demeanor, which we take to be the paradigmatic goals of enhancement, is "natural," that it is encoded in our genes by the evolutionary process. We want to look youthful, attractive, and vigorous because youth, attractiveness, and vigor increase our chances of sexual, and so of reproductive, success. We want to be attractive, in other words, because attractive people have a better chance of having sex, which is a necessary prerequisite (the matters discussed in chapter 5 of this book notwithstanding) to having offspring and perpetuating the lineage, which is "the ultimate goal of all species."[10]

This sociobiological explanation for why we seek to enhance our appearance or demeanor is certainly interesting, and probably partly right—as far as it goes. However, like most sociobiology, it is far too reductionist to be of much help.[11] Its crude misreading of evolutionary theory notwithstanding, this argument is simply inadequate as an explanation of why millions of Americans spend billions of dollars each year to modify their appearance or personality or seek to control the characteristics of their children.[12] For one thing, there are simply too many counterexamples of people who do not conform to these ideals who have had "reproductive success"—the authors of this book among them. And for another, we have yet to hear a satisfying sociobiological argument for why Botox® injections, breast augmentation, and blepharoplasty are "natural," while the changes in the body that typically accompany aging are not.[13]

A second presumption, probably more frequently advanced (if not assumed) at the popular level, is that when enhancement technologies are employed, they are freely chosen by rational, autonomous individuals—that is, they are "lifestyle choices."[14] Undoubtedly, this is true, but only to the extent that we understand that our reason and freedom are shaped, and so limited, by the culture we inhabit, and that the notion "lifestyle choices" is part of the complex web of language and practices that make up our contemporary consumer capitalist society. We choose, in other words, the things we have been shaped by our culture to want. The work of Carl Elliott, who has written the most insightful account of enhancement technologies we know of, [15] leads us to believe that the contemporary embrace of enhancement is largely explicable in terms of two closely related aspects of our world: the extent to which our technological acumen makes possible mass exposure to identical images, and the nature of our political economy.

In pointing to technological acumen, we do not refer so much to our culture's increasingly sophisticated control over the circumstances of our lives (amazing as these are), as to the ways technology in the service of mass communication can make things like enhancement seem "natural." As Elliott observes, ours is an intensely image-conscious world, largely because it is so image-intensive. Current technologies, television being the most obvious, bombard us with visual images, and those images provide an ideal for human appearance and behavior, suggesting that the further we are from this ideal, the less our chances for real happiness.[16]

Television creates for the viewer an "alternate reality" populated by the beautiful women and men we call celebrities, people we long, at some level, to be like (BW, 85). We know celebrities not so much because of their accomplishments, but because of the ubiquity of their images. Celebrities are famous because they are constantly seen.[17] And our constant exposure to their images leads us to think, as Elliott puts it, "that genuine human worth dwells in the phenomenon of being watched" (BW, 85). But the chance that anyone would want to watch us, we are taught to believe, depends on how closely we approximate the ideal projected and sustained by visual media, something most of us need considerable help to accomplish.[18]

Most of us are aware that such help is readily available because the same media that sell the celebrity ideal also suggest to us the means to achieve it. It is hardly accidental that consumer capitalism flourished with the rise of television and other visual media, since "consumer capitalism works, at least in part, by presenting consumers with a vision of the good life. This vision of the good life suggests the ways in which the consumer's life does not measure up, and could be remedied by the consumer product" (BW, 119). One of the central characteristics of such a political economy is its tendency toward what is sometimes called hypercommodification. Not only does consumer capitalism teach us what to want, but also to understand everything we might want, including the ideal form of our own bodies, as available for purchase.

Elliott points to the late-nineteenth-century philosopher Thorstein Veblen and his book *The Theory of the Leisure Class* as the most interesting explanation of this process. Veblen was the first to suggest that people of sufficient means will buy certain things because possessing those things affords to the owner a certain public image:

Conspicuous consumption is Veblen's name for buying not what you need, or even to acquire what you want for utilitarian purposes, but in order to acquire public esteem. This is not merely a matter of trying to impress other people. Consumption is also the basis of *self*-esteem, or, as Veblen says, self-respect—since self-respect depends on the respect of others. In

112

Veblen's world, the point of buying things is not to satisfy your needs but to outrank your friends and neighbors. (*BW,* 102)

It is important to note, however, that conspicuous consumers do not buy in order to stand out or be regarded as exceptional. Rather, the goal is to fit in, not to the undifferentiated masses, but into the particular social circle the consumer regards as most desirable, which is usually just beyond the one currently inhabited. "The motive for this striving, says Veblen, is not greed but emulation: consumers are always trying to outdo those with whom they are in the habit of comparing themselves" (*BW,* 104).[19]

Here of course we are brought back to the influence of visually centered mass media in shaping our desires. We learn from these media, and from the advertisements sponsoring them (the two are increasingly indistinguishable) what to want and whom to emulate. In all cultures, appearance and demeanor "code," meaning they point beyond themselves to suggest social attributes like wealth, power, and sexual desirability (*BW,* 116–17). In the contemporary culture of conspicuous consumption, with its cult of celebrity, the significance of this phenomenon is multiplied. Enhancement technologies offer to the consumer the means to alter his or her appearance or demeanor, and so in one way or another to say to those who might be watching, "My life is good."

Consuming Identity

More surprising, though entirely predictable, is the way in which an image-driven hypercommodification of the self and the body becomes confused with personal identity. As Carl Elliott tells it, he became interested in enhancement therapies in part by reading Peter Kramer's best-selling book *Listening to Prozac.*[20] With the advent of selective serotonin reuptake inhibitors (SSRIs), the critique of enhancements such as cosmetic surgery as "false to the self" came under serious attack. As Kramer documented, patients taking Prozac didn't claim the drug made them feel like a new person; they said it made them feel like themselves (*BW,* 51). For some, but not all, patients on SSRIs, their "true self" was the person on medicine, and Prozac was less a therapy than an identity device. Soon, thousands of people with little or no history of clinical depression were taking Prozac for its effects on personality rather than mood.

But if true identity can be achieved only with the help of a consumer item—in this case a pharmaceutical—which self is "natural": the "true" one on Prozac, or the "false" one without? It would appear that this is a matter for the consumer to decide. Just so, this apparent malleability of the self turns "true personal identity" into one more—perhaps the ulti-mate—consumer item. Sociologist Grant McCracken complains, "There was a time when this self-invention was impossible. We were defined by others. Religion, the community, work, in-laws, husbands, children, our ethnic group, our neighbors were all happy to tell us what to do." Today, however, "We all live lives now of active transformation. This is one of the great accomplishments of our cultural tradition and one of the great joys of our personal lives."[21] Frequent, total transformations of personality are no longer symptoms of the vice of inconstancy, but freedom itself. As Carl Elliott points out, we are to be forgiven for imagining that the subject of McCracken's effusive praise is Enlightenment political thought instead of his real concern, women's hairstyles since the 1950s: "McCracken's book, *Big Hair,* carries the subtitle *A Journey into the Transformation of the Self,* which is a pretty good description of how McCracken sees hair" (*BW,* 115).

But far more is at stake here than beehives and wedges. Identity itself is up for sale, and the market has less to do with what any one person might really want than what's put on the shelf. In what Elliott tellingly calls a "Gnostic truth," he explains: "A market economy has nothing remotely to do with getting what you want. It has everything to do with making yourself feel good about what is available" (*BW,* 135). This is a Gnostic truth indeed, for it trades in and ultimately depends upon there being a radical distinction between the feeling, wanting human subject—that is, the "I" who feels and wants—and the particular, concrete circumstances of any one person's existence.

Seen through the lens of orthodox Christian theology, such a distinc-tion is nothing more than heresy. For what self, apart from the gift of the body, exists to shop the identity market? And if the mind and identity itself can be altered with medications, what part of the disembodied self is making these choices? Apparently there is nothing left to enliven this puppet self but the tiny part of the mind or soul that makes choices. Choosing itself becomes the defining mark of human identity. In remaking identity as a consumer item, the person is whittled away into sawdust, and modernity's precious autonomy is revealed as little more than the triumph of the will.[22]

And the body? In classic Gnostic fashion, it becomes mere clothing for the identity, having nothing to do with the "true self," which can refashion the body as it chooses as the means to do so become available. Thus, in one of Elliott's most disturbing chapters, he talks with apotemnophiliacs, people who feel abnormal with four healthy limbs and seek otherwise unnecessary amputations in order to (re)gain a sense of "wholeness." Elliott is again struck by the use of identity language, for example: "I have always felt I should be an amputee." "I felt, this is who I was." "It is a desire to see myself, as I 'know' or 'feel' myself to be" (*BW,* 211). In short, apotemnophiliacs feel, absent the amputation of one or more limbs, that they are "stuck in the wrong body."

But, as Elliott rightly asks, what can such a statement really mean, when the true self is the one produced by medical science (*BW,* 211)? For orthodox Christians, moreover, what self, apart from the gift of the body indissolubly connected to the spirit, could conceivably be located in the "wrong" container? Unlike most classic Gnosticism, this modern version does not so much hate the body as it instrumentalizes it, making flesh the malleable servant of the will. The vastly superior, incorporeal self decides how the body will conform to the latest chosen self. If version 3.0 demanded liposuction, 3.1 might require a more intriguing cocktail manner and 3.2 a nicely cleft chin.

There are, of course, more serious body-identity dilemmas than slim thighs and enhanced penis size. What of the person who claims to be trapped in a body of the wrong sex? We can claim no expertise in this matter, both of us being insufficiently imaginative to ponder escape from maleness. There may well be a reason to surgically alter genitalia and hormonally reconfigure the body so that flesh conforms to body image. But Paul McHugh, longtime professor of psychiatry at Johns Hopkins University, provides some reason for caution. In an article entitled "Psychiatric Misadventures,"[23] McHugh describes three fashionable attempts to go beyond the limited knowledge base of psychiatry (which McHugh calls "a rudimentary medical art"): schizophrenia viewed as "psychiatric oppression," multiple personality disorder, and gender reassignment surgery. McHugh contends this last "misadventure" uses surgical means to deal with what he considers a psychiatric disorder. "Surely," he says, "the fault is in the mind, not the member."[24] Before debating the factual basis for McHugh's claims, Christians who understand the body as God's unique gift should at least pause to consider his words. Altering the body to conform to the mind or a more socially acceptable mind-body relationship has more than just theological repercussions. Elliott notes:

> Psychiatry and surgery have had an extraordinary and often destructive collaboration over the past seventy-five years or so: clitoridectomy for excessive masturbation, cosmetic surgery as a treatment for an "inferiority complex," intersex surgery for infants born with ambiguous genitalia, and—most notorious—the frontal lobotomy. It is a collaboration with few unequivocal successes. (*BW,* 235)

We fear a similar litany will be all too easy to assemble some decades hence when considering the history of enhancement therapies. More likely, though, as in Huxley's *Brave New World,* or the eugenic dystopia depicted in the film *Gattaca,* we will come to see the new order of things as normal, even desirable.

Discerning Bodies

How is the gathered body, the Christian body, served through enhancement therapies? Historically, cultures have altered bodies not just to improve social desirability, but also to ensure social cohesion. For example, tattoos and other body modifications can indicate status or social commitment. And surely a depressed parent may better serve his family if he takes an appropriately prescribed antidepressant. Once again, we quickly stray into the language of identity, though. Do the secondary social effects of one person's happiness following cosmetic rhinoplasty justify spending large sums of money? Of course, if authentic selfhood is the primary issue, there's little room for argument.

Consider, though, the following statistics. In the United States in 2001, there were 1.8 million vision correction procedures performed (one per eye), mostly LASIK surgery. In a recent Gallup poll, 85 percent of those interviewed who said they were interested in LASIK surgery stated that their primary interest was to "alleviate dependence on eyeglasses or contacts."[25] In other words, they were seeking corrective surgery to replace their "unnatural" glasses and contacts. Some people have found LASIK surgery truly liberating, and we do not condemn outright those who seek or perform it. Perhaps less defensible in light of what is to follow, however, are the 246,633 purely cosmetic eyelid procedures (blepharoplasty) done in 2003.[26]

Now consider the world burden of blindness from just two medical conditions: river blindness (onchocerciasis) and trachoma. River blindness, found in Africa, the Arabian peninsula, and the Americas, is caused by a parasite that currently infects over 18 million people, and has left 300,000 irreversibly blind. Over 125 million people are considered at risk for transmission of the disease. Worldwide prevention of river blindness is technically possible by killing the parasites and controlling the flies that spread them. Trachoma, caused by repeated infections with the microorganism *Chlamydia trachomatis,* which currently infects 150 million people, mostly in areas of extreme poverty, has left 5.9 million people irreversibly blind, making it second only to cataracts as a worldwide cause of blindness. Trachoma can be treated or prevented with surgery, antibiotics, facial cleanliness, and environmental controls.[27]

Are medical and economic resources well used to freshen up sagging eyelids when millions are doomed to readily preventable blindness? We realize that, in macroeconomic terms at least, this is a silly question. But we're not asking as economists or Americans, and we readily admit we have no powerful arguments for economists or Americans as such for either to change the current situation. We ask, however, as Christians, wondering if by entering the communion line with perfect eyelids while the gathered body in the Sudan can't see at all, are we not eating and drinking condemnation on ourselves (1 Cor. 11:29)? Surely such conditions ought at least to give us pause when contemplating cosmetic medical procedures.

Anything for Love?

In every culture, from North America to Sudan, certain appearances and demeanor code for success. But they also code for desirability. They say not simply "my life is good," but also, and by extension, "I am desirable. I am worthy of love." In the end, we believe, the proliferation of enhancement technologies is largely about the desire to be desired, to fit in, to be regarded as worthy by another person. Say what you will about the autonomous subject, about "doing this for myself"; the self for whom we do these things is a self who wants to be wanted, who cares about being cared for. In this visually centered, visually intense world, being wanted is not only expensive, but a lot of work, and it is hardly surprising that we should seek the help of one of the most powerful and technologically sophisticated industries to achieve desirability. Yet the desire to be wanted and the treacherous political machinations necessary for satisfying that desire are anything but new.

For a sense of the dangers and difficulties inherent in what we might call the "politics of security,"[28] we turn to a classic example, found in the opening scene of William Shakespeare's tragedy *King Lear*. This scene is sometimes called the "love-auction."[29] The elderly Lear, having decided to retire and withdraw from public life, decides to divide his wealth among his three daughters, and to do so based ostensibly on the relative magnitude of their public declaration of love for him:

> Tell me, my daughters
> (Since now we will divest us both of rule,
> Interest of territory, cares of state),
> Which of you shall we say doth love us most?
> That we our largest bounty may extend
> Where nature doth with merit challenge.

Almost immediately, the careful reader comes to suspect that Lear's motives are complex and far from selfless. Because he is about to divest himself of his wealth, Lear's future security depends on his daughters' love. Past experience has taught him that his two elder daughters, Goneril and Regan, are selfish schemers who love no one but themselves, and that his younger daughter, Cordelia, is a person of considerable character who cares deeply for him. What Lear wants is for Cordelia to win the auction. This will justify the outcome upon which he has already decided, that she receive the greatest share of his kingdom, thereby assuring him a comfortable and dignified old age.[30] But this outcome depends on her willingness to outdo her sisters. She will have to embarrass herself by flattering her father in public.

As the auction begins, the eldest daughter, Goneril, speaks first, and holds nothing back:

> Sir, I love you more than words can wield the matter;
> Dearer than eyesight, space, and liberty;
> Beyond what can be valued, rich or rare;
> No less than life, with grace, health, beauty, honour;
> As much as child e'er lov'd, or father found;
> A love that makes breath poor, and speech unable.
> Beyond all manner of so much I love you.

The second daughter, Regan, follows, and her declaration is even more lavish than her sister's:

> Sir, I am made
> Of the selfsame metal that my sister is,
> And prize me at her worth. In my true heart
> I find she names my very deed of love;
> Only she comes too short, that I profess
> Myself an enemy to all other joys
> Which the most precious square of sense possesses,
> And find I am alone felicitate
> In your dear Highness' love.

Lear responds to his elder daughters' declarations as he had planned, pledging to each of them a modest share of his kingdom while continuing to rely on Cordelia's willingness to play his game. That is, he depends on her engaging in the same deceitful hyperbole her sisters have already displayed, an activity not at all in keeping with her virtuous character. Lear sets the stage for her to deliver the performance he expects:

> —Now, our joy,
> Although the last, not least; to whose young love
> The vines of France and milk of Burgundy
> Strive to be interest; what can you say to draw
> A third more opulent than your sisters? Speak.

But Cordelia's response is hardly what Lear expected. To Lear's "what can you say," she responds:

> Nothing, my Lord.
> Lear: Nothing?
> Cordelia: Nothing.
> Lear: Nothing can come of nothing. Speak again.
> Cordelia: Unhappy that I am, I cannot heave
> My heart into my mouth. I love your Majesty
> According to my bond; no more nor less.

Lear finds himself now on the horns of a dilemma; he has counted on Cordelia's cooperation to justify giving her the largest share of the kingdom, thereby securing his own future. If he retracts his earlier declaration and divides the kingdom on some other basis, he risks losing face with those gathered to watch, some of whom are men of considerable stature. But if he cannot persuade Cordelia to play along, he exposes himself to the risk of being dependent for the remainder of his days on people who care nothing about him. To Cordelia's terse initial reply, he says, "How, how, Cordelia? Mend your speech a little / Lest it may mar your fortunes." Cordelia's stubbornly honest reply exposes her father's game and her sisters' participation as the deceptions they are, while stating in the clearest possible terms the extent of her love for Lear:

> Good my lord,
> You have begot me, bred me, lov'd me; I
> Return those duties back as are right fit,
> Obey you, love you, and most honour you.
> Why have my sisters husbands, if they say
> They love you all? Haply, when I shall wed,
> That lord whose hand must take my plight shall carry
> Half my love with him, half my care and duty.
> Sure I shall never marry like my sisters,
> To love my father all.

Lear's response is harsh. He decides Cordelia shall receive nothing in the way of an inheritance, with her portion divided among her sisters, and he will live out his retirement alternating between their households. He will maintain his title and the service of a modest number of knights, but otherwise will depend exclusively on his daughters' generosity for his livelihood. It is here that the tragic character of the story begins to unfold.

The elder sisters behave badly toward their father, refusing him not merely the service of his knights, but his title and the honor he believes is due him. Once he is no longer in a position to bless them with power or wealth, their love for him disappears, and they treat him as they might a beggar, offering food and shelter and nothing more.[31] His ungrateful daughters at last revealed as they truly are, their cruelty drives Lear into a madness from which he will not fully recover, a place in which the love he so desperately wanted is nowhere to be seen.[32]

We are hesitant to draw too tight an analogy between the circumstances of *King Lear* and those leading so many in our own world to turn to enhancement technologies to make themselves desirable, and so to secure themselves and their futures against a dangerous and loveless world. Yet some things seem to be characteristic both of Lear's world and of our own. Both are populated by women and men who need to be loved, and both are hard places where love appears scarce. Such scarcity tempts us to strive to make ourselves lovely, sometimes without regard to the costs or consequences of our efforts, or else to despair of love, convinced that we are simply unworthy of another's desire. In this world, as in Lear's, our striving and our despair have about them something of the tragic. Thankfully, we are afforded the possibility of inhabiting a different world, one where love and acceptance are not so scarce.

Is This What Jesus Had in Mind?

At this point we might do well to return to our starting place, Jesus's Sermon on the Mount. We began this chapter considering what Jesus might have meant when he told his disciples to "be perfect," noting that this exhortation has led generations of Christians either to despair their inability to be sinless or to interpretative gymnastics of the sort displayed by Niebuhr and his followers. Both of these alternatives miss the point, for both, says John Howard Yoder, "import a modern concept of perfection where it has no place."[33]

It is possible to render Jesus's words in Matthew 5:48 as "be perfect," but based on the context this is not a good translation.[34] The exhortation occurs at the end of a discourse that may be understood as Jesus's interpretation of the spirit and intent of the second table (the second half) of the Decalogue (the Ten Commandments). Jesus is instructing his followers concerning the proper nature of their relationships—to family members, fellow members of the Christian community, strangers, and enemies. The paragraph concluded by the language in question begins with distinguishing observation of this part of the Sermon: "You have heard that it was said . . . but I say to you . . ." In this paragraph, the particular relationship in question is to the disciples' enemies:

You have heard that it was said, "You shall love your neighbor and hate your enemy." But I say to you, Love your enemies and pray for those who persecute you, so that you may be children of your Father in heaven. . . . For if you love those who love you, what reward do you have? . . . And if you greet only your brothers and sisters, what more are you doing than others? Do not even the Gentiles do the same? Be perfect, therefore, as your heavenly Father is perfect. (Matt. 5:43–48 NRSV)

Beyond the well-known and usually ignored call to love one's enemies, the broader theological point of this paragraph has to do with God's work in the world: God's people are called to reflect, in their life together, God's character. It is God's nature to love not simply the lovely, but the unlovely, as well.[35] And "because God does not discriminate, his disciples are called upon likewise not to discriminate in choosing the objects of their love."[36] To "be perfect" is to abandon the politics of security and immerse oneself in the politics of indiscriminate love.

Admittedly, the application of this notion to the concerns of this chapter is not straightforward—it is not so simple, that is, to say that since God loves ugly, fat, depressed people as much as attractive, athletic, cheerful ones, we shouldn't care about how we look or feel or how others look or feel. But the fact of God's indiscriminate, embodied love does, we believe, give us a perspective from which to look anew at enhancement technology. Just to the extent that our use of enhancement technologies is motivated by the desire to make ourselves, as individuals, desirable or otherwise worthy according to the distorted standards of contemporary culture, it is misbegotten. And just to the extent that we allow our regard for others to be captive to such standards, we fail to love as we have been loved, and so fail to bear witness to the world the nature and extent of the love of God for the creation. We are called to be transformed, but into conformity with an ideal far different from the one reflected in the pale light of the television screen.

8

Frailty and Grief,
Overcome by Hope and Love

■ Wendell Berry's *Jayber Crow* is a beautiful, elegiac novel that tells, according to the subtitle, "the life story of Jayber Crow, barber, of the Port William membership, in his own words."[1] The book is that, certainly, but like all of Berry's fiction, it is much more. *Jayber Crow* is a work of love, a careful meditation on how thoughtful women and men come to discover, love, and pursue—sometimes seemingly in vain—the things in life that matter most, things like truth, love, and a sense of belonging to a place and a community of friends. Berry depicts the wise, reflective Jayber's entire life precisely as such a quest, one that begins in earnest when, as a preministerial student at a small, denominational college, he commences silently to question his teachers' easy embrace of theological simplicities such as literal biblical inerrancy. When his questions grow so ponderous he can no longer keep them to himself, Jayber begins, one by one, to go to his teachers, "starting with the easiest questions and the talkiest professors."[2] Yet the facile answers they offer him are unsatisfying, and their advice to stop asking questions proves impossible for their invincibly earnest pupil.

That earnestness, finally, leads Jayber to approach the one professor he genuinely fears. "I was afraid to go to him," he recalls, "because I knew he was going to tell me the truth."[3] In a burst of emotion Jayber floods the professor's office with difficult theological questions, and then waits intently for a response. But the professor has no answers, or none he is willing to offer, and the two are left staring at each other as the significance of Jayber's predicament grows clear. He can scarcely serve as pastor in a church that proclaims as truth such illogic, and he must, if he is to remain true to himself and his quest for understanding, resign his scholarship and leave the college. "I had this feeling," says Jayber to the professor, "maybe I had been called."

> "And you may have been right. But not to what you thought. Not to what you think. You have been given questions to which you cannot be *given* answers. You will have to live them out—perhaps a little at a time."
> "And how long is that going to take?"
> "I don't know. As long as you live, perhaps."
> "That could be a long time."
> "I will tell you a further mystery," he said. "It may take longer."[4]

And so begins Jayber Crow's quest, which we like to think is a splendid metaphor for the difficult, lifelong task of Christian faithfulness. For the truth of Christianity is not ultimately an idea or a set of propositions to be assented to, but a life to be lived. It is a life that must be lived in constancy in the face of unanswered questions and in spite of sometimes significant uncertainty, and it is a life about which the full truth cannot be known until it is ended. "For now," as St. Paul explains, "we see in a mirror, dimly, but then we will see face to face. Now I know only in part; then I will know fully, even as I have been fully known" (1 Cor. 13:12 NRSV).

Remembering Our Baptism

In the course of a lifetime, we grow into the fullness of faith as we learn to embrace the vital realities established by our baptism. Among these is a paradox: having been joined bodily to Jesus in his death and resurrection, we are freed to live out our lives within the bounds of our creatureliness. This means we are free to accept and even to receive as gifts all that flows from being embodied, including our frailty, our dependence, and finally, our mortality. In so doing, we learn important lessons: our lives as bodies are good gifts from a gracious God, who controls the course and outcome not only of our lives, but of all history. Because we come from God, belong to God, and are destined finally to return to God, we need not fight without restraint to control all the circumstances of our existence, or to preserve our lives as they near their end, or to control absolutely the circumstances of our dying.[5]

Death is an evil—Paul acknowledges in 1 Corinthians 15 that it remains, even after the resurrection of Jesus, an "enemy"—but it is not the worst thing that can happen to us. God is with us in our dying as much as in our living, and we have the promise that Jesus's resurrection from death was the first of many yet to come (1 Cor. 15:20–28). Moreover, as we are freed from seeing death as our ultimate, unvanquished enemy, we are freed as well from the terror of death. As the Orthodox Great Vespers for the Genealogy of Christ proclaims: "Thou didst demolish by Thy Death, O Lord, the gates of Hades; Thou didst dissolve the realm of death; and didst free the human race from corruption, granting the world life and incorruptibility and Great Mercy." In light of this gift and its accompanying freedom from terror, we are able to be with and care for those who suffer and die, offering them the gift of our presence and receiving from them the gift of their passing.[6]

Christianity thus turns out to be not simply about what happens to us after we die, but also about our learning to live together in such a way that our dying—and our caring for others as they die—is the earthly conclusion of a faithfulness we learn and live out along the way. We remain fearful of death, sometimes terribly so. We grieve the loss of those we love, deeply and often inconsolably. Yet our fear and grief are tempered by our vision of an eternal future with God and each other in the communion of saints. Thus we understand that entering into the "face to face" Paul speaks about to the Corinthians is but the completion of a journey begun at, and a trajectory established by, our emergence from the baptismal font, where we are joined to Jesus in his burial and resurrection (Rom. 6:3–11). As Jayber Crow learned from his teacher, this is a journey that takes an entire lifetime, and perhaps even longer. Yet it is a journey we can hope to complete only if we begin now to live into the truth of our baptism.

Denying Mortality in a Culture of Death

The work of embodying Christian faithfulness at the end of life, of learning to die well and to care well for those who are dying, is especially arduous in contemporary North American culture. What Pope John Paul II has called a "culture of death" is in fact a culture of control that characteristically prefers death only as a matter of convenience or of hastening the inevitable.[7] We fear dying, to be sure, but we also prefer not to be present to death, to be reminded of the inevitability of death, or even to talk about death, for such reminders are offenses to our unspoken hope that, with the help of an increasingly able medicine, we might be able to avoid death—at least for a long, long time. Just so, our basic, intuitive fear of death is multiplied as we distance ourselves from the phenomenon of

124

death and from as many reminders as possible of our own mortality, a distancing that is advanced by the very structure of the world we inhabit.[8]

Perhaps the best way to characterize that structure is to say that it is one of dividedness. The structure of the contemporary world distances us from death because it divides us, from each other and from the earth upon which our lives depend. We have, of course, always been divided in these ways, at least to an extent, for such dividedness is among the most conspicuous ways the universal human alienation from God that Christians call "original sin" is manifest in our lives. The twentieth-century Protestant theologian Dietrich Bonhoeffer has a wonderfully succinct way of summarizing the theological meaning of the "fall," explaining that upon alienating himself from God, "Man's life is now disunion with God, with men, with things, and with himself."[9] Yet, until the advent of the modern era, this condition of dividedness was largely understood as something to be overcome, or at least resisted, and social structures tended to reflect that struggle. Contemporary North American culture reflects not simply an abandonment of resistance, but an embrace of the dividedness against which previous cultures struggled.[10]

Most of the ways contemporary culture contributes to our dividedness relate to the ways we are shaped by our generally uncritical participation in the now dominant global political economy. As enthusiastic participants in the endless and ever expanding production, distribution, and consumption of commodities, we are part of an economy of placeless hypermobility. Our desire for the abstract "more" necessary—so we are told—for a better life knows no limit, and we are willing to work very hard in pursuit of it. We leave home to go to work, both in the general sense of leaving the places of our upbringing as we pursue successful careers, and in the particular, pedestrian sense as we "go to work" daily, commuting increasingly longer distances to get there as we achieve the means to own bigger and more luxurious houses farther into the suburbs. Our employment is based on the assumption that any connection we might have to workplace and coworkers is merely contractual. We are taught to see ourselves as rational, self-interested, and acquisitive individuals who temporarily enter mutually beneficial relationships, including the relationship we have with our employer, most often a corporation about which we care nothing and which cares nothing about us. Because we are so driven by aspirations to have more, and because our employers may or may not have a use for us tomorrow, we have to be mobile, ready at all times to move on to the next opportunity, out of either necessity or self-interest.

And so we are like leaves in a windstorm, constantly moving with the gusts of our own ambition or that of the companies for which we work. Rootless, having no place, we lack time to know our neighbors or our extended families. We are alone with our work and the money it produces and the goods and services we can buy with that money. And because of our isolation and our rootlessness, we need to buy more and more, for we are either unable or too short on time to do things for ourselves. We thus grow increasingly dependent upon strangers who are presumably as self-interested and acquisitive as we are and whom we must pay to do many of the things other generations did for themselves. The wisdom and love of community, family, and place are usurped by the technical skill and esoteric knowledge of so-called experts, and we simply assume that they know better than we what is best.

Of course, such assumptions profoundly shape the ways we imagine and deal with the end of life, such that we now almost always associate death and dying not simply with medicine, but with medicine in its most aggressive and technologically sophisticated forms. Admittedly, this is not always the case, and when it is the case it is not unequivocally bad, for aggressive and technologically sophisticated medicine has legitimate uses for which we are thankful. Yet the authors believe the tendency in modern North American culture to associate life's end with hospital and nursing home is generally a profound indicator of the extent to which ours is a culture of death, for such an association indicates our tendency to segregate life from death and the living from the dying. Our lives, after all, are about producing and consuming, and we scarcely have the time to take to visit, much less care for, those no longer involved in production and consumption and no longer able to care for themselves. We assume that caring for the dying is something people are paid to do, and that things have always been this way.

Perhaps this is because we are so unwilling to confront our own mortality. Some of us go to great lengths to avoid every reminder of death in our everyday lives, and to treat death as something unnatural and alien to life. Others attempt to control death by scheduling the precise means and timing of their end. As the chief power that makes possible such avoidance or control, medicine becomes, mostly perchance, the ersatz object of our worship.

In chapter 2, we argued that one of the more important skills Christians need to develop is the ability to discern and resist the powers and principalities in their pretensions toward divinity. But the powers are in this present age important, even indispensable parts of God's good creation, and because they are made to serve us, our resistance is a good deal more complex, and so considerably more difficult than wholesale rejection. We must, as we have said, learn to *use* the powers in service of our pursuit of faithfulness toward God.

As we hopefully have shown, this is hard work, not reducible to rules or principles. It requires those virtues that can be cultivated only by faithful participation in the practices of the gathered body of Christ, and the help of the entire Christian community, both to help us discern what to do in particular situations and, just as important, to make possible, by our life together, appropriate and possibly atypical ways of caring for one another as we approach life's end. Perhaps most important of all, it requires our carefully attending to the examples of those who have been there, struggled with the power of medicine, and found a faithful way through the morass.

A Story of the Extraordinary Faithfulness of Ordinary People

By all accounts, the Haywood family constituted a flourishing household on Maryland's Eastern Shore. In 1999, Harry Haywood was an active fifty-eight–year-old who had recently retired from his job teaching marine and diesel mechanics to students at a local vocational high school. His wife, Ann, was an elementary schoolteacher, and their daughter, Geraldine, was 26 and in her second semester of study at Duke University Divinity School.[11] Harry and Ann lived together in a house they had built themselves when Geraldine was in elementary school, and they remained extremely close to Geraldine. Harry especially enjoyed spending time in his canoe, watching birds, wildlife, and the steady rhythms of the changing seasons on the tidewater of the Choptank River.

In most respects the Haywoods were typical of the people living in their small town. They worked hard, got on well with their neighbors, and were active contributors to the life of the community. While none of them was especially "religious," Christian tradition played a significant role in the way they saw the world. Harry had grown up in the Methodist church, and although he was no longer a regular churchgoer, his upbringing continued in a variety of ways to show itself in his life. Ann was a faithful Catholic actively involved in her local parish. Geraldine had over the years found herself most at home as a Protestant, and was pursuing ordination in the United Methodist Church.

In some very important ways, however, these were extraordinary people, for they took significant time during their life together to talk about important matters. Both Harry and Geraldine had been Peace Corps volunteers, the former in Africa and the latter in the Pacific Islands. In speaking with Ann and Geraldine, one cannot but sense that Harry's African experience had a profound effect on his understanding of how life should be lived. They recall that he spoke frequently of how he learned from the African people a deep appreciation for the wisdom of the elderly, the importance of friendship and extended family, and the significance of every person's contribution to the welfare of the community. Perhaps the most important lesson he learned was to appreciate the natural rhythms of the earth and to regard birth and death as integral parts of those rhythms. Geraldine in particular remarks that the fact of death as a natural occurrence, and the implications of that fact for human life, was a regular topic of the conversations she had with her father. These were the lessons, she remembers, he passed along to her with intention as they walked through the woods surrounding their home or canoed the river, lessons that she and her mother recognized then and recognize now as significant aspects not simply of African culture, but of Christian tradition, as well.

Confronting the Power of Medicine

Until March 1999, Harry had rarely been sick. But when he came in one morning from shoveling after an unexpected late snowstorm, it was clear to Ann that something was wrong. Ann recalls the shock she felt when she looked at his face and eyes, which had in a matter of an hour or so turned a distinct yellow. A trip to the emergency department of the local hospital led to a four-day hospitalization and a series of diagnostic procedures, one of which revealed something wrong with Harry's pancreas. There was no mistaking the doctor's manner when he discussed these findings with Harry and Ann; this was a serious matter that was best dealt with at a larger, more sophisticated facility. He referred Harry to the University of Maryland Medical Center in Baltimore, to consult with a specialist.

Before the trip, Ann remembers, they had an "important conversation" during which they considered the possibility that this was an illness from which Harry would not recover and which might well occasion the use of the "living will" they had signed some years earlier. From Harry and Ann's perspective, such a possibility was sad, and even tragic, while still rather abstract. Yet Harry made it clear to Ann that he believed death was not the worst thing that could happen to him. He said that he was not especially afraid to die, and that no heroic measures were to be taken to maintain his life simply for its own sake. Geraldine was called and informed of the situation, and soon she joined her parents for the trip to Baltimore.

In Baltimore, the Haywoods experienced the intricate complexity of contemporary high-tech medicine, at both its best and its worst. In a tense and awkward meeting with a team of three surgeons, during which the doctors and the Haywoods were wedged almost comically into a tiny examining room, Harry learned his diagnosis of pancreatic cancer and was told that his therapeutic options were limited by the nature and extent of his disease. Ann and Geraldine recall that their initial reaction was shock; they had not anticipated hearing the word *cancer,* and the physicians had assumed the family already knew how serious things were. Needless to say, the next several minutes were awkward as the family struggled to take in the news while the physicians sat shoulder to shoulder, awkwardly looking at their feet and acting, Ann and Geraldine recall, "as if they had never seen anyone cry before."

The awkwardness of the moment gave way soon enough to a resolve, especially on Ann's part, to move forward. The lead surgeon recommended Harry undergo a radical surgical procedure called a "Whipple operation," during which a substantial part of his pancreas and small intestine would be removed. Ann's first and only question, which she put to the physicians quite forcefully, was when the surgery could be completed. After some negotiation—the physicians, Ann and Geraldine recall, were surprised at the Haywoods' assertiveness—the team agreed to clear their schedules and operate on Harry right away. Geraldine recalls an important conversation she and one of the surgeons had while Harry was in the hospital lab for his preoperative blood work; ever the student, she showered the doctor with questions about his work, the hospital, and, of course, her father's diagnosis. "You need to understand," he told her, "how serious this is. Your father has a one-in-four chance of surviving." "Have you told *him* that?" said Geraldine. "No," replied the surgeon. "And I won't, and you mustn't, either. If he knows how slim his chances are, he won't make it."

The burden of bearing such information alone was huge, Geraldine recalls, but short-lived. The surgery was an apparent success, and the physicians were extremely optimistic and more than willing to communicate the reasons for their optimism to Ann and Geraldine. This was in no small part Geraldine's doing. "I had heard," she says, "that at major teaching hospitals they treated everybody like a number or a piece of meat. I know now that's not necessarily true, but at the time, that's what I was thinking. So my goal was to make them see us as people. I started asking them very personal questions. I asked, 'Where did you go to medical school?' and moved to 'Tell us about your family,' and 'What do you do in your spare time?'" These gestures, she says, seemed to shock the hospital staff. "They looked at me like I was crazy. But at the same time, they asked us every personal question about our lives, and they knew everything about us, and yet it's not acceptable to ask them personal questions about their own lives. But why not? They know everything; they know our whole history! So, I decided I was going to 'get to them.' And it worked." Sometimes, resisting the powers can be as simple as engaging their humanity.

Ann and Geraldine were pleased to find the ICU staff compassionate and accommodating. Yet, Geraldine said, even her overtures were to an extent part of her playing a role, trying to fulfill what she believed were the expectations of the physicians and nurses toward her, an educated, "together" person. That evening, when she left the intensive care unit, saying good-bye to her father, who was by then sitting up in bed and speaking, she realized she didn't even know how to get out of the parking garage. "That's when I realized," she recalls, "that there's a lot more to this hospital stuff than I had ever imagined." She had started to become aware of the power of medicine, and like most of us experiencing it for the first time, was overwhelmed by that power.

Faithfulness in the Midst of Hope and Despair

For five days Harry's recovery exceeded everyone's expectations. Ann returned to work and Geraldine returned to school, both anticipating Harry making a full recovery. But then things began slowly to change. Harry's occasional confusion, not unusual for patients in intensive care, began to worsen. In the same telephone conversation she was told the pathology report had declared Harry cancer-free, Ann was informed he had been placed on a ventilator. And although it took time to sink in, this was an indication that something was not right. They returned to the hospital, where they learned the news. What remained of Harry's pancreas had leaked, and the leaking bile had eroded the sutures to the intestine. The procedure had failed, and Harry had developed an infection.

Over the course of the next several days Harry's condition steadily declined. He remained on the ventilator and was apparently unconscious because of heavy sedation. In spite of the fact that his abdomen was being flushed regularly, his laboratory reports indicated his pancreas was still leaking, and he was taken back to surgery in an attempt to repair the leak. Geraldine recalls those days:

> Every other day they were taking him to the OR. There's just this "fight mentality," just like the doctors, and you start buying into the system. But you also start to realize that you're running out of time, and that if this surgery doesn't work, your loved one is going to die. It becomes scarier and scarier, and then you realize you're also being watched [by the hospital staff]. There's so much going on, and it's overwhelming. You start off and there's just the nasal cannula [for oxygen] and one IV, and before you know it, there's the ventilator and his surgical wound is open and packed with gauze and covered with plastic wrap and there is a whole wall full of IV medications.

Ann and Geraldine had begun again to confront the possibility that Harry was going to die. Easter weekend came, and on Sunday they learned that the father of a woman they had come to know in the waiting room had died the night before. The woman left a note for Geraldine, thanking her for her friendship over the past days, and remarking that she was thankful her father had died on Easter. Those remarks, they remember, marked the beginning of a change in how they understood what was happening to Harry. In the midst of the physicians' continued optimism about his chances, and while giving their permission for yet another surgery, they prepared themselves as best they could for his death.

As is sometimes the case, the final surgery was technically successful but medically a failure. The Whipple procedure was undone, and Harry's digestive tract was essentially disconnected, emptying into a series of bags taped to his body or hung from his bed. The plan, Ann and Geraldine learned, was to try to stabilize Harry, get rid of the infection, and then take him back to surgery to salvage as much of his digestive system as possible. Then he developed pneumonia.

Pneumonia in an otherwise healthy person is a serious, but readily treatable illness. But in someone as sick and as weak as Harry, it was a disaster. When Ann and Geraldine met with the surgeon, he was obviously not optimistic and began to allude to the need for them to expect the worst. Yet in the midst of all this ominous frankness, Ann and Geraldine felt they were being told two distinct and conflicting stories. On the one hand, they were being asked indirectly to plan for Harry's death. On the other hand, the physicians continued to hold out the hope of recovery, albeit in some abstract future preceded by a long hospitalization and yet more surgery—at one point, the possibility of a tracheotomy, followed by an interval of time in a nursing home, followed by yet more surgery, was broached. And this made them feel terribly conflicted, for they were concerned, in the midst of their grief, that their grieving was an indication that they were giving up the very hope that was keeping their husband and father alive.

Grief and Hope

The next afternoon, Ann and Geraldine met with the surgeon, and, after a few minutes of talking about "options," Ann produced Harry's living will and asked him to be totally honest about his expectations. Ann recalls him looking at them for a minute, and the reading over the living will, and then saying, as if relieved, "You really do understand, don't you?" They assured him that they did, that Harry had spoken openly with them about his death, and that they had discussed it with each other. They were prepared, they explained, to honor Harry's intentions.

In collaboration with the physician and the head nurse, Ann and Geraldine planned to wait until week's end and then withdraw Harry's ventilator support and allow him to die naturally. While obviously saddened by the implications of this decision, they accepted it as being in Harry's best interests and prepared to grieve his death. The physicians, on the other hand, were shaken deeply by the prospect of Harry's death. In large part, Ann and Geraldine believe, this is because they were good and decent people who cared deeply for their patient. But it was also clear that they were disturbed by the failure represented by Harry's death.

Their distress is reminiscent of Wendell Berry's suggestion that the modern hospital is a juxtaposition, but usually not a convergence, of two worlds, the world of love and the world of technological efficiency. In most cases the former is represented by patients and their families and the latter by physicians and other professional caregivers; both have as their goal the restoration of the patient to health, meaning to family, community, and work. Yet they differ in that the world of love, properly understood, can make a space for death, while the world of efficiency cannot. Says Berry:

> In the world of love, things separated by efficiency and specialization strive to come back together. And yet love must confront death, and accept it, and learn from it. Only in confronting death can earthly love learn its true extent, its immortality. Any definition of health that is not silly must include death. The world of love includes death, suffers it, and triumphs over it. The world of efficiency is defeated by death; at death, all its instruments and procedures stop. The world of love continues, and of this grief is the proof.[12]

But how can something so terrible as death be included in love? And how can love triumph over it? We would suggest that such love is possible because it depends for its power on the love of God for the creation, a love most clearly displayed in the death and resurrection of Jesus and the promise of resurrection for all the dead united to Jesus in baptism. When the day came, Harry's physician spoke apologetically to Ann, telling her he did all he could and wished he could have done more. To this Ann responded, shaking his hand and thanking him, "Doctor, we all have to die. Without death there is no resurrection. We believe in resurrection." The next day, Harry's ventilator support was withdrawn, and he died, in the presence of those who loved him. And Ann and Geraldine, more than five years later, continue to grieve his dying and to be consoled by their hope in the resurrection. Ann continues to work actively as a member of her parish, and Geraldine is a Methodist minister who now serves as a hospital chaplain.

Resurrection and the Communion of Saints

We understand the decision to allow Harry to die as a gesture of witness, rather than fatalism or abandonment. Ann and Geraldine chose the world of love over the world of efficiency. They were able to do so because they believed, and wanted their lives to show, that ultimately only love triumphs over death. Love's triumph over death is manifest in grief, as Berry says, but also in hope. For the Christian, love cannot be severed from hope. Grief comes as we experience what appears to be ultimate separation from those we have loved. Such separation reminds us of how little control we finally have over our own personal histories, much less the history of the world, which often appears to us as the victory of chaos and death over order and life. Just so, it is an occasion for despair. Hope, however, suggests to us that our grief is temporary, that although we cannot control history, the One who raised Jesus from death to life does control it, and indeed already has done so, to the advantage of life and love.[13] And this offers us the possibility of being free to live and to die and to care for each other as we face dying, even though we are not in control. For even as medicine, even medicine at its best and most sophisticated, delays but does not overcome the destruction of our bodies, God's love does precisely that—it overcomes death. Hence, at the center of our life as Christians is our hope in the resurrection of our frail, dependent, mortal bodies, the hope that makes possible our love. As Barth explains:

> We are waiting for our *Body's* redemption; if the body is not redeemed to obedience, to health, to life, then there is no God; then what may be called god does not deserve this name. The truth of God requires and establishes the Resurrection of the Dead, the Resurrection of the Body.[14]

In resurrection we envision the restoration of God's perfect intention for God's good creation, an intention that includes the perfection of the love that binds us to one another in this life. It is therefore not by accident that in 1 Corinthians Paul is ambiguous in his use of the word *body,* using it now to refer to the body of the individual human, then to the presence of Christ in the Eucharist, then to the gathered community of believers. For Paul understands that the perfection of our individual bodies, which is to be accomplished in the resurrection, cannot be separated from the perfection of our love for God and each other. The resurrection is not simply a corporeal, but also a corporate event, through which the God whose name is love "may be all in all" (1 Cor. 15:28). So love, for the Christian, is inseparable not only from hope, but from community as well, as when we proclaim in the Apostles' Creed, "I believe . . . in the communion of saints [and] the forgiveness of sins," we share our conviction that even sin and death cannot sever the relationships we live out in the Christian community.[15] In resurrection, all the forms of human separation that are occasions for grief—the most horrible being death—are overcome.

133

For a glimpse of this hope, we return in conclusion to the story of wise Jayber Crow. Jayber, we learn, spends his adult years not simply as Port William's barber, but also as its gravedigger and its church's janitor. As the years pass, and as he prepares resting places in the yard of the church for the membership's deceased, Jayber develops a special affection for the living and the dead among them. One day, he recalls, when he went up there to work, sleepiness overcame him and he lay down on the floor behind the back pew to take a nap.

> Waking or sleeping (I couldn't tell which), I saw all the people gathered there who had ever been there. I saw them as I had seen them from the back pew, where I sat with Uncle Othy (who would not come any farther) while Aunt Cordie sang in the choir, and I saw them as I had seen them (from the back pew) on the Sunday before. I saw them in all the times past and to come, all somehow in their own time and in all time and in no time: the cheerfully working and singing women, the men quiet or reluctant or shy, the weary, the troubled in spirit, the sick, the lame, the desperate, the dying, the little children tucked into the pews beside their elders, the young married couples full of visions, the old men with their dreams, the parents proud of their children, the grandparents with tears in their eyes, the pairs of young lovers attentive only to each other on the edge of the world, the grieving widows and widowers, the mothers and fathers of children newly dead, the proud, the humble, the attentive, the distracted—I saw them all. I saw the creases crisscrossed on the backs of the men's necks, their work-thickened hands, the Sunday dresses faded with washing. They were just there. They said nothing, and I said nothing. I seemed to love them all with a love that was mine merely because it included me.
>
> When I came to myself again, my face was wet with tears.[16]

Tears are shed because of love, and because of grief. In the end, for those who believe in the resurrection of the dead and the communion of saints, they turn out to be the same.

Conclusion

Medicine As If God Mattered

■ In one sense, our aims in the preceding chapters have been modest. We have simply asked Christians to use medicine in ways consistent with their most basic convictions about God and God's intention for creation as narrated in the stories of Israel, Jesus, and the community called church. In another sense, however, these aims are rather immodest, for we have asked the reader to allow herself or himself to be immersed in a life-changing conversation and its attendant practices with little in the way of specific guidelines for how that conversation should begin or proceed.

In part, this is a function of the nature of Christian faith. While rules and principles are helpful, they are insufficient as guides for living at the intersection of faith and medicine. Something more than "Christians and Medicine for Dummies" is necessary. We have come to see our approach as "using medicine as if God mattered," which has several possible meanings. First, as we stated in the introduction, we hope to join theology—rather than individualized spirituality—with medicine in conversation, or at least to open a space for that conversation to begin. We have no fear that medicine, as currently constituted in North America, will have any trouble holding up its end of any such discussion. What we worry about, though, is that the church will continue to cede to medicine power over the conversation's scope, particulars, and language. The church will have to lose some of its false humility, though a certain amount of prudence in this matter is advisable. The powers, as we have seen, are every bit as reluctant as individual humans to relinquish control, and secular forces are quick to point out—rightly so, we might add—the ways in which Christianity has egregiously abused its power over the centuries. For some Christians, a few lessons in humility would go a long way. In order for

135

Christians to resist the allure of medicine as power, we must do better at living out what we say we believe in our worship. It is in worship, or more specifically in liturgy (*leitourgia:* "the people's work"), that Christians find their first theology. Anything else, from Augustine to Zizioulas, is second-ary.[1] So, rather than urging Christians to leverage a corporate medical buyout, we enjoin Christians to do something at once simpler and much, much more difficult: to live out in community what we acknowledge and embody in liturgy, and to speak—through embodied words and shared action—truth to power, even when that power is medicine.

A second meaning of the phrase "medicine as if God mattered" builds on this. If God matters, so do God's gathered people. The stories Christians share with each other and with the Jews from whom salvation comes make one thing very clear: God chooses to act in creation through com-munity, calling out and gathering the people of Israel, and later, through Christ's saving action, grafting a new people onto that good tree.[2] As we have seen, it is almost exclusively as individuals that medicine and medi-cal ethics urge us to imagine ourselves. Only in community can we resist that power, for only together can we strengthen one another.

Significantly, the community we call the church is far more expansive than our local congregations. We have seen how the boundaries that nations and economies erect are bridged by the body of Christ. Each encounter with the power of medicine must be seen in the light of this gathered people; each decision must be pondered with the possible effects on that people in view. We do not mean to downplay the importance of following one's conscience—in today's hyperindividualized society there is little danger of that being taken seriously—but we do mean to open a respectful conversation between each Christian's conscience and the gathered people to whom we are joined in baptism. We needn't be apolo-getic, then, when asking the doctor to give us some time before making a decision, not only to think it over individually, but to share that burden with our community, in prayer, conversation, and liturgy.

A third way to read our subtitle is to understand the God that matters as Trinity: God is the One whose essence is relationship. Our individual bodies and the body gathered as church are God's good gifts to be used in God's service, and we have explored some of the ways we might do this when dealing with the power of medicine. But there is much more to the Trinity than this. Most Christians in the West are fairly clear—if a bit unorthodox—on God as Father and Son. Outside of Pentecostals and Charismatics, though, most are rather fuzzy on God the Holy Spirit, often envisioning misplaced flames or an aloof white bird when the name comes up. Yet Christians at least claim to believe that the Holy Spirit is, since the Ascension of Christ to the Father, present to us as advocate and helper (see John 16:7–15).[3] One way the church might unlearn some of its false humility is to develop a palpable trust in the power of the Holy Spirit to guide the community through strange and treacherous territory. We hope it is clear by now that, for Christians at least, medicine is just such a place, and that the Holy Spirit may well be the only advocate up to the task of bringing us safely through. We do not mean to inspire a new generation of Savanarolas, stirring the pious into a frenzy of antihospital protests, complete with bonfires of medical records. The trusting, faithful resistance we envision will be quieter and necessarily nonviolent, as we saw in the case of the couple navigating the minefields of assisted reproduction, or in that of the Haywoods, learning to let go of their beloved.

For these, and for the others whose stories we shared, the way through was never clearly marked. Ways of doing things had to be invented at times, but each improvisation was taken up in conversation with the community. We think the word *improvisation,* as used here, is well chosen, because that is very much what sharing in the life of Christ is: creative, celebratory, free play within a structure provided by group and tradition.[4] When a jazz quartet jams, it typically establishes some formal element—twelve-bar blues or a chord progression, for example—and lets each soloist expand and play upon that base while being supported by the others.[5] Each player is expected to know the progression and the modal scales in which the solo will unfold, to have some experience intently listening to and playing with the group, and to have mastered her instrument through a lifetime of practice. Faithful living as a body likewise requires knowledge of the stories and worship we are baptized into, experience living in Christian community, and a lifetime devoted to that community's shared practice.[6] We navigate our way through the maze of modernity without maps, but as Christians we never do so alone. Gathered into the communion of saints—a community not circumscribed by death—we improvise our witness to the powers using ancient themes.

So our descriptions of faithful living have been necessarily partial and allusive, gesturing at the way rather than prescribing it. Still, any jazz player wanting to keep his chops regularly returns to basic exercises. There are, after all, some concrete things Christians can do to encourage faithful witness in medicine's world. We wish to conclude this project by briefly suggesting just a few of these.

First, and perhaps most significantly, all Christians would do well to remember to live as if we are not in this alone. By virtue of our baptism, our bodies have all been made part of the same body of Christ, a community in which we are called to suffer or rejoice together. If we are to make common cause of our suffering and our rejoicing, we must abandon contemporary culture's fetish with privacy and make ourselves available and vulnerable to those with whom we share our lives. For this to happen, we must be willing to take time to be with each other, to learn each other's stories and assess each other's fears, desires, and needs. And so the first concrete thing Christians can do is simply be with each other convivially in conversation and prayer, cultivating relationships within which there eventually develops a space for talking about difficult matters like sickness, frailty, and death. Many strands of the Christian tradition and many local churches already have structures within and practices through which these things might be accomplished; those that do not should create them.

Once we establish the lines of communication by which we might become aware of each other's lives, a second step in the right direction is to recall and enact our obligations to serve each other. "Works of mercy" have always been central to the life of the Christian community, the means by which we try to make visible to the world God's love. Within and beyond the church, people need help when they are sick. They need rides to the doctor or the hospital. They need someone to prepare meals for them and to clean their house. They need someone to help them take their medicines on schedule, to bathe and dress them, to help them go to the bathroom. They need someone to care for their children or their pets. They may need someone to help pay their medical expenses. All of these are things that members of Christ's body should be doing for each other. It may be beyond the capacities of a given local community to employ a full-time parish nurse or to establish a church-funded clinic or an alternative health-care system, but such limits do not preclude more modest forms of service, including the simplest of all—but perhaps the most important—being with our sisters and brothers who are sick.

A third step congregations might take is to make the faithful use of medicine a specific focus of their teaching ministry. Contemporary North American Christianity is largely biblically and theologically illiterate. Against the intimidating complexity of modern medicine, this leaves many Christians completely lost when it comes to thinking about whether a particular use of medicine may be faithful or not to the tradition. Sunday school classes, book clubs, and discipleship groups (to name only a few) all offer forums within which Christians can learn about and discuss the significance of issues ranging from the meaning of baptism to the significance of hospitality to the hope of resurrection, from global health to advance directives to stem cells to health insurance.

These suggestions are not much, but they are a start, in that they are ways of reminding Christians to live differently, because their lives are gifts from a gracious God whose love they are called to display to the world in their love for each other. Our task is at once simple and terribly difficult: to reclaim from the powers our own bodies, and to live in such a way that proclaims the body as God's gift to us and, by God's grace, our gift to the world.

Joel James Shuman
Brian Volck
Lent, 2005

Notes

Introduction

1. Joel Shuman and Keith Meador, *Heal Thyself: Spirituality, Medicine and the Distortion of Christianity* (Oxford: Oxford University Press, 2003).

2. George Bernard Shaw, *The Doctor's Dilemma,* Act I (Baltimore: Penguin, 1954), 116.

Chapter 1 Doctors and Christians

1. Stanley Hauerwas, from the forward to Shuman and Meador, *Heal Thyself,* xi.

2. For a fuller treatment of this phenomenon and the distorted Christianity it both assumes and fosters, see Shuman and Meador, op. cit.

3. *Catechism of the Catholic Church,* paragraphs 1514–15, 1517.

4. Robert Coles, *Harvard Diary* (New York: Crossroad, 1988), 10.

5. Ibid., 11.

6. Stanley Hauerwas, *Dispatches from the Front* (Durham, NC: Duke University Press, 1994), 156. Perhaps the acceptance of incompetently trained priests suggests a widespread appreciation of the validity of sacraments *ex opere operato,* a theological expression referring to the effectiveness of the sacrament quite apart from the one administering it. Given the level of theological discourse in North America, we think this unlikely.

7. *The Princess Bride,* directed by Rob Reiner (Century City, CA: Twentieth Century Fox, 1987).

8. Canadian history, of course, presents an interesting contrast within North America to the problems of authority, with what we know today as Canada constituting itself a dominion in 1867 without benefit of mass military slaughter. That some observers south of the border assume Québecois separatism or east-west political divisions will inevitably lead part or all of Canada to political union with its more populous neighbor may reveal more about the observers (such as their ignorance of Canadian history or their own assumptions about authority) than about Canada.

9. It is important to note that we use "liberal" here in the technical sense, as a description of those theories of government that privilege individual freedom, or liberty, above all other goods. Which is to say we are *not* talking about the position held by those on the so-called left wing of American politics.

10. As Stanley Hauerwas suggests, "If you want to have a sense of what medieval Catholicism felt like, become part of a major medical center" (*Dispatches from the Front,* 27).

11. Having witnessed enough misuses of the fashionable practice of intellectual scapegoating, we should note in Bacon's defense that the stated principle behind his "Great Instauration" was Christian charity. Bacon's failure to thoroughly explore how that charity might limit the aims and means of scientific and technological progress is perhaps mitigated by his inability to envision the scope of human pretensions of control in later centuries and the increasingly attenuated authority of Christian thought. For a critique of the "Baconian Project" in modern medicine, see Gerald McKenny, *To Relieve the Human Condition* (Albany: State University of New York Press, 1997).

12. By "consumer-driven," we mean that spirituality as conceived in modern industrialized culture, in contrast to most of the world through most of its history, is understood to be determined by personal choices and feelings rather than as a vocation or inclusion within the larger, given narrative of a people, so that individual religious belief and practice now flow from previously arrived-at personal convictions. One can, for example, log on to the "Beliefnet" website and find, via a personal-interest survey, which religious tradition is most congenial to one's beliefs. Among its many consequences, this shopper's model makes the moral claims of a tradition subject to individual preference and consent. The harder commands of a particular religion, such as loving one's enemies or leaving one's gift at the altar to reconcile with an estranged brother, fall that much more easily under the control of the individual will. It is hard to imagine, for example, the shape of Archbishop Oscar Romero's life if his primary concern had been to "follow his bliss."

13. See Abraham Maslow, *Motivation and Personality,* 3rd ed. (Boston: Addison-Wesley, 1987). Sometimes known as "Maslow's pyramid," this standard of self-help seminars surely reflects some truth—how else can one explain its popularity?—riddled though it may be with bourgeois assumptions. In a perceptive rebuttal, though, one of our sons, upon returning from a medical trip to an impoverished village in rural Honduras, was appalled at the rude behavior of wealthy travelers in the Houston airport. "Dad," he said in dismay, "People in Honduras seemed a lot happier, and they had a lot less to be happy about."

14. Like Francis Bacon, Constantine deserves a fate better than intellectual scapegoat. In the context of the early-fourth-century Mediterranean world, Constantine recognized that Christians were everywhere, including in high levels of imperial government. Historical data do not support the oversimplified model of the church as healthy and uniformly pure—if occasionally persecuted—until the Edict of Milan, or that "Constantinianism" names a discrete, precipitous fall in Catholic theology and practice. Nonetheless, affixing a *Chi-Rho* atop an imperial standard suggests the risen Christ blesses the empire and its ways of doing things *as is,* rather than judging them and finding them wanting. While it is clear the church changed much in late imperial society, the reverse is just as true. For a helpful account of the effects of "Constantinianism" on Christian consciousness, see John Howard Yoder, "The Constantinian Sources of Western Social Ethics," in

The Priestly Kingdom: Social Ethics as Gospel (Notre Dame, IN: University of Notre Dame Press, 1984), 135–51.

15. We hope the brief discussion of baptism that follows makes clear our understanding that baptism—even infant baptism—is much more than a quaint naming ritual. Properly understood, baptism has all the quaintness of death—or birth. With this is mind, the recovery of the *catechumenate* by various traditions, most notably in the "Rite of Christian Initiation of Adults" and the call for a "post-baptismal *catechumenate*" following infant baptism within the Roman Catholic Church (*Catechism of the Catholic Church,* 1229–1233), is most welcome.

16. The root of the Greek word *baptizein* has many meanings, including "'to dip in or under,' 'to dye,' 'to immerse,' 'to sink,' to drown,' 'to bathe,' (and to) 'wash'" (*Theological Dictionary of the New Testament,* abridged ed., ed. Gerhard Kittel and Gerhard Friedrich [Grand Rapids: Eerdmans, 1985], 92).

17. A comprehensive list of the goods of creation is impossible here. For a remarkable introduction to the tradition of creation and its goods as icon of God, see John Cryssavagis, *Beyond the Shattered Image* (Minneapolis: Life and Light Publishing, 1999).

18. Margaret Mohrmann, *Medicine as Ministry* (Cleveland: Pilgrim Press, 1995), 15–16.

19. Interestingly, nowhere in scripture is the sin of Adam and Eve named "a fall," a kinetic, spatial image which may represent a Platonic gloss on Genesis. Likewise, "original sin" enters the Christian lexicon with Augustine. We have neither the time nor the competence to discuss the interpretations of Genesis 3 and its consequences within the Christian tradition(s), East and West, but we acknowledge without reservation that this interpretative tradition is an authoritative part of the Christian story into which we are baptized. For our present purposes, a detailed account of the efficient cause of this alienation from God is less important than the reality of that alienation as understood by the church.

20. Cf. Augustine, *Confessions* XIII.

21. Precisely because of James's stress on *performing* one's faith, Martin Luther denounced the Letter of James as the "epistle of straw." Much subsequent textual criticism therefore stressed the relative theological unimportance and late composition of James, opinions recently under serious challenge (see Luke Timothy Johnson, *The Letter of James: A New Translation with Introduction and Commentary* [Anchor Bible Series] [New York: Doubleday, 1995]). With five hundred years perspective, perhaps we can see Luther's judgment in its historical and political context, without turning James into a proto-Pelagian, or imagining that James thinks humans are capable of saving themselves.

22. For an illuminating introduction to the interplay between Christian practice and theology in the early church, see Rowan Greer, *Broken Lights and Mended Lives* (University Park: Pennsylvania State University Press, 1986), and Amy G. Oden, *And You Welcomed Me: A Sourcebook on Hospitality in Early Christianity* (Nashville: Abingdon Press, 2001). Michael Polanyi's notion of "indwelling" is also relevant here, as in the following observation: "The extensive dogmatic framework of Christianity arose from ingenious efforts, sustained through many centuries, to axiomatize the faith already practised by Christians" (*Personal Knowledge* [Chicago: University of Chicago Press, 1958], 286).

23. For a history of this phenomenon from the nineteenth century to the 1980s, see Paul Starr, *The Social Transformation of American Medicine: The Rise of a Sovereign Profession and the Making of a Vast Industry* (New York: Basic Books, 1984).

24. "Scientific" evidence for this dates back at least to the thirteenth century, when Emperor Frederick II allegedly conducted an experiment to determine which language (Latin, Greek, or Hebrew) was natural to humanity. He arranged for a cohort of newborns to be cared for by nurses who never spoke in their presence. Reportedly, all the children died before speaking a word. While this may tell us more about infant mortality in medieval Europe than the human need for language, the story is compelling and helps us understand "the state of the question" for investigators in the 1200s. Duplicating these results today would be difficult, considering the current standards of human research committees.

25. Wendell Berry, "Health Is Membership," in *Another Turn of the Crank* (Washington, DC: Counterpoint, 1995), 91.

26. Ibid., 90.

27. See Carl Elliott, *Better than Well: American Medicine Meets the American Dream* (New York: Norton, 2003).

28. Hospital physicians routinely prepare for emergency situations through "advanced life support training" and "mock codes," in which an emergency is simulated for teaching and review. This optimally includes the use of real equipment on life-size dummies especially designed for this purpose. The theory, at least, is that practicing with something as close to the real thing as possible better prepares the team for the actual event. Using unfamiliar equipment in a novel situation invites disaster. Once again we remind the reader that unprepared Christians are no less dangerous than unprepared doctors.

29. The word *patient* comes from the Latin *pati,* "to suffer."

30. David Power, "Let the Sick Man Call," *Heythrop Journal* 19 (1978): 262.

31. Megan McKenna, *Rites of Justice* (Maryknoll, NY: Orbis, 1997), 162–63.

32. It is one of the great ironies of history that a religion purporting to worship a crucified God who invites his followers to "pick up your cross" (a brutal device of torture and death) and "follow me" should, in time, be understood by (some of) its adherents as little more than a way of "being nice." D. Stephen Long explains why "God Is Not Nice," (though he is kind!) in *God Is Not . . . ,* D. Brent Laytham, ed. (Grand Rapids: Brazos Press, 2004).

33. McKenna, *Rites of Justice,* 161.

34. Martin Luther, following Augustine, was fond of saying that Christians are *"simil justus et peccator,"* meaning we are simultaneously made righteous and yet continue frequently to fail in our struggle against sin.

35. While the modern liberal nation-state is not the Roman Empire, this does not render it immune to the withering critique Augustine directs against the latter in *The City of God.* We consider ourselves blessed to live in a modern republic, however flawed, but we are sobered by our reading of Hebrew scripture, in which God's unmerited blessing inevitably brings God's unwanted judgment. In regard to the relationship between the Cities of Man and of God, we concur—with some reservations—with the German rhyme: *"Republikum oder Kaiserreiche; es ist immer die gleiche, immer die gleiche"* ("Republic or Empire, it's all the same, all the same").

36. See, among others, Stanley Hauerwas's *The Peaceable Kingdom* (Notre Dame, IN: University of Notre Dame Press, 1983) and *In Good Company: The Church as Polis* (Notre Dame, IN: University of Notre Dame Press, 1995), as well as Rodney Clapp, *A Peculiar People: The Church as Culture in a Post-Christian Society* (Downers Grove, IL: InterVarsity Press, 1996), William Cavanaugh, *Theopolitical Imagination* (London: T & T Clark, 2002), and Michael Budde and Robert Brimlow, eds., *The Church as Counterculture* (Albany: State University of New York Press, 2000).

37. As always, institutional vocabulary betrays more than it may wish to reveal.

38. The Letter of James, ever the deflator of self-serving sentimentality, warns us how despicably we behave when we pursue what we want instead of what God asks of us: James 4:1–10.

39. Part of the mixed blessing of postmodernism is the opportunity to see claims of "scientific objectivity," from whatever field of human endeavor, as—at the very least—less stable than once supposed.

40. We also purposely use the word *crucial* here, since what the church has to show the world is the cross and the Jesus we nail there.

Chapter 2 Naming the Power of Medicine

1. For a discussion of some of these accounts of power, especially as it pertains to medicine, see Joel Shuman, *The Body of Compassion: Ethics, Medicine and the Church* (Boulder, CO: Westview, 1999), 28–44.

2. Francis Bacon's adage "knowledge is power" (*Meditationes Sacrae,* 1597) implies power to act, to change things. Bacon makes this explicit through his *Great Instauration,* while maintaining that such action must be motivated by charity. If by "knowledge" we mean no more than a collection of facts divorced from action, what power such knowledge yields, however well intentioned, seems suspect. A mother who knew all about her child's needs yet never responded to them might be considered neglectful at best.

3. See, for example, Howard Brody, *The Healer's Power* (New Haven: Yale University Press, 1992).

4. Lorrie Moore, "People like That Are the Only People Here: Canonical Babblings in Peed Onk," in *Birds of America* (New York: Picador USA, 1999; hereafter cited as *PIT*).

5. The ritualized, quasi-religious behaviors of the modern hospital further endow medicine with an aura of power and the promise of "salvation" from illness and pain. As we noted in the previous chapter, Stanley Hauerwas advises that "if you want to have a sense of what medieval Catholicism felt like, become part of a major medical center. You will discover there an exemplification of the Byzantine politics often associated with the papacy in its heyday." (From *Dispatches from the Front* [Durham, NC: Duke University Press, 1994], 27).

6. Claudia Kalb, "Faith & Healing," *Newsweek,* November 12, 2003, 47.

7. The willingness of some Christians to sign on to modern medicine's project in ways dictated by medicine is similar to the high esteem some Christians hold for Carl Jung, who, it is claimed, makes room for religious belief in his psychological theory. While there is certainly insight and wisdom in Jung's work, we suggest that the untrustworthy, envious, and downright creepy God who makes cameo appearances in *Memories, Dreams, Reflections* and who dominates *Answer to Job* might prompt Christians to think hard about exactly what sort of hospitality to belief Jung actually extends.

8. Bringing religious practices into the service of something less than God and God's gathered people—a transgression the Bible names idolatry—has a long, disastrous history Christians would do well to recall: Holy War, pogroms against Jews, colonialism, racism, and even the capitulation of liberal Christianity to the Nazis by the so-called German Christians are all representative of this legacy.

9. For this way of thinking about medicine we are indebted especially to Ross Smillie, who suggested it to one of us some years ago in a seminar in medical ethics at Duke University.

10. Walter Wink, *Naming the Powers: The Language of Power in the New Testament* (Philadelphia: Fortress, 1984), 9.

11. Hendrik Berkhof suggests that the significance of Paul's speaking of fallen angelic and demonic powers in the same passages he speaks of institutional and political powers is that the apostle wants to emphasize what these entities have in common, namely, "that these Powers condition earthly life." Hendrik Berkhof, *Christ and the Powers* (Scottdale, PA: Herald Press, 1977), 19.

12. John Howard Yoder, *The Politics of Jesus* (Grand Rapids: Eerdmans, 1972), 139–40, emphasis ours.

13. An excellent account of the historic origins of the New Testament language of principalities and powers is offered by G. B. Caird, *Principalities and Powers: A Study in Pauline Theology* (Eugene, OR: Wipf and Stock, 2003).

14. Walter Wink, *Engaging the Powers: Discernment and Resistance in a World of Domination* (Philadelphia: Fortress, 192), 65.

15. Yoder, *Politics of Jesus,* 146.

16. Ibid.

17. We are grateful to Alex Sider for directing our attention to the rich history of Christian usages of the language of "power." Although a detailed discussion of that history is beyond the scope of this work, it is worth noting that the language disappears from Christian usage at the end of the Apostolic Period, reemerging in the late fourth century in the work of the Cappadocian Fathers, who use it primarily to refer not to world powers, but to the powers of the human soul. Only in the twentieth century does the explicitly sociopolitical usage of the language reemerge. As we suggest here, however, the two usages are properly interconnected.

18. Caird, *Principalities and Powers,* 9. See also Berkhof, *Christ and the Powers,* 30.

19. Berkhof, *Christ and the Powers,* 32.

20. Yoder, *Politics of Jesus,* 144.

21. Nicholas Lash, *The Beginning and the End of "Religion"* (Notre Dame, IN: University of Notre Dame Press, 1996), 37.

22. Berkhof, *Christ and the Powers,* 34.

23. We take this account of worship from Daniel Hardy, "Worship as the Orientation of Life to God," *Ex Auditu* 8 no. 2 (1992): 55–71.

24. Yoder, *Politics of Jesus,* 147.

25. Berkhof, *Christ and the Powers,* 38.

26. Caird *(Principalities and Powers)* is helpful here when he explains (28) that the redemption of the powers, like the redemption of the Christian, is effected by the cross, and that redemption, or salvation, "is always a past fact, a present experience, and a future hope" (81).

27. Berkhof, *Christ and the Powers,* 29, italics original.

28. Yoder, *Politics of Jesus,* 153.

29. Berkhof, *Christ and the Powers,* 44.

30. For example: Michel Foucault, *The Birth of the Clinic* (New York: Vintage, 1975), and Ivan Illich, *Medical Nemesis: The Expropriation of Health* (New York: Pantheon, 1976).

31. Arthur C. McGill, *Death and Life: An American Theology* (Philadelphia: Fortress, 1987), 18.

32. Lash, *Beginning and the End,* 21.

33. Ibid., 20.

34. McGill, *Death and Life,* 39.

35. For a brief, amusing rebuttal to such Gnostic tendencies, we recommend W. H. Auden's late poem, "No, Plato, No," in *Collected Poems* (New York: Random House, 1976), 669.

36. Margaret Mohrmann, *Medicine as Ministry* (Cleveland: Pilgrim Press, 1995), 15–16.

37. Self-described Christians are every bit as guilty of this tendency as proud secularists. Vigen Guroian, drawing on the work of Philippe Aries and Sherwin Nuland, claims: "Even self consciously religious people tend to respond to death with an other-worldliness that suggests a weakened belief in Providence and no real sense of grace. . . . In many cases, the art of caring for the dying has given way to an art of saving life at all cost. [Nuland] adds that this new science of saving life is mostly concerned with the physician's need to be in control and the patient's need to feel that someone is in control." From *Life's Living toward Dying* (Grand Rapids: Eerdmans, 1996), 12–14.

38. Here see Gerald McKenny, *To Relieve the Human Condition* (Albany: SUNY Press, 1997).

39. Especially where our children are concerned, the general tendencies of our culture toward autonomous individualism, as well as the rise of expert social service agencies, surely contribute to these phenomena. While it is at once overly idealistic, simplistic, and unfair to suggest the role now claimed by social workers of various kinds was once occupied by friends, neighbors, and kin, the modern model certainly differs from the one offered by the Acts of the Apostles or, for that matter, the several historical examples of Christian community in recorded history.

40. Caird, *Principalities and Powers* (hereafter *P&P*), 55.

41. We borrow this notion from Gilbert Meilaender, *Body, Soul, and Bioethics* (Notre Dame, IN: University of Notre Dame Press, 1996), who describes the body as having a "natural history."

Chapter 3 Life as a Body

1. Students of the history of ancient Christianity will recognize this question as a version of Tertullian's critique of Christianity's emerging dependence on Greek philosophy, "What does Athens have to do with Jerusalem?" While Tertullian clearly intended his rhetorical listeners to respond, "Nothing," our retelling of the interinvolvement of theology and medicine requires a different response.

2. *Babette's Feast,* written and directed by Gabriel Axel (New York: Orion Classics, 1988).

3. The Isak Dinesen short story on which the film is based was written at the suggestion of an English dinner companion, who challenged the author to sell a story to the *Saturday Evening Post,* adding that American audiences would be more interested if she chose to "write about food." This literary anecdote is recounted in Ron Hansen's essay "Babette's Feast," from *A Stay against Confusion* (New York: HarperCollins, 2001). By the way, Karen Blixen, writing under the pseudonym Isak Dinesen, lost the bet. Both the *Post* and *Good Housekeeping* rejected the story. A year later, one of the finest short stories of the twentieth century appeared in the pages of *Ladies' Home Journal.*

4. One can, of course, do a perfectly wonderful production of *Romeo and Juliet* as adolescent heat, which Franco Zeffirelli filmed in 1968. One can also make it a play about violence, as in the 1996 Baz Luhrmann movie. Neither exhausts the play's fullness.

5. From "Babette's Feast," in *Anecdotes of Destiny and Ehrengard* (New York: Vintage Books, 1993), 52.

6. Ibid., 54–55; emphasis ours.

7. Ibid., 57.

8. Ibid., 51.

9. For those unafraid of imagining God as artist, see Thomas Schmidt's *A Scandalous Beauty: The Artistry of God and the Way of the Cross* (Grand Rapids: Brazos Press, 2002) and Dorothy Sayers's classic, *The Mind of the Maker* (New York: Harcourt Brace, 1941).

10. The fourth-century Cappadocian fathers describe the relationship between the persons of the Trinity as *perichoresis,* a "dancing around." Modern feminist interpretations of God as relational can be found in Elizabeth Johnson's *She Who Is* (New York: Crossroad, 1994) and Catherine LaCugna's *God for Us* (New York: HarperSanFrancisco, 1991).

11. We realize some scholars translate the Hebrew phrase with which Genesis begins *("Bereshit barah")* as: "In the beginning of creating." This reading does not detract from the complete gratuity of creation.

12. From Thomas of Celano's *Second Life.*

13. In his *Brothers Karamazov* and many other writings, Dostoyevsky, like Friedrich Nietzsche, Herman Melville, and Emily Dickinson, intuited the shape of the twentieth century while inhabiting the nineteenth. Those in the twenty-first century who haven't entirely abandoned questions of meaning still use, for the most part, the language—and thus the categories—of nineteenth-century writers.

14. Jean Vanier, founder of *L'Arche,* describes this process in *Becoming Human* (Toronto: Anansi, 1998). Tracy Kidder's *Mountains beyond Mountains* (New York: Random House, 2003) describes how Paul Farmer, founder of Partners in Health, found adequate expression of the motivation for his "humanitarian work" in explicitly theological language. We will say more about Dr. Farmer in chapter 6.

15. Physician Margaret Mohrmann, reflecting on scripture in this matter, finds no biblical text in which God creates anything called "life": "God created and creates living beings. . . . There is no life except as embodied in living beings" *(Medicine as Ministry* [Cleveland: Pilgrim Press, 1995], 22–23).

16. From Brian Wren, *Bringing Many Names: 35 New Hymns* (Carol Stream, IL: Hope, 1989), no. 16. Copyright © 1989 Hope Publishing Company. Used by permission.

17. From an interview with Ken Myers (*Mars Hill Audio Journal* 41, Nov.–Dec. 1999).

18. Once again, we wish to avoid intellectual scapegoating. Descartes is not the problem, but rather the symptom of the West's profound confusion over the relative place of mind, soul, and body in the created world. Descartes and his contemporaries inherited this confusion, we suggest, from late medieval scholasticism, through the conduits of the Renaissance and the Reformation-era philosophy.

19. *Theological Dictionary of the New Testament, Abridged,* G. Kittel and G. Friedrich, eds. (Grand Rapids: Eerdmans, 1985),1005; italics ours.

20. Ibid., 1148.

21. An excellent treatment of Paul's use of "body language," in 1 Corinthians is Dale Martin's *The Corinthian Body* (New Haven: Yale University Press, 1995). Martin reads Paul with an ear for rhetoric and a familiarity with first-century medical texts.

22. From Wendell Berry, *Sex, Economy, Freedom & Community* (New York: Pantheon Books, 1993), 106.

23. The familiar excerpt from John Donne's *Devotions upon Emergent Occasions, Meditation XVII,* echoes this biblical understanding of human interconnectedness: "No man is an island, entire of itself; every man is a piece of the continent, a part of the main. If a clod be washed away by the sea, Europe is the less, as well as if promontory were, as well as if a manor of thy friend's or of thine own were. Any man's death diminishes me, because I am involved in mankind; and therefore never send to know for whom the bell tolls; it tolls for thee."

24. Devotees of the late Joseph Campbell would, of course, argue there's nothing at all unique in Jesus's story. We lack time and space here to explain why we disagree. One place to begin a response to that claim would be the work of René Girard.

25. By the end of the second century, authorship of Luke's Gospel was credited to the "beloved physician" and companion of Paul mentioned in Philemon 24, Colossians 4:14, and 2 Timothy 4:11. Whether the author was a physician or not, he had a strong body-consciousness.

26. We will explore more Gospel connections between meals and healing in chapter 6.

27. Even if one accepts as authoritative the shorter version of Mark, which omits any physical appearance of the risen Christ, Mark's Jesus still quarrels with the Sadducees over the resurrection (Mark 12:18–27; see also Matt. 22:23–33; Luke 20:27–40; and, in a different context, Acts 23: 6–8). The Greeks' problem with the resurrection of the dead is mentioned in Acts 17:22–34.

28. *Christology* refers to theories about the identity of Jesus as Christ.

29. The author of John's Gospel shows no awareness of Gnostic communities or texts, since the latter are artifacts of the second century. Most of the surviving accounts of Gnostic thought and practice come to us from its opponents, including Irenaeus, whom we shall soon meet. With the discovery of the Nag Hammadi codices in 1947, scholars had a more direct account of early Gnosticism. These latter works have been variously interpreted as proving that "friendlier" alternatives to orthodoxy existed or that the orthodox opponents of Gnosticism were, if anything, kind in their rebuttals. Hans Jonas's *The Gnostic Religion: The Message of the Alien God and the Beginnings of Christianity,* 2nd ed. (Boston: Beacon Press, 1963) had been the definitive scholarly text in English until the translation of Kurt Rudolph's *Gnosis: The Nature and History of Gnosticism* (San Francisco: Harper and Row, 1983). We, of course, write as best we can within the interpretive traditions of orthodox Christianity, while recognizing there may be other ways to understand and describe the many, often contradictory, forms of Gnosticism. Elaine Pagels has gained considerable fame for advocating Gnostic sensibilities based on her "good parts version" reading of Nag Hammadi texts. Bart Ehrman, by contrast, advances a more scholarly, historical interpretation of "Lost Christianities." While we acknowledge the second and third centuries were theological messes, we do not accept the notion that "orthodoxy" merely names an ideological winner of a power struggle within early Christianity. Perhaps we lack the special *gnosis* to be persuaded to this point of view.

30. Nowadays, unfortunately, *Orthodox* and *Catholic* suggest denominational identities. We prefer the term *orthodox* for two reasons. First, we wish to emphasize the still unappreciated debt Western Christianity owes the Orthodox East, especially in the latter's appreciation of the embodied nature of Christian worship. Second, we hope to avoid the suggestion that we are advancing a particularly "Roman" Catholic theology, rather than one we believe common to the whole of Christian tradition.

147

31. In contrast to the modern obsession with egalitarianism, in theory if rarely in practice, the ancient mind was fascinated by elites. In our own time, each side in the reawakened struggle between orthodoxy and "alternate Christianities" accuses the other of arrogant elitism. While we hope to remain orthodox, we are unhappy with the demonization of theological opponents, which, historically, leads almost seamlessly into persecution, often of the grossest sort. Orthodox poet Scott Cairns concludes his poem "Adventures in New Testament Greek: *Hairesis*":

> Even heretics love God, and burn
> convinced he will love them too.
> Whatever choice, I think they will have failed
> to err sufficiently to witness less
> than appalling welcome when—just beyond
> the sear of that ecstatic blush—they turn.

From *Philokalia* (Lincoln, NE: Zoo Press, 2002), 18. Used by permission of the author.

32. Hamlet's first soliloquy (act 1, scene 2) begins in the First Folio, "O, that this too too solid flesh would melt, / Thaw, and resolve itself into a dew!" while some early quartos read, "O, that this too too sallied [i.e., "sullied" or defiled] flesh would melt." In either case, Hamlet is in a terrible predicament, having been charged with avenging his father's death, while the murderer has married Hamlet's mother and occupies Denmark's throne. Hamlet's already considering suicide in Act I to be free of material torment, the "mortal coil" from which he wishes to have "shuffled off," in his later, more famous soliloquy. In Act I, Hamlet continues, wishing:

> The Everlasting has not fix'd
> His canon 'gainst self-slaughter! O God, God,
> How weary, stale, flat and unprofitable
> Seem to me all the uses of the world!
> Fie on't, ah fie! Tis an unweeded garden
> That grows to seed. Things gross and rank in nature
> Possess it merely.

Even taking Hamlet's circumstances into account, his words hint at lasting Gnostic influences within Christian Europe centuries after the apparent victory of orthodoxy.

33. Such as the aeons and emanations that would eventually get Origen into trouble.

34. As in the heresy known as Docetism, from the Greek *dokein,* "to seem."

35. A brief, fairly painless introduction to the life and writing of Irenaeus is Hans Urs von Balthasar's *The Scandal of the Incarnation: Irenaeus against the Heresies* (San Francisco: Ignatius Press, 1990).

36. Ibid., 54.

37. This restoration, like the "kingdom of God," is eschatological, meaning it is at once "now" and "not yet," truly won for us through God's saving action, but waiting for its fullness when all things are gathered in Christ.

38. This book would not have been written without the Internet. We both use e-mail and search engines frequently, and our description of chat rooms betrays at least some familiarity with the practice. We both use cars, too, knowing how

they generate pollution, injure countless people, and turn near-neighbors into strangers. Technology can't help but be two-edged, blessing even as it harms. As struggling Christians, we hope to use these mixed blessings as wisely as possible, knowing how easily they corrupt.

39. J. K. Rowling, *Harry Potter and the Sorcerer's Stone* (New York: Scholastic Press, 1997), 214.

40. It is interesting to note how the camps in this debate have moved. Where, in Irenaeus's time, the orthodox position emphasized the body against the Gnostic exaltation of spirit, now it is orthodoxy that is accused of being overly spiritual and life-denying. What truth lies in this accusation is, we suggest, the consequence of retained threads of Gnostic thought within orthodox tradition. If the spirit is far more important than the body, then either the body must be punished through obsessive ascetic practice or it is powerless and irrelevant and can be used to libertine excess. Both paths have been followed in the history of Gnostic (and quasi-orthodox) practice, although the latter is clearly the preferred form today.

41. Catherine Wallace, *Selling Ourselves Short* (Grand Rapids: Brazos Press, 2003), 54. See also Peter Brown, *The Body and Society: Sexual Renunciation in Early Christianity* (New York: Columbia University Press, 1988). Wallace's synopsis comes within a discussion of the gender dualism that plagues Western thought even as Christian compassion has largely succumbed to the forces of capitalist competition. As Wallace points out, even many feminists assume and absorb the dualism arising from the Greco-Roman stew she describes.

42. Things were never so simple, of course. A marvelous survey of Christian speculation about just this phrase in the creed is Caroline Walker Bynum's *The Resurrection of the Body in Western Christianity, 200–1336* (New York: Columbia University Press, 1995).

43. See *Sources of the Self: The Making of the Modern Identity*, by Charles Taylor (Cambridge: Harvard University Press, 1992).

44. Bruce Malina, *The New Testament World: Insight from Cultural Anthropology* (Atlanta: John Knox Press, 1981), 54–55, emphasis in original. As the following citations demonstrate, even biblically literate moderns can't discuss community except in contrast to individuality.

45. Wayne Meeks, *The Origins of Christian Morality: The First Two Centuries* (New Haven: Yale University Press, 1993), 45.

46. Alexander Schmemann, *For the Life of the World: Sacraments and Orthodoxy* (Crestwood, NY: St. Vladimir's Seminary Press, 1998), 25.

47. Gerhard Lohfink, *Does God Need the Church?: Toward a Theology of the People of God* (Collegeville, MN: Liturgical Press, 1999), 52.

48. Ibid., 218.

49. The nature of the Eucharist is, of course, a matter of contention among various Christian traditions, and the Eucharist has often been a source of division rather than unity, as epitomized in the 1529 Marburg Colloquy between Luther and Zwingli. What most traditions appear to agree on, however, is that Eucharist is in some way holy and that it is a gift. Contemporary singer/songwriter Peter Mayer describes how his understanding developed, in his song "Holy Now":

When I was a boy, each week,
On Sunday, we would go to church
And pay attention to the priest
He would read the Holy Word
And consecrate the holy bread

And everyone would kneel and bow
Today the only difference is
Everything is holy now

("Holy Now," from *Million Year Mind,* Blue Boat Records, 1999.) Used by permission of the author.

We hear Mayer's words, not as an opposition between the Eucharist's (or the Word's) holiness and that of the creation, but rather that, in truly encountering the Holy in Word and Eucharist, one can begin to see how all creation is holy, too.

50. Or, in Feuerbach's failed attempt to dismiss what he considered idealistic speculation by means of a pun, *"Man ist was er isst"* ("Man is what he eats").

51. From "The Liturgical Shape of the Christian Life: Teaching Christian Ethics as Worship," in Hauweras, *In Good Company: The Church as Polis* (Notre Dame, IN: University of Notre Dame Press, 1995), 156.

52. Aidan Kavanaugh, *On Liturgical Theology* (Collegeville, MN: Liturgical Press, 1984), 158–59. For an account of how liturgy challenges the world's violence, specifically that of Pinochet's Chile, see William Cavanaugh's *Torture and Eucharist* (Oxford: Blackwell, 1998).

53. Stanley Hauerwas, "Worship, Evangelism, Ethics: On Eliminating the 'And,'" in Hauerwas, *A Better Hope* (Grand Rapids: Brazos Press, 2000), 159.

Chapter 4 The Shape of What's Given

1. "Journey of the Magi," in T. S. Eliot, *The Complete Poems and Plays, 1909–1950* (New York: Harcourt, Brace and World, 1971), 69.

2. Chinua Achebe takes Eliot's words for the title of his novel of cultural disruption in colonial Africa. *No Longer at Ease* is set two generations after his first novel about the collision of cultures, *Things Fall Apart,* the title of which comes from W.B. Yeats's poem "The Second Coming."

3. Alasdair MacIntyre defines a practice as "any coherent and complex form of socially established and cooperative human activity through which goods internal to that form of activity are realized in the course of trying to achieve those standards of excellence which are appropriate to, and partially definitive of, that form of activity, with the result that human powers to achieve excellence, and human conceptions of the ends and goods involved, are systematically extended." *After Virtue* (Notre Dame, IN: University of Notre Dame Press, 1984), 187.

4. In the traditional Catholic and Orthodox understanding of the sacraments (or mysteries, in Orthodox parlance), baptism, confirmation, and Eucharist are sacraments of initiation. The Orthodox still celebrate them at the same time, so that even infants are baptized and chrismated and partake of the Eucharist in the same liturgy. The word *chrismation* should alert us to the powerful transformation one undergoes (and is expected to live out) by incorporation into the body of Christ. *Chrismation* comes from *chrisma,* or anointing. In Israel, priests, kings, and prophets were anointed as a sign of their calling (see Zech. 4:14; 1 Sam. 16:13; 2 Sam. 2:7; 1 Kings 1:34, 19:16). Our word *Christ* comes from the Greek *Christos* ("anointed"), a translation of the Hebrew *masiach.* By extension, then, the anointing that is chrismation can be understood as "en-Christ-ing."

5. There is a persistent theme in Eliot's poetry of birth and death mingling in the shadows of human experience, often associated with water imagery. One could trace this from "Prufrock" ("Till human voices wake us, and we drown") to a culmination in "Four Quartets" ("The wave cry, the wind cry, the vast waters / Of the petrel and the porpoise. In my end is my beginning"). That this association

appears for Eliot years before his conversion suggests how Christian imagery remained a force, however attenuated, in Western culture at the beginning of the twentieth century. A lot has changed in a hundred years.

6. Edwin Abbot, *Flatland,* 7th ed. (New York: Dover, 1952).

7. In Act V of Shakespeare's *Hamlet,* Hamlet tells Horatio that "there is a divinity that shapes our ends, / Rough-hew them how we will," and later, "There is a special providence in the fall of a sparrow. If it be now, 'tis not to come; if it be not to come, it will be now; if it be not now, yet it will come. The readiness is all." While this can be read as more Stoic than Christian, we rather like the Christian resonances. What makes the first quotation even more likeable is the plainness of its words. To "rough-hew" and "shape ends" are terms used by trimmers of hedges.

8. Guroian, *Life's Living toward Dying,* 37.

9. Ibid., 37–38.

10. In *The Stories of John Cheever* (New York: Alfred Knopf, 1979), 429–37. We are indebted to Vigen Guroian for calling our attention to this story.

11. Ibid., 431.

12. Ibid., 435.

13. Ibid., 437, emphasis ours.

14. Epistle to Diognetus 5:5–7, in *The Apostolic Fathers* (Grand Rapids: Baker, 1999), 541.

15. Stanley Hauerwas explores how theodicy is not a Christian problem, while "anthropodicy," theodicy's secular offspring, remains at the heart of contemporary technological medicine. See his *God, Medicine, and Suffering* (Grand Rapids: Eerdmans, 1990), originally released with the title *Naming the Silences.*

16. The passage "entertaining angels unawares," which recalls Abraham's hospitality at Mamre (Gen. 18:1–15) has been misused at times to suggest a sort of divine lotto, encouraging everybody to stay in the hospitality game since, every so often, someone wins big. We think the subsequent reference to the body in the materially thankless task of visiting prisoners and the oppressed sufficient to counter this.

17. Greer, *Broken Lights and Mended Lives,* 123. In the fourth century, Julian the Apostate's attempts to reverse the Christianization of his empire included the planned establishment of pagan institutions of hospitality modeled after the efforts of his Christian opponents. Julian's letter to Arsacius, pagan high priest of Galatia, urges the Galatian pagans to be exemplary in their lives, and particularly to establish "hospices" where the poor and sick will be cared for. That Julian's "Letter to the Galatians" emphasizes the importance of works as a counterexample to ascendant Christianity supports Greer's contention that Christianity drew converts more through better lives than better arguments. Fifteen hundred years later, Nietzsche proposed to destroy Christianity not by challenging its creeds, but rather by subverting its ethic. The domestication of Christian practices by the powers has immeasurably advanced Nietzsche's project.

18. Quoted in Amy Oden, *And You Welcomed Me: A Sourcebook on Hospitality in Early Christianity* (Nashville: Abingdon, 2001), 58–59.

19. Ibid., 187.

20. A proper understanding of autonomy as an expression of human dignity and freedom under God is certainly appropriate. Is overvaluation of autonomy, in addition to being misguided, also a sin? Here's Scott Cairns:

The heart's *metanoia,*
on the other hand, turns
without regret, turns not
so much *away,* as *toward,*
as if the slow pilgrim
has been surprised to find
that sin is not so *bad*
as it is a waste of time.

From "Adventures in New Testament Greek: *Metanoia*" in *Philokalia* (Lincoln, NE: Zoo Press, 2002), 15. Used by permission of the author.

21. Elaine Scarry, *The Body in Pain: The Making and Unmaking of a World* (New York: Oxford University Press, 1985).

22. Ibid., 4.

23. Ibid., 35.

24. Ibid., 4.

25. In this and the following discussion, we are indebted to M. Therese Lysaught's insightful essay "Patient Suffering and the Anointing of the Sick," which first appeared in *The Cresset,* Feb. 1992, 15–21.

26. See Arthur Kleinman, *The Illness Narratives: Suffering, Healing and the Human Condition* (New York: Basic Books, 1988) for an anthropologically informed attempt by a physician to recover the language of embodied experience.

27. Lysaught, "Patient Suffering and the Anointing of the Sick," anthologized in *On Moral Medicine,* 2nd ed. (Grand Rapids: Eerdmans, 1998), 361.

28. See Megan McKenna, *Rites of Justice: The Sacraments and Liturgy as Ethical Imperatives* (Maryknoll, NY: Maryknoll, 1997), and Alexander Schmemann, *For the Life of the World: Sacraments and Orthodoxy* (Crestwood, NY: St. Vladimir's Seminary Press, 1998).

29. National Council of Catholic Bishops, *Study Text 2: Pastoral Care of the Sick and Dying* (Washington, DC: Office of Publishing Services, USCC, 1984), 20.

30. Though defining what constitutes "productive" is usually left to the individual, the thrust of North American life suggests a great deal of getting and spending will necessarily be involved.

31. Lysaught, "Patient Suffering," 362.

32. Ibid., 362–63.

33. Precisely how the Greek *arête* became "virtue" (from the Latin *vir,* for "male") and, much later, became synonymous with a stereotyped "feminine" passivity is explored in Alasdair MacIntyre's *After Virtue,* 2nd ed. (Notre Dame, IN: University of Notre Dame Press, 1984). See particularly chapter 16, "From Virtue to Virtues to After Virtue." In regard to waiting for good things to come, MacIntyre points out how that most unfeminine of institutions, the nation-state, urges its citizens to do precisely that even as they give their lives for the state's ends. See MacIntyre's "A Partial Response to My Critics," in *After MacIntyre: Critical Perspectives,* ed. John Horton and Susan Mendus (Notre Dame, IN: University of Notre Dame Press, 1994), 303.

34. We owe an obvious debt here to John Howard Yoder, who wrote, "People who bear crosses are working with the grain of the universe" (from "Armaments and Eschatology," in *Studies in Christian Ethics* 1, no. 1 (1988): 58.

35. Wendell Berry has written so extensively on the difference between good and harmful work that it's hard to know which of his books to begin with. Pick up any of his essay collections, and you'll find this theme explicitly developed. His stories and poems, of course, reveal the same wisdom in less didactic fashion.

36. Ernesto Cortes, Southwest regional director of the Industrial Areas Foundation (IAF), talks about pairing the Golden Rule with the Iron Rule: "Never do for others what they can do for themselves."

37. From Stanley Hauerwas and Charles Pinches, "Practicing Patience," anthologized in *The Hauerwas Reader* (Durham, NC: Duke University Press, 2001), 356.

38. "Old Folks Boogie," by L. George and B. Payne.

39. *The Life of Brian,* directed by Terry Jones (London: Python (Monty) Pictures, 1979).

40. James F. Keenan, S.J., draws on Jewish and African-American womanist models of lament and "sassing" in his essay "Suffering and the Christian Tradition," available online at http://info.med.yale.edu/ intmed/hummed/yjhm/spirit2003/ suffering/jkeenan1.htm.

41. Hauerwas and Pinches, "Practicing Patience," 365.

42. Ibid.

43. Ibid.

44. Ibid.

45. Jean-Claude Larchet, *The Theology of Illness* (Crestwood, NY: St. Vladimir's Seminary Press, 2002), 104–5.

46. Ibid., 117.

47. Ibid., 120.

48. Ibid., 122.

49. Ibid., 123.

50. Liberation theologian Gustavo Gutiérrez warns: "Emphasis on the practice of justice and solidarity with the poor must never become an obsession and prevent our seeing that this commitment reveals its value and ultimate meaning only within the vast and mysterious horizon of God's gratuitous love" (Gustavo Gutiérrez, *On Job: God-Talk and the Suffering of the Innocent* [Maryknoll, NY: Orbis Books, 1987], 96).

51. From "Sinsick," in Stanley Hauerwas, *A Better Hope: Resources for a Church Confronting Capitalism, Democracy, and Postmodernity* (Grand Rapids: Brazos Press, 2000), 199.

Chapter 5 What Are Children For?

1. George Orwell, in *1984,* understood that a limited language (i.e., "Newspeak") limits the imagination. If there is no word to express "resistance," resistance itself is unsustainable, and if each word has only one approved meaning, there will be no variability of opinion or belief. Aldous Huxley, in *Brave New World,* understood that a people given everything they want will come to love their servitude.

2. Jackson Lears, *No Place of Grace: Anitmodernism and the Transformation of American Culture, 1880–1920* (Chicago: University of Chicago Press, 1981), 144.

3. From "An Interview with Amy Laura Hall," in *The Other Journal,* no. 4; italics ours.

4. We hope our debt to Wendell Berry is obvious here. His essay collection, *What Are People For?* (New York: Farrar, Straus, and Giroux, 1990), is one among many places in which he steps back from the modern enthrallment to technology and asks, "To what end are we doing this? Whom does this serve?"

5. Owen P. Phillips, Sherman Elias, Lee P. Shulman, et al., "Maternal Serum Screening for Fetal Down Syndrome in Women Less than 35 years of Age Using Alpha-fetoprotein, HCG, and Unconjugated Estriol: A Prospective Two-Year Study" *Obstetrics and Gynecology* 80 (1992): 353–58.

6. Thomas Elkins and Douglas Brown, "The Cost of Choice: A Price Too High in the Triple Screen for Down Syndrome," *Clinical Obstetrics and Gynecology* 36, no. 3 (1993): 532–40. In their discussion, Elkins and Brown cite Barbara Katz Rothman's largely ignored warning: "The technologies of prenatal diagnosis are offered to people in terms of expanding choices. However, it is always true that although new technology opens up some choices, it closes down others. . . . Prenatal diagnosis serves as a technology of quality control, based on a given society's ideas about what constitutes 'quality' in children. The ability to control the 'quality' of our children may ultimately cost the choice of not controlling that quality. . . . Issues of basic values, beliefs, and the larger moral questions will be lost in this narrowing of choices as decisions become more pragmatic, often clinical, and always individual" (From Barbara Katz Rothman, "Prenatal Diagnosis," in J. M. Humber and R. F. Almoder, eds., *Bioethics and the Fetus: Medical, Moral and Legal Issues* [Totowa, NJ: Humana Press, 1991], 173–75.)

7. Hard statistics are difficult to come by, but almost every review acknowledges that the vast majority of prenatal diagnoses of Down syndrome result in abortion. The U.K., which documents this far better than the U.S., had a 92 percent abortion rate between 1989 and 1997 (David Mutton, Roy Ide, Eva Alberman, "Trends in Prenatal Screening for and Diagnosis of Down Syndrome: England and Wales 1989–1997," *British Medical Journal* 317 [1998]: 922–23.) A 91 percent rate was observed at Boston's Brigham and Women's Hospital between 1988 and 1990 (T. M. Caruso and L. B. Holmes, "Down Syndrome: Increased Prenatal Detection and Dramatic Decrease in Live Births: 1972–1990," *Teratology* 49 (1994): 376.) Prenatal diagnosis is more frequently offered to "older" women, who have a statistically higher risk of bearing a child with Down syndrome (see *Morbidity and Mortality Weekly Report* 43 [33]: 617–23.)

8. Margaret Sanger, the founder of Planned Parenthood, spoke in a less politically correct era when she advocated the segregation and sterilization of "human weeds," while encouraging the planned breeding of "human thoroughbreds," as in *The Pivot of Civilization* (New York: Brentano's, 1922). Sanger's embrace of and complicity in the American eugenics movement is briefly reviewed in chapter 7 of Edwin Black's *War against the Weak: Eugenics and America's Campaign to Create a Master Race* (New York: Four Walls Eight Windows, 2003). Black's book catalogs in painstaking detail the "scientific" origins of eugenics, its champions throughout American secular progressive movements, and its deliberate exportation to other countries, particularly Germany. How "liberal" and "progressive" American Protestants enthusiastically embraced this movement—which involuntarily sterilized more than 60,000 of the "unfit" in the United States—is documented in Christine Rosen's *Preaching Eugenics: Religious Leaders and the American Eugenics Movement* (Oxford: Oxford University Press, 2004).

9. From "Abortion, Theologically Understood," in Hauerwas and Pinches, *Hauerwas Reader,* 618.

10. Such bodies include our own, those of our loved ones, our enemies, and the animals, plants, fungi, and unicellular organisms with which we share this planet.

11. Karl Barth, *Church Dogmatics*, III/4: The Doctrine of Creation, G. W. Bromiley and T. F. Torrance, eds. (Edinburgh: T & T Clark, 1961), 266. Italics ours.

12. Greer, *Broken Lights and Mended Lives,* 104.

13. Compare this to the Stoic extinction of the passions. Stoics typically understood producing heirs as a duty proper to the virtuous man—a virtue that, of course, required the participation, if not necessarily the cooperation, of women.

It's interesting here to recall that the Stoic philosopher-emperor Marcus Aurelius rejected the practice of adopting a suitable heir to the imperial throne—a practice that fostered the political stability necessary to create the admittedly mixed blessings of "Pax Romanum"—in favor of his biological son, the megalomaniacal Commodus, whose reign was anything but virtuous. In a modern Christian context, Hauerwas notes, "the 'sacrifice' made by the single is not that of 'giving up sex,' but the much more significant sacrifice of giving up heirs. There can be no more radical act than this, as it is the clearest institutional expression that one's future is not guaranteed by the family, but by the church" (from "Sex in Public: How Adventurous Christians Are Doing It," in Hauerwas and Pinches, *Hauerwas Reader,* 498).

14. Greer, *Broken Lights and Mended Lives,* 116.

15. Nor can the Christian be satisfied with Kahlil Gibran's vague and airy references to children as "Life's longing for itself."

16. Those familiar with contemporary adoption practices and parlance know how quickly "correct" terminology comes and goes, yet people have adopted children for millennia. Apparently the practice still mystifies us enough to fall back on scientific-sounding euphemisms.

17. *Catechism of the Catholic Church,* no. 1255. English trans. (Vatican City: Libreria Editrice Vaticana; Chicago: [distributed by] Loyola University Press, 1994).

18. "A Good Man Is Hard to Find," in Flannery O'Connor, *The Collected Stories* (New York: Farrar, Straus, and Giroux, 1971), 132.

19. Ibid., 130.

20. Ibid., 132.

21. Ibid., 132.

22. We owe this insight to Gil Bailie.

23. O'Connor, "A Good Man," 133.

24. "Institutional review boards" are the committees that review human research proposals for practical and ethical concerns within a hospital, university, or corporation.

25. The following quotations are taken from a private communication and used with permission from the original author. Names are withheld for reasons of privacy.

26. GIFT is an acronym for gamete intra-fallopian transfer, a technological procedure requiring ovarian stimulation and egg retrieval—rather like in vitro fertilization (IVF), but without fertilization outside the body. Instead, the collected ova are placed directly into the woman's fallopian tubes along with the man's sperm.

27. Ibid. The reference to Hagar, of course, recalls Abram's "technological fix" to the problem of Sarai's infertility, an approach that Sarai herself suggested, then regretted (Genesis 16). Margaret Atwood's *The Handmaid's Tale* (New York: Anchor, 1998) skillfully imagines an American theocracy where fertile "handmaids" are forced to bear children for infertile "mistresses." In this case, the biblical reference is to Rachel's infertility, and her suggestion that Jacob bear children through her maid, Bilhah. We await a similarly well-told novel of the dystopia we have already entered, in which the wealthy buy the means to desirable offspring while selectively exterminating the undesirable, even as the poor are vilified for having "unwanted children" and left to fend for themselves. We hope it is clear by now that this is a problem the church must decisively respond to.

28. Ibid.

29. Raymond Brown, *The Birth of the Messiah* (New York: Doubleday, 1993), 73.

30. Is it still possible to write satire in an age where none blink at restoring the "normal" through expensive, intricate, and artificial means? As one of us is fond of saying, "No wonder Kurt Vonnegut doesn't write much anymore."

31. While a bit grim, it's worth remembering how the still-disguised Wesley rebukes Buttercup in *The Princess Bride,* "Life is pain, Highness. Anyone who says differently is selling something."

32. In this respect, the King James translation of Mark 10:14, "Suffer the little children to come unto me," takes on special resonance.

33. William H. Willimon, *What's Right with the Church?* (New York: Harper and Row, 1985), 65.

34. Cf. James 1:22. Read as an entirety, the Letter of James is a powerful rebuttal to the Gnostic claims of the powers, particularly those of medicine. As we noted in the previous chapter, even the sick person's body is reclaimed from alienation through anointing and prayer.

35. Bill Tilbert, from an unpublished sermon cited by Richard B. Hays in *The Moral Vision of the New Testament* (San Francisco: HarperCollins, 1996), 458.

36. Like pacifism, embodied witness to real abortion alternatives is largely dismissed in North American society as "unrealistic," often painted as "doing nothing" in the face of horrible circumstances. Unlike pacifists, though, many so-called conservatives fit the bill of their detractors, frequently ignoring women's lived experiences and imagining that answers to such conditions are simple or available with the stroke of a presidential pen. Liberals have a better record of listening to women in crisis, but are—in our view—overly fond of technological solutions. If the gathered body is to respond to the realities of North America culture, it will need to begin its lived witness long before crises occur, showing children there is more to intimacy than genitals, that "what people do in their bedrooms" is deeply connected to the health of the community, and discussing openly, honestly, and with respect for both communal tradition and real circumstances, roles for contraception and abstinence. The rest of this chapter will gesture at the community's responsibility once children are begotten. To do justice to this communal witness across generations would take an entire book, but we can suggest some places for the interested to start their reading. Years before Hillary Clinton stumbled upon the idea that pro-choicers and pro-lifers might work together to reduce the number of abortions, Frederica Mathewes-Green and others were already engaging in that conversation. The news industry predictably ignored such endeavors in favor of juicier stories, but Mathewes-Green's book *Real Choices: Listening to Women; Looking for Alternatives to Abortion* (Ben Lomond, CA: Conciliar Press, 1997) is well worth reading. Wendell Berry's conviction that nothing, not even food or sex, falls outside community concern, runs throughout his work. We particularly recommend the title essay in his collection, *Sex, Economy, Freedom & Community.* Anne Tyler's wonderful novel *Saint Maybe* (New York: Fawcett Columbine, 1991) describes how costly responsibility for another's children might be embodied.

37. "Assisted Reproduction Technique Surveillance—United States, 2001," *Morbidity and Mortality Weekly Report,* April 30, 2004/53 (SS01), 1–20.

38. Alan Guttmacher Institute, www.agi-usa.org/presentations/abort_slides .pdf.

39. From *Foster Care National Statistics,* National Clearinghouse on Child Abuse and Neglect Information (HHS), 2003, www.nccanch.acf.hhs.gov/pubs/factsheets/foster.cfm.

40. UNICEF Child Mortality Statistics, www.childinfo.org/cmr/revis/db2.htm.

41. Robert E. Black, Saul S. Morris, and Jennifer Bryce, "Where and Why Are 10 Million Children Dying Every Year? *Lancet* 361 (2003): 2226–34.

42. Brendan Kramp, "Rural Texas Church Makes Adoption a Community Affair," available through the North American Council on Adoptable Children, www.nacac.org/newsletters/faith/texaschapel.html. All subsequent references to Bennett Chapel are from this article.

43. Fyodor Dostoyevsky, *The Brothers Karamazov,* trans. Constance Garnett, rev. Ralph E. Matlaw (New York: Norton, 1976), 49. Even more troubling is the warning a few paragraphs earlier:

> The more I love humanity in general, the less I love man in particular, that is, separately, as single individuals. In my dreams . . . I have often come to making enthusiastic schemes for the service of humanity, and perhaps I might actually have faced crucifixion if it had been suddenly necessary; and yet I am incapable of living in the same room with anyone for two days together, as I know by experience. As soon as someone is near me, his personality disturbs my self-esteem and restricts my freedom. In twenty-four hours I begin to hate even the best of men: one because he's too long over his dinner, another because he has a cold and keeps blowing his nose. I become hostile to people the moment they come close to me. But it has always happened that the more I detest men individually the more ardent becomes my love for humanity. (Ibid., 48–49)

Chapter 6 A Body without Borders

1. Matthew says, "Indeed . . . (Jesus) . . . said nothing to them without a parable" (Matt. 13:34).

2. Jesus was an observant Jew. Except for healing the sick, Saturday was his day off. (See Matt. 12:9–13.)

3. Since he's half dead, there's still a story to be told. If he were completely dead, there would be nothing left to do but "look through his pockets for loose change," as Miracle Max in *The Princess Bride* advises. Completely dead bodies figure prominently in mystery stories. As we will soon see, this too is a mystery story, but of a different sort, offering more possibility of redemption than the typical detective tale.

4. Once again, our complacent piety emasculates Jesus's stories, shielding the modern hearer from the bitter tasks of conversion by rendering divine demand impotent. Jesus's parables are masterpieces of edgy social commentary, and in that sense at least, Jesus can be understood as the Lenny Bruce of first-century Palestine. That Jesus's social criticism arises from the heart of Torah places him in the perilous tradition of the prophets, whom Abraham Joshua Heschel calls "the most disturbing people who ever lived" (Abraham Joshua Heschel, *The Prophets: An Introduction,* vol. 1 [New York: Harper and Row, 1962], ix).

5. We realize Luke's Gospel is the reigning favorite among socially conscious exegetes, though it was not ever thus. John Howard Yoder's masterpiece *The Politics of Jesus* (Grand Rapids: Eerdmans, 1972) provides a close reading of Luke precisely because the dominant reading of Luke in the 1950s and 1960s saw Luke's editorial purpose as "apologetic," reassuring his reader that Christians were not a threat to the empire (2nd ed., 53). Since our purpose in this chapter is to prophetically widen the body's vision beyond borders, Luke is a logical fit. Were we

to emphasize the perilous tasks of discipleship or the authority of Christ and his church, we may well have turned to Mark or Matthew, respectively.

6. Space limitations preclude a thorough survey here. Exemplary healings can be found in Luke 5:12–24, 7:1–10, 7:11–16, 8:26–39, 9:37–43, and 17:11–19. Note the absence of distinction between healings and the exorcisms in Luke 4:40–41, 6:18, 8:26–39, and 9:37–43; Luke builds no Cartesian wall between body, mind, and spirit. Meal stories in Luke include 6:27–32, 7:36–50, 14:1–24, 19:1–10, 22:14–23, 24:13–35, and 24:36–53. The other synoptic Gospels include parallel themes. Charles Amjad-Ali observes that healing miracles in Mark bring the marginalized back into full political, economic, social, and religious participation within the community. See Charles Amjad-Ali, *Passion for Change: Reflections on the Healing Miracles in Saint Mark* (Rawalpindi: Christian Study Centre, 1989). Meals and healings are signs of the eschatological "kingdom of heaven" in Matthew, as in Matthew 22:1–14 and 12:22–28. Special thanks to Father Greg Schaffer for helping us set Lukan accounts in broader synoptic context.

7. Wendell Berry, "Healing," in *What Are People For?* (New York: North Point Press, 1990), 9.

8. See his chapter, "Meals Are Where the Magic Is," in Luke Timothy Johnson, *Religious Experience in Earliest Christianity* (Minneapolis: Fortress Press, 1998).

9. As Matthew's Gospel tells it, the kingdom's banquet extends an invitation to many. Sadly, few respond, and even among these few, at least one is turned out for not changing into a wedding garment. As we once heard J. Glenn Murray, S.J., say, "Jesus was promiscuous about whom he ate with, but he invited tax collectors, prostitutes, and sinners to the table precisely so they would not leave as tax collectors, prostitutes, and sinners."

10. See Laurie Garrett, *Betrayal of Trust: The Collapse of Global Public Health* (New York: Hyperion, 2001), and Paul Farmer, *Infections and Inequalities: The Modern Plagues* (Berkeley: University of California Press, 2001).

11. As in the estimated "cost to society" for raising a child with Down syndrome we mentioned in the previous chapter.

12. We readily acknowledge that contemporary medical ethics is far more complicated than this brief taxonomy suggests. One happy arrival on the scene is so-called intrinsic ethics, owing much to the work of Alasdair MacIntyre. As we read the literature, though, highly individualistic accounts of utilitarianism and deontology dominate the field, with the ghosts of John Stuart Mill and Immanuel Kant still haunting the machine of medical ethics.

13. Having been on both the giving and receiving end of the highly ritualized legal transaction of informed consent, we find the claims made about the process largely illusory. One of us once heard a seasoned clinician warn, "If you're not a little frightened about what you can persuade a patient or her representative to do, you're not very observant." Real consent is a much longer, far more complicated relational process than a rehearsal of "risks and benefits" followed by a signature at the bottom of a printed form—rather like marriage, actually! Graduate medical education rarely acknowledges this. The bare ritual is followed by the respective parties, leaving "each in the cell of himself . . . almost convinced of his freedom" (from "In Memory of W. B. Yeats," W. H. Auden, *Collected Poems* [New York: Random House, 1976], 197).

14. Paul Farmer, *Pathologies of Power: Health, Human Rights, and the New War on the Poor* (Berkeley: University of California Press, 2003), 21. Farmer and Nicole Gastineau Campos provide a sustained, withering critique of medical ethics'

neglect of the world's poor in "Rethinking Medical Ethics: A View from Below," *Developing World Bioethics* 4, no. 1 (2004): 17–41.

15. Black, Morris, and Bryce, "Where and Why," *Lancet* 361 (2003): 2226–34.

16. *AIDS Epidemic Annual Report 2004,* U.N. Programme on HIV/AIDS, www.unaids.org/wad2004/report.html.

17. Colin McCord and Harold P. Freeman, "Excess Mortality in Harlem," *New England Journal of Medicine* 322 (1990): 173–77. Similar statistics for infant or neonatal mortality should be viewed with caution. Very different approaches to premature infants in the United States and in "developing countries" skew the numbers significantly.

18. Carmen deNavas-Walt, Bernadette Proctor, Robert J. Mills, *Income, Poverty, and Health Insurance Coverage in the United States: 2003* (Washington, DC: U.S. Government Printing Office, 2004), 14.

19. Though not entirely so. Márcio Fabri dos Anjos, who tellingly writes from the perspective of liberation theology (of which we will say more in our discussion of Paul Farmer), asks, "To what level of quality can medical ethics aspire, if it ignores callous discrimination in medical practice against large populations of innocent poor? . . . How effective can such theories be in addressing the critical issues of medical and clinical ethics if they are unable to contribute to the closing of the gap of socio-medical disparity?" (Márcio Fabri dos Anjos, "Medical Ethics in the Developing World: A Liberation Theology Perspective," *Journal of Medicine and Philosophy* 21 (1996): 629–37.

20. See Wendell Berry's short story "Fidelity" in *Fidelity: Five Stories* (New York: Pantheon, 1992) and his less mordant, downright funny "Watch with Me," in *Watch with Me and Six Other Stories of the Yet-Remembered Ptolemy Proudfoot and His Wife, Miss Minnie, Née Quinch* (New York: Pantheon, 1994).

21. See again Edwin Black, *War against the Weak* (New York: Four Walls Eight Windows, 2003).

22. See Susan M. Reverby, ed., *Tuskegee's Truths: Rethinking the Tuskegee Syphilis Study* (Chapel Hill: University of North Carolina Press, 2000), and Allan M. Brandt, *No Magic Bullet: A Social History of Venereal Disease in the United States since 1880* (New York: Oxford University Press, 1987).

23. See Thomas C. Quinn, Maria J. Wawer, Nelson Sewankambo, et al., "Viral Load and Heterosexual Transmission of Human Immunodeficiency Virus Type I," *New England Journal of Medicine* 342 (2000): 921–29, a study that identified and observed couples in Uganda in which only one partner was HIV-positive, in an effort to see which factors contributed to heterosexual transmission of the virus. Marica Angell's editorial in the same issue noted, with dismay, "It is important to be clear about what this study meant for the participants. It meant that for up to 30 months, several hundred people with HIV infection were observed but not treated" ("Investigators' Responsibilities for Human Subjects in Developing Countries," *NEJM* 342 (2000): 967–69). See also a troubling chapter in contraceptive research in Ana Regina Comes Dos Reis, "Norplant in Brazil: Implantation Strategy in the Guise of Scientific Research," *Issues in Reproductive and Genetic Engineering: Journal of International Feminist Analysis* 3 (1990): 111–18.

24. While we shall soon see how explicitly Farmer grounds his work in theological language and convictions, we owe a great debt to M. Therese Lysaught for providing a larger theo-political framework in which to understand those convictions. Lysaught's unpublished lectures delivered at the Church and Culture Conference at Valley Covenant Church, Eugene, Oregon, in 2004, entitled "Anointing the Sick: A Christian Politics of Medicine," are particularly helpful in this regard.

25. Paul Farmer, "Political Violence and Public Health in Haiti," *New England Journal of Medicine* 350, no. 15 (2004): 1483–86.

26. Kidder, *Mountains beyond Mountains,* 241–60.

27. Ibid., 78.

28. Ibid., 85.

29. Rights talk and God talk aren't mutually exclusive, but they are, in Wittgensteinian terms, very different language games.

30. The history of this phrase is briefly recounted by one of its leading proponents, Gustavo Gutiérrez, in an interview in Daniel Hartnett, "Remembering the Poor: An Interview with Gustavo Gutiérrez," *America,* Feb. 3, 2003, available online at: www .americamagazine.org/gettext.cfm?articleTypeID=1&textID=2755&issueID=420.

31. Farmer, *Pathologies of Power,* 155. While we retain a healthy skepticism toward governmental solutions in health matters, we acknowledge the remnants of goodness within the powers and seek to further that goodness without becoming enthralled. Consider how the debate over universal health care might play out in the United States (which, except for South Africa, is the only "developed" nation that does not guarantee some level of health care to its citizens) if Farmer's vision were more common. Rather than complaining about long waits for certain procedures (as in Canada), we might rather focus on finally making such procedures available to the millions of Americans now denied them.

32. From remarks made at an International Health Medical Education Consortium Conference, La Antigua, Guatemala, February 2004. In the larger context of the health of the body, we hear echoes of Wendell Berry here: "To be creative is only to have health: to keep oneself fully alive in the Creation, to keep the Creation fully alive in oneself, to see the Creation anew, to welcome one's part in it anew. . . . The most creative works are all strategies for this health" (Wendell Berry, "Healing," in *What Are People For?* 9).

33. Dr. Greg Schaffer, from a personal telephone conversation with one of the authors.

34. Much of this information comes from Encarncion Ajcot's delightful *Maltiox Tat: A History of Father Gregory Schaffer and the San Lucas Toliman Mission,* privately published and available through the Diocese of New Ulm, Minnesota.

35. The sad and disturbing history of United States involvement in the coup that precipitated the civil war can be found in Stephen Schlesinger and Stephen Kinzer's *Bitter Fruit: The Story of the American Coup in Guatemala,* expanded ed. (Cambridge MA: Harvard University Press, 1999), and Nicholas Cullather's *Secret History: The CIA's Classified Account of Its Operations in Guatemala, 1952–1954* (Stanford, CA: Stanford University Press, 1999). Daniel Wilkinson explores the unspeakable violence of the ensuing war in his *Silence on the Mountain: Stories of Terror, Betrayal, and Forgetting in Guatemala* (Boston: Houghton Mifflin, 2002). In the 1950s, the Roman Catholic hierarchy in Guatemala supported the U.S. forces. By the 1990s, that—and quite a few other things—had completely changed. In April 1998, seventy-five-year-old auxiliary bishop Juan José Gerardi Conedera released the 1,440-page church report on the war, "Guatemala: Nunca Mas" (Never Again). It estimated that, of the 200,000 casualties in the civil war, more than 80 percent had been killed or "disappeared" by the U.S.-supported (and often U.S.-trained) Guatemalan military. Two days after the report reached the public, Bishop Gerardi was murdered in his garage, beaten to death with a concrete block used to crush his skull.

36. Related to us by personal communication from Father Greg Schaffer.

37. "What is wrong with you?" is, of course, the question Parzival, the Grail Knight, finally asks the wounded King Anfortas, but only after long suffering following his (much regretted) missed opportunity. That hospitality and compassion lie at the heart of this medieval epic speaks volumes about the poverty of virtue in the tales we tell today. The adventurous might well seek out Chretien de Troyes's *Perceval,* or Wolfram von Eschenbach's *Parzival,* though shorter attention spans will be rewarded by reading Katherine Paterson's delightful retelling, *Parzival: The Quest of the Grail Knight* (New York: Lodestar Books, 1998).

38. Hilfiker's Minnesota experiences and his decision to move to Washington are documented in his book *Healing the Wounds: A Physician Looks at His Work* (New York: Pantheon, 1985). Two of the chapters originally appeared in the *New England Journal of Medicine.*

39. David Hilfiker, "The New American Hopelessness: A Kingdom Response," in *Upholding the Vision: Serving the Poor in Training and Beyond,* 2nd ed., David Caes, ed. (Philadelphia: Christian Community Health Fellowship, 1996).

40. David Hilfiker, *Not All of Us Are Saints: A Doctor's Journey with the Poor* (New York: Ballantine, 1994), 11 (hereafter *NAUAS*).

41. Any critique of medical care for the poor in the United States must take this abandonment into account. Anyone who has worked within the bureaucracies meant to serve the poor knows how quickly the best of hearts grow heavy with cynicism arising when, despite one's best effort, things do not change. The people working within such systems are, for the most part, truly compassionate and willing to sacrifice something of their own material comfort for the good of others. As a people, though, the United States has permitted the poor to be abandoned. We trust God will judge us accordingly.

42. See David Caes, ed., *Caring for the Least of These: Serving Christ among the Poor* (Scottdale, PA: Herald Press, 1992), and David Caes, ed., *Upholding the Vision: Serving the Poor in Training and Beyond,* 2nd ed. (Philadelphia: CCHF, 1996).

43. See John Perkins's *Restoring At-Risk Communities: Doing It Together and Doing It Right* (Grand Rapids: Baker, 1995) and *Beyond Charity: The Call to Christian Community Development* (Grand Rapids: Baker, 1993). Perkins plays an important role in Charles Marsh's *The Beloved Community: How Faith Shapes Social Justice, from the Civil Rights Movement to Today* (New York: Basic Books, 2005).

Chapter 7 Perfection Money Can't Buy

1. We realize such an effort would, for a host of reasons, be doomed from the start.

2. Even the title framing the scene comes from an extrabiblical source. "Sermon on the Mount" was first used to designate Matthew 5:1–7:29 by St. Augustine.

3. That is, the scriptures. Even today, the "Jewish Bible" is called *Tanakh,* an elision of the words *Torah* (Law), *Neviim* (Prophets), and *Ketuvim* (Writings).

4. According to John Howard Yoder, *The Politics of Jesus* (Grand Rapids: Eerdmans, 1972), 119: "The AV rendering of verse 48 . . . has for years been made the key to the whole Sermon on the Mount." We shall return to Yoder's analysis of this passage momentarily.

5. Reinhold Niebuhr, "The Relevance of an Impossible Ethical Ideal," in *An Interpretation of Christian Ethics* (San Francisco: Harper and Row, 1963), 62–83.

6. "The Ethic of Jesus," in ibid., 22.

7. While definitions here are somewhat fluid, cosmetic surgery is, strictly speaking, a subset of plastic surgery. Cosmetic surgeries, such as breast augmentation, facelifts, and "tummy tucks," take normal structures and "improve" their

appearance. Reconstructive surgery, another subset of plastic surgery, alters an abnormal body part to improve function or appearance. Examples of this would include cleft lip or palate surgery, revisions of disfiguring scars, and skin grafting after burns.

8. From an ASPS press release dated March 8, 2004, at www.cosmeticsurgery-news.com/article2108.html.

9. See chapter 3, above.

10. David Sarwer, Leanne Magee, and Vicki Clark, "Physical Appearance and Cosmetic Medical Treatments: Physiological and Socio-cultural influences," *Journal of Cosmetic Dermatology* 2, no. 1 (January 2003): 29–39, at 29.

11. For an excellent critique of sociobiology, we recommend Wendell Berry, *Life Is a Miracle: An Essay against Modern Superstition* (Washington, DC: Counterpoint, 2000).

12. To their credit, the authors of this study do not restrict their account of why people desire enhancement to evolutionary biology.

13. Until recently, all such "enhancement therapies" targeted a single generation and could not be inherited. Thus, evolutionary defenses of enhancement could be further distorted into a Lamarckian misreading of neo-Darwinism (Jean-Baptiste Lamarck argued that acquired traits are passed on to subsequent generations). Now that "progressive science" has the tools to alter germ lines in the name of consumer eugenics, scientists can soon make future generations in their own image.

14. Here we refer the reader again to the ASPS press release cited above.

15. Carl Elliott, *Better than Well* (hereafter *BW*).

16. Americans' love of television is thoroughly documented and well publicized; according to Elliott, the average American household spends about seven hours per day watching television (83–84).

17. "Hence," says Elliott, "Daniel Boorstin's famous remark that celebrity is the quality of well-knownness for being well-known" (86).

18. If the reader has any doubts about this description, we encourage him or her simply to watch an episode of MTV's *I Want a Famous Face.*

19. Here again, the remarkable work of René Girard is profoundly insightful.

20. Peter Kramer, *Listening to Prozac* (New York: Viking Penguin, 1993).

21. Grant McCracken, *Big Hair: A Journey into the Transformation of the Self* (Woodstock, NY: Overlook Press, 1996), 2.

22. Our allusion to Leni Reifenstahl's movie celebrating the 1934 Nuremberg Rally is intentional.

23. Paul McHugh, "Psychiatric Misadventures," *American Scholar* 61, no. 4 (1992): 497–510.

24. Ibid.

25. Source: "Refractive Surgery—Statistics," available at http://www.allaboutvision.com/resources/statistics-laser-eye-surgery.htm.

26. Source: "Eyelid Surgery (Blepharoplasty)," available at http://www.plasticsurgery.com/Eyelid_Surgery_(Blepharoplasty)/default.htm.

27. Sources: "What Is River Blindness?" available at http://www.sightsavers.org/html/eyeconditions/river.htm, and "Prevalence of Trachoma," available at http://www.sightsavers.org/html/eyeconditions/trachoma_extent.htm.

28. We learned this phrase from our friend Professor Willie Young.

29. In reading *King Lear* this way we depend to a significant extent upon Michael Ignatieff's *The Needs of Strangers* (New York: Picador, 1984), 25–53.

30. Ibid., 37.

31. Ibid., 35–37.

32. Appearance and true identity, as well as seeing and blindness play important thematic roles in *Lear.* Only when Edmund betrays Gloucester and the latter is blinded can the father recognize Edgar as his true son.

33. Yoder, *Politics of Jesus,* 118.

34. The sense of the Greek word *teleios* has to do with conforming to one's *telos,* or true nature. It may also be rendered "complete," "full," "whole," or "undivided." Here see Gerhard Kittel, et al., eds., *Theological Dictionary of the New Testament Abridged in One Volume,* Geoffrey Bromiley, trans. (Grand Rapids: Eerdmans, 1985), 1164–1165.

35. John Howard Yoder, "The Political Axioms of the Sermon on the Mount," in *The Original Revolution* (Scottdale, PA: Herald Press, 1971), 50.

36. Yoder, *Politics of Jesus,* 120.

Chapter 8 Frailty and Grief, Overcome by Hope and Love

1. Wendell Berry, *Jayber Crow* (Washington, DC: Counterpoint, 2000); hereafter *JC.*

2. Ibid., 52.

3. Ibid., 53.

4. Ibid., 54.

5. Here, as is so frequently the case, Jesus serves as our example (John 13:1–20).

6. The love that is the basis for all Christian faithfulness is inextricably connected with the resurrection of the dead. Here we follow Karl Barth, *The Resurrection of the Dead* (Eugene: Wipf and Stock, 2003), to which we will refer much more later.

7. John Paul II, "Evangelium Vitae," *The Encyclicals of John Paul II,* ed. Michael Miller (Huntington, IN: Our Sunday Visitor, 1996). Our way of characterizing the Pope's description of our culture is, we believe, consistent with his intent.

8. For a more extensive account of this phenomenon than we are able to provide here, see Joel Shuman, "The Last Gift: The Elderly, The Church, and the Gift of a Good Death," in *Growing Old in Christ,* ed. Stanley Hauerwas, Carole Stoneking Bailey, Keith Meador, et al. (Grand Rapids: Eerdmans, 2003), 151–66.

9. Dietrich Bonhoeffer, *Ethics,* ed. Eberhard Bethge (New York: Macmillan, 1965), 21. While the public debate about whether religious symbols or messages should be posted in public places in the United States is still being waged, we suggest that the opening pages of Bonhoeffer's *Ethics* might prove an especially helpful corrective to our society's overwhelming hubris.

10. Michael Baurmann, *The Market of Virtue: Morality and Commitment in a Liberal Society* (New York: Kluwer Law International, 1996), 1–6, 19–30.

11. We came to know the Haywoods and learn of their story by virtue of the fact that one of us had the good fortune to teach Geraldine when she was a student at Duke. Her willingness to share her story gave rise to our consideration of the Haywoods' example here.

12. Wendell Berry, "Health Is Membership," *Another Turn of the Crank* (Washington, DC: Counterpoint, 1995), 105.

13. Here we turn again to Barth, who says in his exposition of 1 Corinthians 15: "Christ as the second Adam is the beginning of the resurrection of the dead. Perfection is the resurrection also of his own. . . . This perfection is, as the abolition of death generally, His highest and at the same time his last act of sovereignty (*Resurrection of the Dead,* 164).

14. Ibid., 197.

15. Many of Wendell Berry's stories and novels of the "Port William Membership" narrate how this conviction is lived out. For further insights into relationships maintained through and despite illness and death, we particularly recommend his short stories "Fidelity" and "Watch with Me."

16. Berry, *Jayber Crow,* 165.

Conclusion

1. See Aidan Kavanaugh's *On Liturgical Theology* (Collegeville, MN: Liturgical Press, 1984). Rather than accepting the tag line, *Lex orendi, lex credendi* ("law of prayer, law of belief"), Kavanaugh uses Prosper of Aquitaine's more specific aphorism: *Ut legem credendi lex statuat supplicandi* (the law of supplication establishes the law of belief).

2. See Gerhard Lohfink's *Does God Need the Church?: Toward a Theology of the People of God* (Collegeville, MN: Liturgical Press, 1999).

3. For the role of the Holy Spirit in the life of the church, see Yves Congar, *I Believe in the Holy Spirit* (New York: Crossroad Herder, 1997).

4. Here we find helpful Samuel Wells's book *Improvisation: The Drama of Christian Ethics* (Grand Rapids: Brazos Press, 2004).

5. Even Ornette Coleman's "harmolodic theory" of free jazz improvisation established a shared, albeit freely shifting, basis upon which the gathered instrumentalists could improvise.

6. There has been a blossoming of literature on ecclesial practice as performance, with Dietrich Bonhoeffer appearing rather often as a case study. See, for example, Stanley Hauerwas, *Performing the Faith: Bonhoeffer and the Practice of Nonviolence* (Grand Rapids: Brazos Press, 2004), and "Living and Dying in the Word: Dietrich Bonhoeffer as Performer of Scripture," in Stephen Fowl and L. Gregory Jones, *Reading in Communion: Scripture and Ethics in Christian Life* (Grand Rapids: Eerdmans, 1991). Bonhoeffer's reference to *cantus firmus* and counterpoint in the polyphony of the faithful Christian life is particularly relevant in this regard. See his letter to Eberhard Bethge of May 20, 1994, in *Letters and Papers from Prison,* enl. ed. (New York: Collier, 1971), 302–3.

Acknowledgments

I first learned of this book when Joel Shuman told me I was writing it with him. He didn't know what we had to say about theological claims on the practice of medicine, but he was quite certain I would help him find out. Whether Joel's confidence was well-founded is for the reader to judge. In any case, this book was his idea, and I remain the somewhat bewildered beneficiary of his generosity. Best of all, the two of us deepened an already good friendship along the way, and I learned a few new and shockingly funny jokes to boot.

I owe a great debt to Stanley Hauerwas for introducing me to Joel, who studied with Stanley at Duke University. Stanley, whom I met first through books and later through delightful correspondence which continues to this day, has a near-perfect sense for connections begging to be made. His reply to my first letter began, "I hope you will forgive me for addressing you personally, but I have the feeling you have just started a long friendship." He was right. Friendship is something Stanley Hauerwas takes quite seriously, which must explain why he's so good at it. We—and from this point on, the first person plural will serve—both expanded our circle of friends by taking his advice, starting conversations with people we might otherwise have passed by.

As for friendships in the traditional, Artistotelian sense: enjoying one another's company, being useful to one another, and sharing a common commitment to the good, there could be no better school for friendships than the Ekklesia Project, which we endorse, and through which we have received countless blessings. To all our friends at EP, many who listened to and encouraged us while we were still unsure if we had anything to say, our many thanks.

Both of us trained and worked in health professions before venturing—one formally, the other on the sly—into theology. Our first fields demand—even if they do not always elicit—exceptional honesty from practitioners and patients. Perhaps only in religious ministry do near strangers so regularly confide such intimate life details. It is in such encounters, and not in the pages of books, that one learns the art of medicine, which is merely one genre of the art of being present to another person. To our many patients and colleagues, we owe the incalculable debt a student owes the best of teachers.

We learn many lessons from our students in and out of the classroom, not least of which is that insights we find penetrating and lucid strike many others as dim-witted and opaque. To the extent we successfully explain and illustrate arguments in this book, we must thank those students who had the nerve to say, "I just don't get what you're saying, Doc." The best students are often those who ask legitimate questions unconstrained by the conventions of established disciplines. Coming out of deep left field when we're busy with "serious work," these can be terribly annoying. For precisely that reason, they can also gesture toward neglected escapes from the intellectual cages that the powers tell us are given and immutable.

To those friends who allowed us to tell their stories—especially to Ann and Geraldine Haywood, whose hospitality has been a blessing—we are more than grateful. It is our hope that readers will find their witnesses as encouraging as we have.

Several audiences listened attentively to presentations derived from the arguments and stories contained here, in such venues as the annual gathering of the Ekklesia Project, King's College, and the Program in Theology and Medicine at Duke University. We appreciate their patience as well as their many helpful questions.

Our worship communities, Bellarmine Chapel in Cincinnati and Christ United Methodist Church in Mountain Top, Pennsylvania, support us in many ways, not least of all by regularly gathering to celebrate liturgy well. Churches, like people, are wonderful messes of humanity for which we are often less grateful than we should be. The stories we've included here are only part of the gifts we've received.

Rodney Clapp of Brazos Books believed in this project when it was still an essay and provided detailed and insightful comments on the manuscript, making this a better book. Rebecca Cooper guided us along the book process and dealt with our occasional shocks and surprises—some large, some small—with remarkably good humor. We are delighted for this association with Brazos, their wonderful staff, and the remarkable company they keep.

Book writing is a pursuit best suited to the introvert. Those who've lived with an author know the stretches of time spent at the keyboard, away from standard duties and commitments. Our professional colleagues in medicine and education graciously granted us time and space in which to work out the matters in this book. Our children: Jessie, Amos, and Isaac Shuman, and Will, Peter, and Maria Volck, made greater sacrifices, putting up with absences and closed doors. We hope it's not too late to make it up to them. A man should consider himself blessed when his wife is smarter, better organized, or simply a better person than he. We are both blessed with spouses who are all three at once. To Chris Shuman and Jill Huppert, who offered continued encouragement and support, even while picking up the slack we left them, we offer our deep appreciation and gratitude.

Index

168